Contents

Introduction

Overview of the Series

Grammar Form and Function is a three-level series designed to ensure students' success in learning grammar. The series features interesting photos to help students accurately recall grammar points, meaningful contexts, and a clear, easy-to-understand format that integrates practice of the rules of essential English grammar (**form**) with information about when to apply them and what they mean (**function**).

Form is the structure of a grammar point and what it looks like. Practice of the form builds students' accuracy and helps them recognize the grammar point in authentic situations, so they are better prepared to understand what they are reading or what other people are saying.

Function is when and how we use a grammar point. Practice of the function builds students' fluency and helps them apply the grammar point in their real lives. Abundant practice in both form and function is key to students' success.

Each of the three levels (Beginning, Intermediate, and High Intermediate to Advanced) has four components: Student Book, Workbook, Teacher's Manual with Unit Quizzes, and Website. Used in conjunction, these tools provide students with ample opportunity for practice and teachers with multiple occasions for assessment.

- ❖ The **Student Books** feature engaging photos to ensure comprehension of form and function. Each level contains 14 units of varying length that proceed through grammar points from basic to complex. Book 1, the beginning level, starts with the present tense of *be* and ends with the present perfect tense. Book 2, the intermediate level, begins with a review of the present tenses and ends with reported speech and conditional clauses. Book 3, the high intermediate to advanced level, starts with a review of the present tenses and ends with conditional sentences. The Self-Test in every unit encourages student independence and increases competence in following standardized test formats.

- ❖ The **Workbooks** follow the scope and sequence of the student books and contain additional practice of both form and function of every grammar point. The Workbooks also feature Self-Tests in every unit to provide additional assessment opportunities and the chance for learners to monitor their own progress.

GRAMMAR
Form and Function

Teacher's Manual

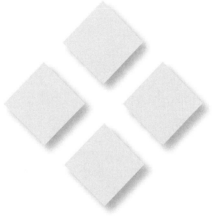

Milada Broukal
Carol Piñeiro

Grammar Form and Function 3 Teacher's Manual

Published by McGraw-Hill ESL/ELT, a business unit of The McGraw-Hill Companies, Inc., 1221 Avenue of the Americas, New York, NY 10020.

 This book is printed on recycled, acid-free paper containing 10% postconsumer waste.

ISBN-13: 978-0-07-008315-8
ISBN-10: 0-07-008315-0

Editorial director: Tina B. Carver
Executive editor: Erik Gundersen
Developmental editors: Annie Sullivan and Arley Gray
Production manager: MaryRose Malley
Cover design: Preface, Inc.
Interior design: Preface, Inc.

McGraw-Hill

- ❖ The **Teacher's Manuals** provide unit overviews, answer keys for the Student Book and Workbook, teaching tips and techniques, notes on culture, usage, and vocabulary, and answers to frequently asked questions about the grammar structures. Teacher's Manuals also include Unit Quizzes comprised of two formats—standardized multiple choice and writing—along with quiz answer keys.

- ❖ The **Website** introduces students to grammar-based reading and listening activities. While viewing fresh, contextual photos, learners read texts and listen to conversations that bring form and function to life. Strategic reading and listening tips are given in case students need help with comprehension. Once the exercises are completed, immediate feedback is available, giving learners the opportunity to view correct-answer explanations. Quizzes help students develop proficiency in taking standardized tests like the TOEFL. In addition, the quiz scores can be electronically accessed by teachers so they are aware of how many units the students have completed and how well they have done.

Teaching Guide for the Student Book

Format

For each grammar point, *Grammar Form and Function 3* Student Book follows a consistent format:

- ❖ The text presents the complete form, or formal rule, along with several examples for students to clearly see the model. Relevant photos help illustrate the grammar point.

- ❖ It explains the function of the grammar point, or how it is used, along with additional examples for reinforcement.

- ❖ It provides diverse exercises to practice the form and function together. Practice moves logically from more controlled to less controlled. **Review** provides a set of exercises that brings key grammar points together.

- ❖ It asks students to apply the grammar point in open-ended communicative activities. **Your Turn** requires students draw from and speak about personal experiences, and **Writing** provides a variety of writing assignments that rely on communicative group and pair discussions. Expansion activities in the Teacher's Manual provide additional creative, fun practice for students.

Using Photos

The high-interest photos in the presentations and exercises capture students' attention. When they see a photo aligned with a grammar point, the photo helps them remember and contextualize the grammar. The photos reinforce the learning and the grammar point. For example, to learn the present progressive, students read, "She is drinking coffee" while looking at a photo of a woman drinking coffee. Later, students are more likely to recall the grammar point because they have formed a mental picture. You can use photos in a variety of ways:

Pre-teaching: to establish a context
- ❖ call on students to describe the photos
- ❖ ask students to name the characters, perhaps using names of classmates

Teaching: to make a connection between image and form/function
- ❖ instruct students to complete the practices associated with the photos according to directions
- ❖ have students work on the expansion activities connected to the photos in the Teacher's Manual

Post-teaching: to reinforce the grammar point
- ❖ review the photos at the end of the unit, eliciting the grammar points
- ❖ have students write a few sentences about the photos on their own or with a partner

Using Grammar Charts

At the beginning of each section, the form of the grammar point is clearly illustrated in a clear, traditional grammar chart. The comprehensive charts include affirmative and negative forms, contractions, and question and answer forms. A photo, or illustration, and example accompany the chart to provide meaningful context. Various functions, or uses, of the grammar point are then simply and clearly explained. Another photo may accompany the explanation of the function. You can use the grammar charts in different ways, and it is a good idea to vary your use of the charts throughout the unit. Some students may need the explicit nature of the chart to feel comfortable at the beginning of a lesson. Others may want to start the exercises without spending too much time on the chart, so balancing the needs of everyone in the class is an important consideration when planning a lesson. Here are a few ideas on how to use the charts:

Pre-teaching: to preview the lesson
- ❖ tell students to look over the chart for homework and then present it in class the next day
- ❖ give students a diagnostic quiz to see how much they know and then introduce the chart, concentrating on the areas they might not have understood

Teaching: to introduce a lesson

❖ elicit oral examples of the structure before students see the chart

❖ put samples of the form on the board before using the chart

❖ explain the grammar point and then go over the examples on the chart

❖ go over the examples and points in the chart one by one before explaining the grammar point

Post-teaching: to reinforce grammar points

❖ using the photos, elicit key sentences to illustrate form and function when you finish a unit

❖ before the Self-Test or Unit Quiz, review the charts in each section

❖ ask students to write the form and function of each structure on the board as a review at higher levels

Teacher and Student Roles; Individual, Pair, and Group Work

Teachers and students can play a variety of roles in the classroom. At lower levels, teacher-directed activities generally work better until students feel comfortable with each other and the material. These include asking questions about photos, introducing grammatical structures, explaining items on charts, dividing students into pairs or groups, giving instructions, and checking answers. However, as students become more comfortable in the classroom and attain higher levels of proficiency, they can take over various aspects of these teacher tasks quite competently. For example, students (individually or in pairs) can be responsible for making up questions about photos, adding additional examples to charts, dividing themselves into pairs or groups, or checking each other's answers, consulting you when they have questions or don't agree.

While students should be required to do some work individually so that they become competent in grammar, pair and group work allow them to learn from each other, communicate with each other, and feel comfortable speaking English. Because no two students are at exactly the same level, they can learn from each other during pair and group work because if one student gets the correct answer, he or she can share it with the others who may not know it. Some agreeing, disagreeing, or other types of negotiation may take place. While trying to figure out answers, students have the opportunity to communicate with each other about natural "information gaps." Eliciting information, supplying information, making suggestions, and responding to suggestions are just a few of the speech acts that take place during these interactions. Finally, they may feel more comfortable speaking with each other than with you; they may assume you want to hear the correct answer, which may cause them to feel nervous or inhibited. Speaking with classmates is generally more relaxing and enjoyable, especially if you have fostered a comfortable learning environment.

Using the Exercises in Class

General exercise types

The exercises fall into several types that range from tightly to loosely controlled. At the beginning of a section, there are fill-in-the blanks, substitution, transposing, matching, labeling, choosing items from a list, sorting items into a list, and writing statements or questions. The answer keys in the Teacher's Manual list the answers for these exercises. At the end of some sections, there are **Your Turn** and **What Do You Think?** exercises that are more open-ended and allow for personal opinions, predictions, or other sorts of creative communication. The answer keys give suggestions as to what these answers might be, but they will vary with each student.

Oral exercises, written exercises, and exercises that can be either

Most of the exercises are designed to include writing practice so that students not only see and hear the structures, but write them as well. You can also use these exercises as oral practice in several ways; if they are easy tasks, students can take turns saying them aloud while writing in a small or large group setting. If they are more difficult, allow students to complete the exercise before checking the answers. If they are working in small groups, they can easily check among themselves and ask questions if they are not sure of the answers. If time is a constraint, you can simply give the answers after students complete the exercise, stopping every now and then to see if everyone agrees.

Using *Your Turn* and *What Do You Think*?

The purpose of these exercises is to encourage students to express opinions, make predictions, and solve problems, using the grammar point recently learned. Students' answers will vary greatly in these open-ended activities. Students can discuss the topics in pairs or small groups as you circulate around the classroom, listening and answering questions. The activities often ask students to then respond in writing. Later, you can go over some of the answers with the entire class if time allows or if a large-group discussion is warranted. Sample answers are given as models in the Teacher's Manual.

Using the Review Section

This section provides exercises that incorporate the key grammar points of a unit. You can present them with the same techniques outlined in Using the Exercises above.

Using the Writing Section

In this section, students are given a model in the first few units, such as a simple postcard or letter. In later units, models are not given, as students should be familiar with the format, and they are asked to write a more complex piece, such as a description, comparison, narration, or process. In pairs, they do pre-writing activities, asking each other questions about the topic and jotting down the answers. Then they rewrite their answers following the format suggested. Finally, they edit the paragraph according to a checklist, monitoring spelling, punctuation, vocabulary, and grammar, and make a final copy to hand in. This approach to guided writing specifies topic and format so students are not at a loss for words; at the same time, it allows them to activate their background knowledge and experience and to communicate personally and creatively with a reader (their partner or teacher). While the entire writing assignment can be completed in class, other options include doing the question-answer pairwork in class and the writing and editing at home, or doing the writing at home and the editing in class the next day. The flexibility of this section allows you to determine the method that best fits your class schedule and needs.

Using the Self-Tests

Each unit contains a two-part Self-Test to assess grammar points that have been taught and practiced in the unit. The first section has ten multiple-choice items similar to one of the structure sections in the TOEFL in which students have to identify the correct answer and darken one of four ovals (A, B, C, or D). The second section has ten multiple-choice items similar to another structure section in the TOEFL in which students have to identify the incorrect answer. Students have the opportunity to complete the Self-Test before taking the Unit Quiz in the Teacher's Manual. They will therefore benefit from the chance to evaluate their understanding of the material and to study areas they are unsure of before taking the Unit Quiz. The Self-Test answers are found at the end of each unit in the Teacher's Manual, so students have to consult you when they are finished. You can review the answers in class or write them on the board and then field any questions they may have about the items.

Using the Appendices

Appendices as grammar and writing reference handbook

The Appendices contain grammar terms, numbers and calendar information, irregular verbs, spelling rules for endings, capitalization rules, punctuation rules, and writing basics. It is a good idea to introduce the students to the appendices the first time you encounter each of these areas in a unit so that they are aware of them and learn how to use them. Rather than paging through the Student Book looking for a certain section, students will be able to locate the information they need quickly and efficiently.

Appendices as material for extension activities

You can also use this material for extension activities in class; for example, when one punctuation mark is being introduced, you can show the students how it fits in with other punctuation marks. Or, when teaching irregular past tense verb forms or irregular past participles, you can ask students to turn to the list of irregular verbs in Appendix 2. Have groups of students choose five verbs. Each group gives its list to another group. The groups must then think of a situation in which each of the verbs on their list can be used, and they write a dialogue or short paragraph using the verbs.

Teaching Guide for the Workbook

Each unit of the Student Book has a corresponding unit in the Workbook, so that students have the opportunity for additional practice of forms and functions outside the classroom. Ideally, you can finish most of the material in the Student Book during class time and assign sections of the Workbook for students to complete at home. The Workbook gives students the opportunity to work independently—or in study groups if they so choose—to perfect their understanding of English grammar. Students can check the answers in pairs or small groups in class and then ask you questions if they are not sure of them. You will find the Workbook Answer Keys in the last section of the Teacher's Manual, after the Unit Quiz Answer Keys.

As in the Student Book, the Workbook includes photos. In the Workbook, photos are used to provide context for activities.

At the end of each Workbook unit, there is a Self-Test modeled on those in the Student Book. These Self-Tests provide an additional opportunity for students to assess what they have learned and review what they have not.

Complete answer keys for the Workbook are found in the final section of the Teacher's Manual.

Teaching Guide for the Teacher's Manual

Format

The Teacher's Manual consists of five sections, in the following order:
1. Introduction
2. Student Book Answer Keys and Teaching Tips
3. Unit Quizzes
4. Unit Quiz Answer Keys
5. Workbook Answer Keys

Introduction

The Introduction provides a general series overview. It also provides teaching tips and explains how to use the key elements in the Student Books, such as the photos and the grammar charts.

Student Book Answer Keys and Teaching Tips

Each unit of the Teacher's Manual opens with a table of contents listing the grammar points and corresponding notes and activities, followed by a brief unit overview. Next, the unit provides answer keys for the Student Book exercises, featuring corresponding notes and activities. The notes include information on culture, pronunciation, usage, vocabulary, and frequently asked questions. The activities include introductions, dictations, comparisons, chants, and pronunciation, appropriate for each grammar point. These are for your benefit; you can choose to simply read through them or do them in class if time permits. Some of the activities invite student participation in boardwork, games, or chants. You might use these to liven up the class and get their energy (and yours) flowing after a long stretch of oral or written work.

Multiple Intelligences and Styles of Learning

There are many kinds of intelligences (linguistic, logical, kinesthetic, spatial, musical, interpersonal, and intrapersonal, to name a few) as well as many styles of learning. Instructors should try to use a variety of techniques in the classroom to accommodate various kinds of intelligence and different styles of learning. The following is a list of the types of activities that support each of the intelligences.

Linguistic: compositions, debates, dictations, discussions, journal keeping, proverbs, scavenger hunts, speeches, stories, word games, and worksheets

Logical: acronyms, calculations, logic games, puzzles, scientific demonstrations, and sequential tasks

Kinesthetic: cooking, crafts, creative movement, hands-on activities, miming, "Simon Says" game, and "Twister" game

Spatial: artwork, charts, diagrams, drawings, graphic organizers, imaginative stories, maps, movies, slides, treasure hunts, videos, and visualizations

Musical: appreciating music, chanting, "Hokey Pokey" song/dance, listening to music, playing musical instruments, and singing

Interpersonal: board or card games, group brainstorming, conflict resolution, cooperative activities, creating and performing role-plays

Intrapersonal: goal setting, independent activities, individual projects, interest stations, journal keeping, reflective learning activities, and self-esteem projects

Many of these activities are reflected in the exercises in *Grammar Form and Function* and the suggestions in the Teacher's Manual. Including a variety of them is the best way that instructors can ensure that students' different intelligences are being addressed in the language classroom.

Unit Quizzes

The 14 Unit Quizzes are found in the section following the Student Book Answer Keys.

Each Unit Quiz is two to three pages long and printed on reproducible pages so that you can make photocopies for your class. These quizzes are more challenging than the Student Book and Workbook Self-Tests, because they contain both a standardized test section and one or more writing sections, where students must apply the grammar structures. The writing sections are similar to exercises in the Student Book, so it is easy to determine if students can not only recognize, but also produce the grammar forms and functions of each unit. After each section, there is a space to tally the number of correct items, so it is easy to score at the end.

Unit Quiz Answer Keys

Complete answer keys for the Unit Quizzes are provided in the Teacher's Manual in the section immediately following the Unit Quizzes.

Workbook Answer Keys

Complete answer keys are provided for the Workbook in the final section of the Teacher's Manual.

Teaching Guide for the Website

The Website provides students with another medium to reinforce the form and function of the grammar points that they have learned, this time through reading and listening comprehension. Short texts and brief conversations on high interest topics at the basic level, followed by questions that check comprehension, engage students, and encourage them to continue developing their skills. Longer texts and listening passages on more academic topics are presented at higher levels. Tips for strategic reading and listening are available if students choose to access them; immediate feedback after completion of exercises is supplied so that students can repeat sections if they need or want to. After finishing each unit, students take quizzes and their scores are reported to you so that you are aware of their progress.

THE PRESENT TENSES

	Unit Sections	Notes/Activities	Student Books 3 and 3A page	Teacher's Manual page
1a	The Simple Present Tense and The Present Progressive Tense	World Leaders Activity	2	2
1b	Stative Verbs and Action Verbs	Dictation Activity	8	3
1c	The Present Perfect Tense and The Present Perfect Progressive Tense	Harry Potter Activity	11	4
❖	Review	Review Answer Key	20	6
❖	Writing	Writing Expansion	24	7
❖	Unit 1 Student Book Self-Test	Unit 1 Self-Test Answer Key	25	7

Unit 1 reviews the present tenses first by contrasting the forms of the simple present tense and the present progressive tense in affirmative and negative statements, yes/no questions, short answers, and wh- questions. A chart illustrates the functions of the two tenses by demonstrating usage through clear examples; these are followed by exercises that range from easier to more difficult, from fill-in-the blanks to open-ended questions.

Then the forms and functions of stative and action verbs are reviewed, with explanations about verbs that can be used either way, followed by exercises to help students distinguish the difference.

Next, this unit presents the forms of the present perfect tense and the present perfect progressive tense in affirmative and negative statements, yes/no questions, short answers, and wh- questions. The functions of the two tenses are illustrated in a chart with clear examples provided. Exercises in which students have to choose one or the other tense (or both) follow.

The writing activity is a letter to a friend, and an expansion activity follows, further extending the students' practice of these tenses.

1a The Simple Present Tense and The Present Progressive Tense

Student Books 3 and 3A p. 2

1 Practice

1. are you doing **2.** 'm/am taking **3.** 'm/am working **4.** Do you like **5.** do
6. 're giving **7.** train **8.** work **9.** don't/do not get **10.** 'm/am learning
11. 'm/am looking **12.** 's/is becoming **13.** are looking **14.** Are you learning
15. am **16.** does the course run **17.** runs **18.** 'm/am doing **19.** Are they giving
20. are **21.** are giving

2 Practice

1. 's/is staying **2.** 'm/am sleeping **3.** 's/is staying **4.** get up **5.** go
6. doesn't/does not get up **7.** eats **8.** drinks **9.** makes **10.** doesn't/does not eat
11. doesn't/does not drink **12.** 's/is using **13.** 's/is driving **14.** 's/is always making
15. 's constantly taking **16.** asks **17.** 's/is becoming **18.** 's/is not staying

3 Practice

1. a **2.** f **3.** d **4.** b **5.** e **6.** c

4 Practice

G **1.** People watch a lot of television.

C **2.** People are going to the movies a lot these days.

G **3.** The seasons change four times a year.

C **4.** The weather is changing these days.

G **5.** Wild animals live in the forests.

C **6.** Many wild animals are becoming extinct.

G **7.** Men work to take care of their families.

G **8.** Women work to take care of their families.

C **9.** Men and women are living longer.

C **10.** Computers are making our lives easier these days.

5 Your Turn

Answers will vary. Sample answer:
In my country, more and more people are moving to the cities, so the cities are getting
larger. Construction companies are building more houses so people can find places to live.
The people are buying cars so the streets are getting more crowded, and the pollution
is increasing.

❖ To provide students further practice with the present simple and present progressive tenses, you can lead an activity that starts by putting the names of regional or world leaders on the board. Alternatively, you can ask students from different regions of the world to go to the board and write the names of some of their leaders.

❖ Under the names, tell students to write a sentence in each of the present tenses. Here are some examples:

> *Arnold Schwarzenegger* **lives** *in the governor's mansion in Sacramento, California.*
> *This week he* **is meeting** *with lawmakers to discuss the state's tax laws.*
>
> *President Bush* **receives** *advice from his Cabinet.*
> *Right now he* **is talking** *with the Secretary of Education about new programs.*
>
> *Queen Elizabeth* **spends** *a few weeks each summer at Balmoral Castle in Scotland.*
> *Today she* **is preparing** *for her annual trip and* **making** *sure everything is ready.*

❖ After the sentences are on the board, students can take turns asking each other yes/no and wh- questions about the leaders.

1b Stative Verbs and Action Verbs

Student Books 3 and 3A p. 8

6 Practice

1. have **2.** has **3.** see **4.** is **5.** love **6.** know **7.** has **8.** don't/do not cost
9. 'm/am going **10.** sounds **11.** 'm/am thinking **12.** don't/do not know **13.** smells
14. are you cooking **15.** 'm/am making **16.** 's/is turning **17.** think **18.** Do you want

7 Your Turn

Answers will vary. Sample answers:

1. I expect to have a large family.

2. I doubt I will be rich.

3. I love cooking.

4. I like to be lucky.

5. I wonder how I will look in 20 years.

❖ Put the students into pairs and have them all go to the board. They should take a copy of the book with them.

❖ One student in each pair chooses a verb from the list of stative verbs in section 1b.

❖ The other student writes a sentence using the verb in the stative form (simple present tense). If the verb can also be used to describe an action, they should write another sentence (present progressive tense).

> For example, if the verb is *know*, the students can only write a sentence with the verb in the stative form: **I know** *your phone number*.

> However, if the verb is *feel*, the students can write two sentences, one in the stative form and the other in the active form: **I feel** *upset today* or **I'm feeling** *better today than yesterday*.

❖ The student who dictated the verb offers corrections.

❖ The students then switch roles. They dictate more verbs and write more sentences.

❖ After the pairs have written sentences with four to six of the verbs, have the pairs look at each others' sentences and offer corrections.

1c The Present Perfect Tense and The Present Perfect Progressive Tense

Student Books 3 and 3A p. 11

8 Practice

A. **1.** has been   **2.** have played/have been playing   **3.** have been
   4. have competed/have been competing

B. **1.** has been   **2.** have competed/have been competing   **3.** has become
   4. has practiced/has been practicing   **5.** has won   **6.** have been watching

9 Practice

A. Reading

B. **1.** 's/has just finished   **2.** 's/has already traveled   **3.** 's/has already done
   4. still hasn't acted   **5.** ...yet?   **6.** So far...   **7.** still hasn't given up
   8. still hasn't/has not had

10 Practice

A. Reading

B. **1.** What have you written?

2. Why is he special?

3. Where do you live?

4. Have you lived

5. How many languages have your books been translated into?

6. How many of your books have been sold?

7. What is the most important thing you've done?

11 Practice

A. **1.** He's/has climbed many mountains in the Himalayas in his career.

2. He's/has climbed Mt. Everest.

3. Has he been in the hospital many times?

4. Has he been climbing a lot this year?

B. **1.** He's/has been on tour in the United States and Europe.

2. He's/has sold two million CDs a year for five years.

3. Has he won any Grammy awards?

4. Has he appeared on television yet?

C. **1.** She's/has been interviewing many famous people since she became a journalist.

2. She's/has been traveling all over the world in her career.

3. She's/has met the president.

4. Has she ever had her own show on television?

Student Books 3 and 3A p. 20

12 **Your Turn**

Answers will vary. Sample answers:

The man is wearing traditional Arabic dress. He's just finished a trip across the desert. Maybe he's been traveling all day.

❖ Write these titles of the first five Harry Potter books on the board.

Harry Potter and the Sorcerer's Stone
Harry Potter and the Chamber of Secrets
Harry Potter and the Prisoner of Azkaban
Harry Potter and the Goblet of Fire
Harry Potter and the Order of the Phoenix

❖ Tell the students the background of the story within the books very briefly: Harry Potter is an orphan sent to live with some relatives, but he knows that he is different from them. On his 11th birthday, he receives an invitation to study at Hogwart's School of Witchcraft and Wizardry. There he learns that his parents were wizards killed by Voldemort, the Lord of Darkness, and that he has inherited their magic powers.

Below are sentences about Harry Potter. Write each sentence on a piece of paper. Make enough copies for every pair or group of students. Cut the sentences in half at the slash marks shown below. Put each set of sentence halves in an envelope. Give one envelope to each pair or small group of students. Ask them to put the words together in the correct order so that they make a logical sentence.

❖ After the students put the sentences together, tell them to write them on the board.

a) Harry Potter has been living / with his aunt, uncle, and cousin for several years.

b) He has not been happy at their house / because they do not treat him very well.

c) He has been sleeping in a tiny room / and doing much of the housework.

d) He has been receiving a lot of mail delivered by owls, / but his uncle throws it away.

e) He has finally read one of the letters, / which is an invitation to a school for wizards.

f) He has slowly begun to realize / that he is different, and the school will be good for him.

g) He has met a stranger / who helps him buy the supplies he needs for school.

h) He has left his aunt's house / and is trying to find the train that goes to the school.

i) He has met a boy on the train / who will be a classmate at Hogwart's.

j) He has arrived at the wonderful magical school / and feels immediately at home.

❖❖❖ # Review

Student Books 3 and 3A p. 20

| 1 | ## Review (1a–1c) |

1. 've had **2.** 'm sailing **3.** are 4. 've been sailing **5.** wake **6.** sit **7.** eat
8. rings **9.** know **10.** is **11.** go **12.** am **13.** love **14.** listen **15.** have
16. take **17.** know **18.** haven't had **19.** never know **20.** are always **21.** 'm not
thinking **22.** work **23.** love **24.** came **25.** 've taken/'ve been taking **26.** 've
studied/'ve been studying **27.** 'm sitting **28.** are riding **29.** is **30.** has been blowing
31. seems **32.** see **33.** are getting **34.** is coming **35.** need **36.** are getting

2 | Review (1a–1b)

1. are **2.** have **3.** 's **4.** is always going **5.** is **6.** 's not **7.** is **8.** 've been trying
9. isn't **10.** 's **11.** are you doing **12.** 'm buying **13.** are you buying **14.** have
15. worry **16.** 's **17.** need **18.** are coming **19.** 've been looking **20.** 've been
talking **21.** Do you know **22.** 's **23.** 's **24.** don't want

3 | Review (1a–1c)

1. Where does the Hubble travel?

2. How far does the Hubble travel above Earth?

3. How long has the Hubble been in space?

4. What does the Hubble do every day?

5. What do the pictures show us?

6. How many pictures has the Hubble taken?

7. What has the Hubble done for scientists and astronomers all over the world?

4 | Review (1a–1c)

1. is **2.** 'm calling **3.** are enjoying **4.** I'm looking **5.** 's **6.** sounds **7.** Have you
been **8.** 've already been **9.** Have you ever been **10.** love **11.** 'm already thinking

Writing Expansion

Student Books 3 and 3A p. 24

Collect the letters and then give them out to students at random, making sure no student
has his or her own letter. Ask students to pretend that they have just received the letter
and want to write an answer, following the correct format.

Unit 1 Student Book Self-Test

Student Books 3 and 3A p. 25

A. **1.** C **2.** B **3.** C **4.** A **5.** D **6.** A **7.** A **8.** C **9.** C **10.** D

B. **1.** A **2.** B **3.** A **4.** B **5.** C **6.** B **7.** A **8.** C **9.** B **10.** A

UNIT 2

THE PAST TENSES

Unit 2 reviews the past tenses first by contrasting the forms of the simple past tense and the past progressive tense in affirmative and negative statements, yes/no questions, short answers, and wh-questions. A chart illustrates for students the functions of the two tenses by demonstrating usage through clear examples; these are followed by exercises that range from easier to more difficult, from fill-in-the blanks to open-ended questions.

Next, the forms and functions of the past perfect tense and the past perfect progressive tense are given in affirmative and negative statements, yes/no questions, short answers, and wh- questions. A chart illustrates the functions of the two tenses and provides clear examples. Exercises in which students have to choose one or the other tense (or both) follow.

Then the form and function of *used to* + base verb and *would* + base verb are reviewed, with explanations about when one or the other should be used; these are followed by exercises to help students distinguish the difference.

The writing activity is a narrative about a person's life, designed to encourage students to write longer pieces. An expansion activity follows, which further extends their practice of these tenses.

2a The Simple Past Tense and The Past Progressive Tense

Student Books 3 and 3A p. 28

1 Practice

A. **1.** was waiting **2.** saw **3.** was talking **4.** was driving **5.** wasn't/was not paying **6.** turned **7.** was crossing **8.** stopped

B. **1.** fell **2.** was running **3.** screamed **4.** noticed **5.** jumped **6.** pulled **7.** stopped **8.** called

C. **1.** was sitting **2.** was watching **3.** was feeling **4.** was thinking **5.** heard **6.** seemed **7.** turned **8.** took **9.** started **10.** heard **11.** froze **12.** were shaking **13.** called

2 What Do You Think?

Answers will vary. Sample answer:
When I heard the police car outside, I opened the door. A policeman and policewoman came in, and I showed them to the stairs. They were holding their flashlights and climbing up slowly. All of a sudden, a bat flew down the stairs. They ducked and I ran to open the door. The bat was flying all around the room, but finally it flew out the door. We all started laughing, and I thanked them for helping me get rid of the bat.

3 Practice

1. was **2.** decided **3.** bought **4.** called **5.** needed **6.** cut down **7.** used **8.** left **9.** was sailing **10.** stopped **11.** gave **12.** was traveling **13.** met **14.** returned **15.** wrote **16.** started **17.** disappeared **18.** heard

4 Practice

1. gave **2.** stood **3.** was playing/played **4.** saw **5.** was learning/learned **6.** knew **7.** hit **8.** made **9.** woke **10.** was sleeping **11.** went **12.** was studying **13.** performed **14.** played **15.** heard **16.** began **17.** was playing/played **18.** continued **19.** applauded **20.** saw **21.** started

5 Practice

Answers may vary. Probable answers:

1. Did his father teach him to play the piano?

Yes, he did.

2. Did he study in Vienna?

Yes, he did.

3. Did he meet Mozart one day?

Yes, he did.

4. Did he hear the music in his last performance?

No, he didn't.

5. Did he cry when he saw the audience?

Yes, he did.

6 Practice

1. Why did Beethoven go to Vienna?

2. Who did he entertain?

3. When did he begin to lose his hearing?

4. What did he continue to do while the audience was applauding?

5. How many people went to his funeral?

7 Practice

1. When Beethoven didn't like an audience, he didn't perform.

2. When he ate in restaurants, he sometimes didn't pay the bill.

3. He didn't eat or sleep while he was working.

4. While he was writing his music, he didn't bathe or clean his room.

5. While Beethoven was conducting the orchestra, he couldn't hear the music.

6. When people cried because his music was beautiful, he laughed at them.

7. Over 20,000 people went to Beethoven's funeral when he died at age 57.

8 Practice

1. named **2.** taught **3.** started **4.** played **5.** won **6.** has helped **7.** has earned **8.** got

9 Your Turn

Answers will vary. Sample answer:
John Lennon was born in Liverpool, England, in 1940. He liked to draw and write, and when he was 15, he formed a band with two of his friends, Paul McCartney and George Harrison. Later, Ringo Starr joined the group, which called itself the Beatles. They were an instant success in England, and in 1964, they traveled to the United States, where "Beatlemania" caught on.

❖ Here are the last names of several composers—from classical to modern—with the letters scrambled. Put them on the board and see if students can unscramble them. The first ones to get the names written out correctly can write them on the board.

Classical composers from Europe/Russia		**Modern composers from the United States**	
cahb	Bach (1685-1750)	toperr	Porter (1893-1964)
zortam	Mozart (1756-1791)	nergwish	Gershwin (1898-1937)
tovehbeen	Beethoven (1770-1827)	ginletnol	Ellington (1899-1971)
cavtoshikyk	Tchaikovsky (1840-1893)	danepolc	Copeland (1900-1990)
snivartyks	Stravinsky (1882-1971)	sinretbe	Bernstein (1918-1990)

❖ If students are able to figure out the composers, you can also ask about some of their famous compositions. If they aren't able to figure out the names, you can tell them, and then do a mini-lesson on one of the compositions you are familiar with.

❖ Students can also look up their favorite popular composers on the Internet and give a report to the class, playing a CD of one of their songs.

2b The Past Perfect Tense and The Past Perfect Progressive Tense

Student Books 3 and 3A p. 36

⟦10⟧ Practice

1. had arrived **2.** got **3.** had already begun **4.** was **5.** had already started **6.** walked **7.** took **8.** didn't/did not finish **9.** 'd/had started **10.** had studied **11.** wanted **12.** had left **13.** decided **14.** didn't/did not like **15.** 'd/had wanted **16.** had never had **17.** called **18.** had seen **19.** didn't/did not want **20.** called **21.** had read **22.** hadn't/had not liked **23.** called **24.** 'd/had already made **25.** heard **26.** did/had done **27.** had never done **28.** went/had gone

⟦11⟧ Practice

1. She looked tired because she had been working too much.

2. She looked tired because she hadn't/had not slept the night before.

3. She looked tired because she hadn't/had not been eating well lately.

4. She looked tired because she had been worrying about her parents.

5. She looked tired because her baby had been sick for a few days.

6. She looked tired because she had been grading exams all night.

12 Practice

A. Reading

B. **1.** Why did the shepherd boy think of a plan to have fun?

He thought of the plan because he had been getting bored.

2. What did his master tell him?

He told him to call for help when he saw a wolf near the sheep.

3. What did he decide to do one day?

He decided to play a trick on the villagers.

4. Did he see a wolf?

No, he didn't see a wolf.

5. What did the villagers do?

They left their work and ran to the field.

6. Why did the boy laugh?

He laughed because he had played a trick on them.

7. What did the boy do a few days later?

He did the same thing.

8. Did he laugh at the villagers again?

Yes, he did laugh at them again.

9. What did the boy do when the wolf really came?

He shouted, "Wolf! Wolf!"

10. What did the villagers do this time?

They heard him, but they didn't run to help him as they had done before.

13 What Do You Think?

Answers will vary. Sample answer:
I think the moral of this fable is that you shouldn't pretend you're in danger unless you really are. Otherwise, people won't come to help you when you really are in danger.

14 Practice

1. 've/have been waiting   **2.** 'd/had been waiting   **3.** has been hurting
4. had been hurting   **5.** 've/have been taking   **6.** 'd/had been taking
7. 'd/had been hoping   **8.** 've/have been going   **9.** has been working
10. 'd/had been working

15 What Do You Think?

Answers will vary. Sample answer:
The patient made a noise and waved his/her hand. The dentist stopped. The patient asked for more local anesthetic to stop the pain.

16 Your Turn

Answers will vary. Sample answers:

1. When I got to class, the teacher hadn't arrived.

2. When I got to class, the teacher was taking attendance.

3. When I got to class, the class had begun.

4. When I got to class, the teacher had collected the homework.

5. When I got to class, all the students had arrived.

17 Your Turn

Answers will vary. Sample answers:

1. By the time I was 16, I had met several government officials.

2. By the time I was 16, I had traveled to many countries in the region.

3. By the time I was 16, I had learned to ride a motorcycle and drive a car.

4. By the time I was 16, I had learned a lot of English.

Small Group Activity

❖ Students can work in small groups to summarize the sentences they have written, trying to find commonalities. For example, they might find that by the age of 6, everyone in the group had started school. Or perhaps by the age of 10, everyone could swim.

❖ When each group has summarized the sentences, they can either say them aloud to the rest of the class or write them on the board.

2c *Used To* + Base Verb and *Would* + Base Verb

Student Books 3 and 3A p. 44

18 Practice

1. used to watch   **2.** used to wear   **3.** would not fight   **4.** used to have   **5.** became
6. came **7.** used to scream   **8.** used to be   **9.** am used to listening   **10.** used to be

19 Practice

1. Bruno used to live in Brazil, but now he lives in Canada.

2. He used to be single, but now he's married.

3. He used to be a student, but now he's an architect.

4. He used to play soccer, but now he plays hockey.

5. He used to weigh 160 pounds/72 kilos, but now he weighs 200 pounds/90 kilos.

6. He used to like movies and dancing, but now he likes watching TV.

7. He used to speak Portuguese, but now he speaks Portuguese and English.

8. He used to be carefree, but now he's serious (for example).

 20 ## What Do You Think?

Answers will vary. Sample answer:

Young people used to listen to folk music at outdoor concerts.

21 ## Your Turn

Answers will vary. Sample answers:

Questions	As a Child	Now
What TV shows did you use to like?	cartoon shows	comedies
What shows do you like now?		
What books did you use to read?	mystery books	novels
What books do you read now?		
What food did you use to like?	French fries	vegetables
What food do you like now?		

Survey Activity

❖ Tell the students to conduct a survey about the answers given in **Your Turn 21.** Divide the class into two groups; one group will collect answers from the *As a Child* column, and the other group will collect answers from the *Now* column.

❖ You can appoint a group leader to take charge of the survey. He or she can assign a pair of students to collect and record the answers, another pair to graph the answers (pie chart or bar graph), and another pair to report on the answers.

❖ When both groups are finished graphing the answers on the board, they can report to the class.

 # Review

Student Books 3 and 3A p. 49

1 ## Review (2a–2b)

1. saw **2.** knew **3.** weren't **4.** was **5.** had overslept **6.** arrived **7.** had been waiting **8.** had wanted **9.** didn't let **10.** was **11.** were hiking **12.** was **13.** was **14.** had looked **15.** was **16.** hadn't slept **17.** came **18.** knew **19.** had hiked **20.** expected **21.** had been **22.** hadn't hiked **23.** had changed **24.** was waiting **25.** told **26.** walked **27.** walked **28.** ended **29.** had **30.** had been walking **31.** were **32.** was going **33.** was getting **34.** did I tell **35.** was **36.** hadn't felt

37. heard **38.** was **39.** laughed **40.** looked **41.** was walking **42.** were
43. had come

2 Review (2a)

1. were **2.** came **3.** were livng **4.** came **5.** arrived **6.** were/had been **7.** decided
8. passed **9.** landed **10.** had been living/had lived **11.** replaced **12.** were **13.** built
14. needed **15.** was **16.** had **17.** fought **18.** didn't have **19.** did they teach
20. told **21.** were **22.** respected **23.** cared **24.** didn't destroy **25.** had
26. believed **27.** had **28.** began **29.** decided **30.** realized

3 Review (2a–2b)

Answers will vary.

4 Review (2a–2c)

1. was **2.** lived/used to live **3.** told/used to tell **4.** didn't let/wouldn't let/didn't used
to let **5.** had heard **6.** were/used to be/would be **7.** finished/had finished **8.** hadn't
thought **9.** started **10.** was **11.** had already started **12.** was showing **13.** walked
14. was putting **15.** shook **16.** wouldn't let/didn't let **17.** had danced **18.** didn't
believe **19.** had been/was **20.** were driving **21.** were/used to be **22.** drove **23.** were
learning **24.** packed up/used to pack up **25.** went **26.** asked/used to ask/would ask

Writing Expansion

Student Books 3 and 3A p. 53

When the students finish writing their narratives, they can give them to a partner to read. The partner should make sure the story is told in chronological order and that important details are included. If they notice that facts are out of order or missing, they should make notes on the paper so that their partner can revise it. Then the students can rewrite their papers and turn them in.

◆ Unit 2 Student Book Self-Test

Student Books 3 and 3A p. 54

A. **1.** B **2.** C **3.** A **4.** B **5.** B **6.** C **7.** A **8.** B **9.** B **10.** D

B. **1.** C **2.** D **3.** D **4.** A **5.** D **6.** B **7.** A **8.** C **9.** C **10.** A

UNIT 3

THE FUTURE TENSES

Unit 3 reviews the future tenses by contrasting *be going to* + base verb and *will* + base verb in a chart illustrating the forms and functions of the two tenses and providing clear examples of each. A range of exercises, from easier to more difficult and from fill-in-the blanks to open-ended questions, allows students to practice the tenses in different contexts.

Next, time clauses and conditional sentences are explained so that students are able to understand the tenses and do the exercises that follow. Present tenses with future meaning demonstrate the use of present simple for fixed schedules and present progressive for specific times in the future, followed by a variety of exercises similar to those already completed.

Other expressions for future time are presented in a helpful chart, and students practice each one in different ways. Finally, the forms and functions of the future perfect and future perfect progressive tenses are explained, with charts and exercises to give students a clear understanding of both.

The writing activity is an essay with a topic sentence and supporting examples about life in the future. An expansion activity follows, which further extends students' practice of these tenses.

3a *Be Going To* and *Will*

Student Books 3 and 3A p. 58

 ## Practice

1. are you going to do   **2.** 'm/am going to see   **3.** 'll/will stay   **4.** 'll/will be
5. 'll/will go   **6.** 're/are going to leave   **7.** will get   **8.** 'll/will

2 Practice

A. Reading

B. Answers may vary. Probable answers:

1. Are cities like Tokyo going to be very crowded in the future?

2. Where are the architects going to build this city?

3. What will the shape of the city be?

4. How high will the pyramid be?

5. What will the pyramid be made of?

6. Will it have residential areas?

7. Will it have cars?

8. How will people travel?

9. Will the weather always be nice?

10. What do the architects hope?

3 What Do You Think?

Answers will vary. Sample answers:

Yes, I'd like to live in a city like this because everything would be very convenient.

No, I wouldn't like to live in a city like this because it would be very high, and I'm afraid of heights. I also think it would be boring after a while because everything would be the same.

 ## Your Turn

Answers will vary. Sample answers:
There will be no cars in the center of the city. People will travel on special chairs with wheels.
These chairs won't use gas; they'll be solar-powered and very clean and quiet.

❖ Divide students into groups according to regions of the world, and tell them to think of a major city where they come from. Each group should make a list of the positive things that they want to remain in the city 100 years from now and the negative things they want to change. For example:

Rome	ancient monuments	traffic and pollution
	fountains and gardens	graffiti and trash
Istanbul	mosques and bazaars	cars and smog
	ferries and waterfront restaurants	polluted water

❖ Then, each group will make up a few sentences using future tense and write them on the board; you can help with vocabulary. For example:

One hundred years from now, Rome will still have ancient monuments, but it won't have traffic and pollution. All the cars will be solar-powered, and the air will be very clean.

One hundred years from now, Istanbul will still have ferries and waterfront restaurants, but it won't have polluted water. The government will clean up the Bosphorous and the people will keep it clean.

❖ When they finish writing the sentences on the board, students from each group should read them to the class.

3b Time Clauses and Conditional Sentences in the Future

Student Books 3 and 3A p. 63

5 Practice

A. Reading

B. 1. Matt wants to be a famous rock singer in the future.

2. He'll become a famous rock star before he's 25.

3. He'll have a lot of money when he's 30.

4. He'll retire as soon as he becomes a millionaire.

5. He wants to travel after he leaves school.

6. He'll save some money before he travels.

7. He'll go to Africa as soon as he has enough money.

8. He'll leave Africa after he's seen the main cities and gone on a safari.

9. He'll visit his friend Hong in China.

10. He'll visit Japan before he comes home.

11. He'll go back to his hometown.

12. He'll go to college if his parents want him to.

6 Your Turn

Answers will vary. Sample answers:
1. I'll get a job as soon as I can.
2. I'll live with my parents until I find an apartment.
3. I'll get to travel a lot if I get an interesting job.
4. I'll buy a house or an apartment when I win the lottery.

7 Your Turn

Answers will vary. Sample answers:
1. What will you do if you hurt yourself?   I'll call for help on my cell phone.
2. What will you do if it rains?   I'll put on my poncho.
3. What will you do if you get hungry?   I'll eat the food in my backpack.
4. What will you do if it gets dark?   I'll use my flashlight.
5. What will you do if you get lost?   I'll look at the map and use my compass.

Sports Activity

❖ Put students in groups of four. Write the following situations and prompts on the board. Each group will choose a situation and ask and answer questions (as in **Your Turn 7** above) using the prompts.

>   Biking: fall off your bike / can't stop / get lost / can't unlock your bike
>
>   Bowling: can't knock down pins / drop the ball on your toes / have a low score
>
>   Rollerblading: go too fast / can't stop on a hill / fall down / can't skate
>   back home
>
>   Sailing: have no wind / get seasick / sail too far away / get caught in a storm
>
>   Skiing: go downhill too fast / lose your ski poles / fall and lose a ski / can't stop
>
>   Swimming: swim too far from shore / see someone in trouble / get tired / see
>   a shark

3c   Present Tenses with Future Meaning

Student Books 3 and 3A p. 67

8 Practice

1. arrives   2. 's/is having   3. 's/is meeting; 's/is seeing   4. 's/is practicing
5. 's/is meeting; starts; ends   6. 's/is going; has   7. 's/is resting   8. 's/is playing; starts
9. 's/is flying; takes off

3d The Future Progressive Tense

Student Books 3 and 3A p. 70

11 Practice

1. At 9:00, she'll be talking to Jack Simms.

2. At 9:30, she'll be writing the status report.

3. At 10:30, she'll be having a conference call with other managers.

4. From 12:00 to 1:00, she'll be having lunch with Peter Jones.

5. At 1:30, she'll be interviewing Janet Pratt for a job opening.

6. At 2:00, she'll be meeting with Steve to talk about the problems.

7. At 2:30, she'll be showing the staff the new sales software.

8. At 4:30, she'll be answering email.

12 Practice

1. will be waiting   **2.** will I recognize   **3.** 'll/will recognize   **4.** won't/will not miss
5. 'll/will be wearing   **6.** won't/will not worry   **7.** 'll/will be sitting   **8.** 'll/will enjoy
9. 'll/will be eating   **10.** 'll/will/have   **11.** will you do   **12.** Will you buy **13.** 'll/will pay
14. won't/will not cost   **15.** 'll/will be   **16.** 'll/will be   **17.** 'll/will get   **18.** 'll/will be
working   **19.** will you be leaving   **20.** 'll/will call   **21.** 'll/will be waiting

13 | Your Turn

Answers will vary. Sample answers:
1. At 7:05, I'll be drinking a cup of coffee.
2. At 7:30, I'll be getting dressed.
3. At 8:00, I'll be waiting for the bus.
4. At 8:55, I'll be walking into the classroom.
5. At 9:15, I'll be sitting in class.
6. At 1:20, I'll be finishing lunch.
7. At 4:00, I'll be talking to my friends.
8. At 6:15, I'll be making dinner.

Planning Activity

❖ Tell students to make timelines of their lives with five-year intervals and explain the timelines to partners in the future progressive tense.

2005	Study for a master's degree and get a job
2010	Get married
2015	Have a child
2020	Get a better job
2025	Have another child
2030	Open my own business

❖ Then, they should take turns asking and answering questions about future plans.
For example:

A: What will you be doing in 2005?
B: In 2005, I'll be getting my master's degree. What about you?
A: I'll be working at my first job. What about in 2010?
B: I'll be getting married. What about you?
A: I'll be having my first child.

3e Other Expressions of the Future; The Future in the Past

Student Books 3 and 3A p. 74

14 | Practice

1. Albert Einstein was going to be a violinist, but instead he became a physicist.

2. Mahatma Gandhi was going to be a lawyer, but instead he became a great political leader.

3. George Washington Carver was going to be an artist, but instead he became a chemist and botanist.

4. Hans Christian Anderson was going to be an actor, but instead he became a fairy tale writer.

5. Frida Kahlo was going to be a doctor, but instead she became an artist.

6. Sigmund Freud was going to be a doctor, but instead he became a psychoanalyst.

Practice

1. was about to do   **2.** were about to drive   **3.** was about to make   **4.** were about to do
5. were about to ring   **6.** was about to tell   **7.** was about to give   **8.** was about to scream

 Practice

1. is to visit   **2.** is about to begin   **3.** is about to enter   **4.** is to give   **5.** is to help
6. is about to introduce

 Your Turn

Answers will vary. Sample answers:
My sister was going to get married last month, but she didn't.
I was going to be her maid of honor, but I wasn't.
She and her fiancé were going to go to Greece on their honeymoon, but they didn't.

Famous Person Activity

- ❖ Continue **Practice 14** by asking students if they know of anyone who changed his or her career.
- ❖ If they cannot think of anyone, have them use the following information to write sentences about famous Americans on the board:

Eleanor Roosevelt	writer	diplomat/activist
Elvis Presley	choirboy	singer/actor
John F. Kennedy	senator	president
John Lennon	artist	guitar player/songwriter
Hilary Rodham Clinton	lawyer	senator

3f The Future Perfect Tense and The Future Perfect Progressive Tense

Student Books 3 and 3A p. 77

 Practice

1. will have driven   **2.** will have helped   **3.** will have played   **4.** will have finished
5. will have studied   **6.** will have started   **7.** will have decided   **8.** will have spent
9–12. Answers will vary.

 Practice

1. are planning   **2.** are going to send   **3.** will be   **4.** are going to be/will not be
5. will be preparing   **6.** are leaving   **7.** will be doing   **8.** will be looking
9. will be collecting   **10.** will have been living   **11.** will have taken   **12.** will have been
13. will have learned   **14.** will be

20 Your Turn

Answers will vary. Sample answers:
By the time I am 40, I will have gotten married.
By the time I am 40, I will have bought a house.
By the time I am 40, I will have had two children.
By the time I am 40, I will have worked for 20 years.

21 Your Turn

Answers will vary. Sample answers:
1. By the end of the year, I will have been attending this school for two semesters.
2. By next July, I will have been living in my apartment for almost a year.
3. By the end of the school year, I will have been studying English for 10 years.
4. By the end of the year, I will have been wearing these shoes for three months.
5. By the end of this year, I will have studied with my present teacher for one semester.
6. By the end of the year, I will have been using this book for four months.

Budget Activity

❖ Ask students what they spend money on. Make a list of their items on the board:

Books	Computer	Housing	Transportation
Clothing	Food	Telephone	Tuition

❖ Then, ask them to estimate how much they will have spent on each item by the time they finish their schooling. For example:

By the time I finish school, I'll have spent $10,000 on tuition.
By the time I graduate, my parents will have spent $2,500 on transportation.

❖ Review

Student Books 3 and 3A p. 82

1 Review (3a, 3f)

1. Will human beings ever go 2. will achieve 3. will happen 4. will help 5. are traveling 6. will be working 7. will have found 8. will have prepared 9. will have joined 10. will have been 11. will have given 12. will the first travelers 13. will know 14. will give 15. will put 16. will know 17. will have discovered 18. will have created 19. will have discovered 20. will no longer be 21. will be 22. Will you be 23. will have traveled 24. will they have visited 25. will they have gone/gotten

2 Review (3a, 3c–3d)

1. 'm flying 2. 'll be 3. 'll be flying 4. 'm traveling 5. 'll see 6. 'll have visited 7. 'll have taken 8. 'll be 9. 'll be working 10. 'll get 11. 'll have been studying/'ll have studied 12. is leaving/leaves 13. 'm going

3 | **Review (3a, 3c)**

1. was about to start   **2.** 'm not doing   **3.** 'm going   **4.** was going to ask   **5.** am I going to do/will I do   **6.** don't have   **7.** You're going to sit/You'll sit   **8.** 'll have bought
9. I'll help   **10.** 'm   **11.** 'll buy   **12.** are we leaving/are we going to leave/do we leave
13. 'll get   **14.** 'll be/'s going to be   **15.** 'll have been relaxing   **16.** 'll be swimming
17. closes   **18.** 'll meet   **19.** finish   **20.** Will you be/Are you going to be

4 | **Review (3a, 3c–3d, 3f)**

Answers will vary.

Writing Expansion

Student Books 3 and 3A p. 86

When students finish writing their essays, have them illustrate what they have written by drawing a sketch or finding a picture in a magazine or on the Internet. After they write their final draft, they should attach the drawing or picture to their essay and put it on a bulletin board for other students to read. Or, if you have a class webpage, you can put the essays and illustrations there.

Unit 3 Student Book Self-Test

Student Books 3 and 3A p. 87

A. **1.** B   **2.** C   **3.** A   **4.** A   **5.** C   **6.** A   **7.** B   **8.** D   **9.** C   **10.** C

B. **1.** A   **2.** A   **3.** A   **4.** D   **5.** B   **6.** A   **7.** D   **8.** A   **9.** D   **10.** C

UNIT 4 ◆

NOUNS AND EXPRESSIONS OF QUANTITY

Unit 4 reviews the forms of regular and irregular plurals of nouns in helpful charts, followed by exercises that allow students ample practice. Possessive nouns with *'s* and *of...* are then presented, accompanied by exercises in which students match form and function.

Compound nouns are the focus of the next section, and students are able to practice them in a variety of interesting ways, including matching, fill-in-the-blank, and open-ended question exercises. Count and noncount nouns follow, with illustrations of instances in which some nouns can be in either category or both. From there, the shift is to the quantifiers *some* and *any*.

Quantifiers are continued with *much, many, a lot of, little,* and *few* in affirmative and negative questions and statements. Finally, *each, every, both,* and *all* are explained, and students discern which forms can be used with which functions.

The writing activity is a descriptive essay about a distinct feature of students' countries, such as architecture, food, or vacation spots. An expansion activity in which students compile their writing into a travel brochure follows.

25

4a ▸ Regular and Irregular Plural Nouns

Student Books 3 and 3A p. 90

 Practice

1. feet **2.** teeth **3.** hobbies **4.** photos **5.** watches **6.** pets **7.** mice **8.** fish
9. canaries **10.** wives **11.** children **12.** lives

2 **Practice**

1. is **2.** is **3.** are **4.** are **5.** are **6.** are **7.** are **8.** are **9.** are **10.** is

3 **Your Turn**

Answers will vary. Sample answers:

I agree that the news on the Internet is more up-to-date because it can be changed every minute of the day.

I don't agree that bacteria are only spread through physical contact because they can also be spread through the air, by coughing or sneezing.

Vocabulary Notes

❖ Here are a few more Latin and Greek words that students may come across in later studies. You can put them on the board and explain them; students should add to the list if they know more expressions.

Latin	Greek
alumnus – alumni = former student/s (m)	criterion – criteria = data on which to judge
alumna – alumnae = former student/s (f)	phenomenon – phenomena = fact or event
radius – radii = half of diameter	schema – schemata = framework
stratus – strata = layer, level	
vertebra – vertebrae = backbones	

4b ▸ Possessive Nouns; Possessive Phrases with *Of*

Student Books 3 and 3A p. 93

4 **Practice**

The words in bold are the answers.

This is a photo of my **grandparents'** wedding. My **grandmother's** wedding dress is made of real lace. It used to be her **mother's.** The color of the **bridesmaids'** dresses matches the flowers. My **grandfather's** expression is very serious. He borrowed his **brother's** best suit for the wedding and it is a little too tight. **Men's** suits are less formal nowadays. **Women's** hairstyles are also more casual. I like this photo because it reminds me of the old days.

5 | Your Turn

Answers will vary. Sample answers:
The sleeves of her dress are very wide.
The bride's veil is long.
The people's faces look happy.

6 | Practice

1. Jack's sister   **2.** the name of the restaurant   **3.** Tony's Place   **4.** the name of the street   **5.** side of the street   **6.** Mike's Pizza   **7.** The freshness of the food   **8.** the size of the portions   **9.** The price of the main courses   **10.** the daily specials

7 | Your Turn

Answers will vary. Sample answers:
1. The price of a suit is more important to me than the style or color.
2. The fit of a sweater is as important as the material.
3. The quality of a pair of shoes is more important than the style.
4. The name of the designer isn't as important as the way the clothes look on me.
5. The style of a coat isn't as important as the thickness.

Notes on Culture

❖ Students may come across references from holy books (Torah, Bible, Koran) in everyday situations; here are a few examples with their meanings, which you can either write on the board or post on the bulletin board. You or they can add to the list:

❖ *Religious references using the possessive:*

Adam's rib – The first woman, Eve, was supposedly made from the rib of the first man, Adam, in the garden of Eden.

Noah's ark – A large boat saved Noah, his family, and pairs of animals from a great flood.

David's reign – A long, peaceful era in Israel under King David

The patience of Job – Job was afflicted with many ills, which he bore patiently.

The courage of Delilah – Delilah cut Sampson's hair while he was sleeping and took away his strength.

The wisdom of Solomon – Two women were fighting over a baby, and Solomon resolved the dispute by saying that the baby should be cut in half.

4c Compound Nouns

Student Books 3 and 3A p. 97

8 Practice

1. sixteen-year-old son **2.** three-week computer course **3.** ten-speed bicycle
4. driver's license **5.** two-door car **6.** five-year-old car **7.** car salesperson
8. five-minute test drive **9.** two thousand-dollar car **10.** five-year loan

9 Practice

1. an alarm clock **2.** a camera case **3.** coat hangers **4.** coffee mugs
5. a computer keyboard **6.** a hair brush **7.** a lamp shade **8.** a neck tie
9. a pencil sharpener **10.** a screw driver **11.** a tea pot **12.** tennis shoes

10 Your Turn

Answers will vary. Sample answers:

baby blanket	computer cable	post office	high-heeled shoe
telephone number	bicycle rider	head hunter	loose-leaf paper
subway station	lunch time		

Compound Noun Activity

❖ Here are more nouns that students might come across in different subject areas. You can write them on the board, and they should go to the board in groups and make as many compound nouns as possible. Or, you can put them on index cards in an envelope, and then in small groups students can manipulate the nouns to make as many compound nouns* as possible

Business	Science	History	Geography
account	animal	agenda	basin
bank	data	campaign	coast
bond	electron	economic	desert
investment	experiment	election	level
issue	laboratory	era	mountain
market	microscope	funds	ocean
report	organism	government	plain
sale	procedure	period	range
stock	report	politics	sea
turn	research	speech	temperature

* Students may have to use an adjective form instead of a noun form for some phrases:
political era instead of ~~politics~~ era
coastal plain instead of ~~coast~~ plain

4d Count Nouns and Noncount Nouns

Student Books 3 and 3A p. 100

11 Practice

1. glasses **2.** an experience **3.** hair **4.** time **5.** experience **6.** a glass/glasses
7. hairs **8.** times **9.** glass

12 Practice

1. much **2.** much **3.** many **4.** much **5.** much **6.** many **7.** much **8.** little **9.** few
10. many

13 Your Turn

Answers will vary. Sample answers:

You: I think we have too many tall buildings in our city.
Your partner: I agree, and I think that there are too few parks and trees.
You: I think there is too much traffic and too much noise.
Your partner: I agree. If we had more cycle paths, more people would ride bicycles to work.
You: Then there would be less traffic and less noise.
Your partner: Yes, and if we had fewer stores, there would be more open space.

Nonsense Activity

- ❖ Tell students to look at the charts in section **4d,** #2 and #3, and make 10 phrases using the nouns in the charts.
- ❖ Then tell them to make 10 "nonsense" phrases using the same nouns. For example, if they wrote *a gold watch,* they could write *a gold nose,* or *chocolate bars* and *chocolate sneakers*
- ❖ Those with the silliest phrases should be encouraged to read them aloud to the class.

4e *Some* and *Any*

Student Books 3 and 3A p. 103

14 Practice

1. any **2.** some **3.** Any **4.** some **5.** any **6.** any

15 Practice

1. some **2.** any **3.** any **4.** some **5.** any **6.** some **7.** some **8.** some
9. some/any

16 Your Turn

Answers will vary. Sample answers:

You:	Can you go to the store for me? I need some eggs and some flour because I want to make pancakes tonight.
Your partner:	Sure! Are there any other things that you need?
You:	Well, I don't have any syrup. Could you get some maple syrup?
Your partner:	Of course, a small bottle? Oh, what kind of maple syrup do you want?
You:	Oh, any kind of maple syrup will do... as long as it's from Canada.
Your partner:	Can you make sausages to go with the pancakes?
You:	Good idea! Get some sausages and some butter, just in case we don't have any.

Guessing Game

❖ Students will play a quick guessing game with the contents of their backpacks or bags. Divide them into small groups, and tell one student to answer while the others ask questions containing plural or nouncount nouns. For example:

> B: Do you have any gum in your backpack?
> A: No, I don't have any.
> C: Do you have any mints?
> A: Yes, I have some.
> D: Do you have any money?
> A: Yes, I have some.
> E: Do you have any credit cards?
> A: No, I don't have any.

❖ Continue until all students have had a turn answering the others' questions.

4f *Much, Many, A Lot Of, A Few, Few, A Little, and Little*

Student Books 3 and 3A p. 106

17 Practice

1. much/a lot of **2.** a lot of **3.** many **4.** much **5.** many **6.** many/a lot of
7. much/a lot of **8.** much

18 Practice

1. a little **2.** few **3.** few **4.** a few **5.** little **6.** a few **7.** a few **8.** a little
9. a few **10.** a little

19 Your Turn

A. Answers will vary. Sample answers:

1. I don't have much time to socialize because I'm working hard to finish my degree this year.
2. I spend too much money on eating out and buying clothes, and then I have to pay too much interest on my credit card.
3. I have too many employees in my company, and I don't have enough money to pay them, but I don't want to lay them off.
4. I have too much furniture and too little space to store other things in my apartment.

B. Answers will vary. Sample answers:

You: I'm having trouble with money. I spend too much, and I charge a lot of things on my credit card.

Your partner: How many credit cards do you have?

You: Three. And I owe a lot of money on all of them.

Your partner: That's a real problem. Can you start spending less?...

Recipe Activity

❖ Tell students to get together in regional groups and think of a typical dish from their part of the world, writing down the basic ingredients.

❖ Then they should meet with another group and ask questions like the following:

A: *Do you need much rice to make sushi?*
B: *No, only a little.*
B: *Do you need many eggs to make a Spanish tortilla?*
A: *No, you need only a few eggs but a lot of potatoes.*

❖ To summarize, the opposite group repeats what they were told about basic ingredients:

A: *So you need only a little rice and a little fish to make sushi.*
B: *Right. And you need a few eggs and a lot of potatoes to make a tortilla.*
A: *You've got it.*

4g *Each, Each (One) Of, Every, Every One Of, Both, Both Of, All, and All Of*

Student Books 3 and 3A p. 110

20 Practice

1. d
2. e
3. b
4. a
5. c

Nouns and Expressions of Quantity

21 Your Turn

Answers will vary. Sample answers:
Both Maria and Marta are wearing red sweaters today.
Each student has his or her grammar book.
Every one of the students is studying grammar now.

· Picture Activity

❖ Cut out pictures with people in them from magazines. Some can have two people, but most should have many. Give one picture to each student and ask them to write five questions about their picture using the words from section **4g**. For example:

Are all the people wearing suits?
What does every student have on his or her feet?
Where are both people standing?

❖ After they finish writing the questions, tell them to exchange pictures and papers with another student. Looking at the new picture, they should write the answers to the questions.

❖ When they finish, they can return the paper to the other student to read and correct.

Review

Student Books 3 and 3A p. 112

1 Review (4a–4b, 4d–4f)

1. was **2.** a few **3.** much **4.** coffee **5.** is, pollution **6.** each **7.** little **8.** much
9. children **10.** some, cacti **11.** makes **12.** any **13.** looks **14.** train stations
15. ideas **16.** Nancy's house **17.** Few **18.** any **19.** much **20.** cause of the accident
21. wives **22.** much **23.** memoranda **24.** some, any **25.** is, a little

2 Review (4a–4b, 4f)

1. bats **2.** feet **3.** creatures **4.** people **5.** theses **6.** titles of the papers **7.** was
8. books **9.** bats **10.** knowledge **11.** experience **12.** facts **13.** people **14.** like
15. people's ideas **16.** are **17.** aren't **18.** animals **19.** is **20.** clean **21.** time
22. cats **23.** species **24.** drink **25.** types **26.** animal **27.** blood **28.** eat
29. fruit **30.** pollen **31.** insects **32.** spiders **33.** animals **34.** bats **35.** insects
36. plants **37.** forests **38.** seeds **39.** nature's friends/friends of nature

3 Review (4a, 4c, 4e–4f)

1. people 2. has 3. have 4. brothers-in-law 5. ice 6. times 7. bags
8. vegetables 9. celery 10. tomatoes 11. rice 12. potatoes 13. starch
14. things 15. has 16. fruit 17. peaches 18. nuts 19. can openers
20. Aren't two can openers 21. pot holders 22. tooth paste 23. has 24. teeth
25. things 26. Time

4 Review (4a, 4c, 4f–4g)

Tina: Guess what? I'm going to explore the Amazon! It doesn't cost ~~many~~ *much* money.

Marie: Really? I know there are a lot of ~~travels~~ *travel* bargains right now, but the Amazon?

Tina: Oh, yes. I've always wanted to go there. How ~~much~~ *many* times have I told you that? All

of ∧ *the* people I know are surprised. I don't know why.

Marie: Only a few ~~person is~~ *people are* that adventurous. Don't forget to pack lots of ~~mosquitos~~ *mosquito* spray.

Tina: Don't worry. The travel agent gave me a few ~~book~~ *books* to read. Each book ~~have~~ *has* a list

of ~~thing~~ *things* to bring.

Marie: Well, I don't have ~~a little~~ *much* to do today. Can I help you buy some ~~equipments~~ *equipment*?

Tina: Sure. I need to buy so ~~much~~ *many* things. I understand there will be a lot of ~~rains~~ *rain*. I'll

need two ~~cameras bags~~ *camera bags* for my two cameras.

Marie: You know, every one of your vacations ~~have~~ *has* been an adventure. I think I've been to

every one of your after-vacation ~~party~~ *parties* and listened to all your ~~story~~ *stories*. You should start

your own tour company and call it "~~The Adventure of Tina.~~ *Tina's Adventures*"

Tina: That's a great idea. All of ∧ *the* people I know would come. They'd give me a lot

of ~~businesses~~ *business*.

Marie: I have a few ~~idea~~ *ideas* of my own. We can be partners. Both ∧ *of* us know a lot about travel.

Tina: Yes! Every one of your ideas ~~are~~ *is* great. How about Brian? Maybe he can give us some

~~offices~~ *office* ~~product~~ *products*. You know, ~~papers~~ *paper*, ~~pen~~ *pens*, and maybe a few ~~computers keyboard~~ *computer keyboards*.

Marie: I don't know. Brian never has any ~~times~~ *time*. He's so busy with all his own ~~works~~ *work*.

Tina: Well, there's too ~~many~~ *much* work for just the two of us, don't you think?

Marie: I don't think so. I have almost a ~~month~~ *month's* vacation coming to me. I can start doing a few ~~thing~~ *things* while you're gone. Maybe I can get some ~~advices~~ *advice* about starting a business. I know a ~~little~~ *few* people who can help us. With a ~~few~~ *little* effort, we'll have our own business!

Writing Expansion

Student Books 3 and 3A p. 116

After writing their essays, students can design a travel brochure in groups. Tell them to organize their descriptions in a logical way, drawing pictures or cutting them out of magazines to illustrate what they have written. After students have finished their brochures, they can share them with the class.

Unit 4 Student Book Self-Test

Student Books 3 and 3A p. 117

A. **1.** B **2.** D **3.** D **4.** A **5.** C **6.** B **7.** D **8.** D **9.** A **10.** A

B. **1.** A **2.** C **3.** A **4.** A **5.** D **6.** C **7.** A **8.** A **9.** C **10.** D

UNIT 5

PRONOUNS AND ARTICLES

Unit 5 reviews the forms and functions of subject and object pronouns and possessive adjectives and pronouns by presenting easily understood charts and a variety of exercises; the exercises, designed to help students identify the correct pronoun in usage, include fill-in-the-blank, underlining, and rewriting activities. Indefinite pronouns and explanations about formal and informal uses of *his/her* and *their* after indefinite pronouns are also presented. Reflexive pronouns are then reviewed followed by helpful exercises, similar to those mentioned above.

Next, *other* as an adjective and as a pronoun is presented with examples that clarify form and function. Finally, the indefinite and definite articles are reviewed in charts with numerous examples that clarify the ambiguities of their use.

The writing activity is a movie review with a suggested topic for each paragraph to help students construct it logically. An expansion activity follows, which further extends their practice of these pronouns and articles.

5a Subject and Object Pronouns; Possessive Adjectives; and Possessive Pronouns

Student Books 3 and 3A p. 120

1 Practice

1. it **2.** it **3.** they **4.** them **5.** She **6.** her **7.** He **8.** him **9.** it/he/she **10.** it/he/she **11.** We **12.** us

2 Practice

1. my **2.** Her **3.** mine **4.** mine **5.** hers **6.** Our **7.** theirs **8.** Their **9.** ours **10.** My **11.** hers **12.** yours

3 Practice

A. 1. your **2.** my **3.** mine **4.** I **5.** yours **6.** me **7.** I **8.** you

B. 1. Our **2.** theirs **3.** Our **4.** theirs **5.** Their **6.** them **7.** they **8.** ours **9.** us **10.** we **11.** us **12.** they **13.** our

C. 1. He **2.** her **3.** Her **4.** she **5.** her **6.** his **7.** hers **8.** her **9.** him **10.** She **11.** His **12.** he **13.** She **14.** it **15.** her **16.** She **17.** them **18.** Her

19. Answers will vary. Sample answer:

...sushi, so he ordered a huge tray of sushi and took it over to Anna's dorm. Her roommate answered the door and invited him in. When he put the tray on the table, Anna's eyes lit up. "Oh George, how did you know that the way to a woman's heart is through her stomach?" George just smiled, and the three of them ate the sushi with gusto. Since then, George has been taking Anna out for sushi every week, and she has never refused a date.

4 Practice

1. *All students* are required to hand in *their assignments* on time. If *students do* not understand the assignment, *they* must ask the instructor for further help. If *students borrow* or *copy* another person's work and *submit* this as *their* work, the instructor may require *them* to withdraw from the course.

2. If my son calls this afternoon, please tell him to call me on my cell phone. I will be unable to speak to any other *callers* unless *their* business is extremely urgent.

3. To play this game, *players* will need to move *their markers* around the board and answer the question in the square *they land* on. If *players do* not know the answer to a question, *they have to go* back to the previous square.

5 Practice

1. their **2.** his or her **3.** they **4.** them **5.** he or she **6.** his or her **7.** they **8.** him or her

❖ Tell students that they are going to practice with the **Indefinite Pronouns** on page 123, #9. Write two example questions and answers like the following on the board to illustrate the assignment:

Questions	**Answers**
Does anyone in the class like spaghetti?	*Everyone does.*
Can anybody in the class dive well?	*No one can.*

❖ Have one student read the first question and another student read the answer. Then do the same with the second question.

❖ Tell the students to think of a similar question. One by one, they can go up to the board and write their question and then call on another student to write an answer to it using an indefinite pronoun. Continue until all students have gone to the board.

5b Reflexive Pronouns

Student Books 3 and 3A p. 128

6 **Practice**

e	1.	a) yourself
g	2.	b) by itself
a	3.	c) themselves
c	4.	d) by himself
d	5.	e) yourselves
b	6.	f) ourselves
f	7.	g) myself

7 **Your Turn**

Answers will vary. Sample answers:
Student A: Do you cut your hair yourself?
Student B: No, I usually go to the hairdresser. Do you fix your car yourself?
Student A: No, I usually take it to the mechanic.

❖ Two very unusual animals are the lemur and the chameleon, both found in Madagascar, which is introduced in section **5e.** Give the students a mini-lecture on this subject, after which you can ask questions like those below to practice reflexive pronouns. You could also write the questions on the board before the lecture. If possible, bring in photos of these animals.

❖ Lemurs are primates (therefore, related to monkeys, apes, and humans) that live in Madagascar and other nearby countries. They have long arms and short legs, which means they are especially good at swinging from tree to tree. They are also quite good at hopping around on the ground. They live in family groups dominated by females, who guard the group, search for food, and choose a mate. The males usually live alone and join the group only during mating season. Lemurs groom themselves—comb each other's hair and remove insects—and carry their babies around on their backs.

Does the male lemur live with the group?   *No, he lives by himself.*
Who guards the females?   *They do it themselves.*
Who carries the females' babies around?   *The females do it themselves.*

❖ Chameleons are lizards that also live in Madagascar. They have eyes that can rotate separately, so one eye can be looking forward and the other eye backward at the same time. They come in many colors: black, blue, brown, green, red, white, and yellow, and can even change colors. Many people believe this change is for protection, but actually it is due to temperature, light, and mood. When chameleons are calm, they are usually green, but when they are angry, they turn yellow. They also have long sticky tongues that they flick out to catch insects.

What is different about chameleons' eyes?   *Each eye can rotate by itself.*
Do chameleons change color to protect   *No, they change colors to show their*
themselves?   *moods.*
How do chameleons feed themselves?   *They flick out their tongues to catch*
                                               insects.

5c *Another, Other, Others, The Other,* and *The Others*

Student Books 3 and 3A p. 130

8 Practice

1. the other   **2.** each other   **3.** each other   **4.** others   **5.** every other   **6.** Another
7. other   **8.** the others   **9.** the other

9 Your Turn

Answers will vary. Sample answers:
1. One man is walking with a cane. Others are standing or sitting.
2. Some of the buildings are large. Others are smaller.
3. One person on the bench to the right is reading. The other seems to be holding a child.
4. Most of the people are sitting down. The others are standing.

❖ You can extend the activity in **Practice 8** and **Your Turn 9** by bringing in pictures and distributing them to pairs of students. There should be several people, animals, or things in each picture so that students can write a short paragraph using definite and indefinite adjectives and pronouns using the chart on page 130, #1 as a guide.

❖ After the students finish writing, have them join another pair and share their sentences, checking them for grammatical accuracy. Alternatively, you could circulate and check the sentences as they finish.

5d The Indefinite Articles A and *An;* One and *Ones*

Student Books 3 and 3A p. 133

10 Practice

1. a/an **2.** a/a **3.** an/a **4.** an/a **5.** a/a **6.** an/a **7.** a/an **8.** an/an

11 Practice

A. 1. a **2.** One **3.** a **4.** ones **5.** a **6.** a **7.** a **8.** a

B. 1. He was a chef. **2.** He made thin ones. **3.** Because a customer complained about the regular, thick ones. **4.** Each person eats seven pounds of potato chips.

12 What Do You Think?

Answers will vary. Sample answers:

Potatoes contain a lot of water. When they are fried in oil, the water evaporates and makes them lighter. That's why it takes four pounds of potatoes to make one pound of potato chips.

13 Practice

1. this one **2.** that one **3.** The one **4.** the white ones **5.** one **6.** one/the other
7. Which ones **8.** The ones **9.** The small ones **10.** ones

14 Your Turn

Answers will vary. Sample answers:
You: I'd like a cake please.
Your partner: What kind?
You: One with chocolate frosting.
Your partner: A big one or a little one?
You: A big one with red roses in the middle.
Your partner: Is this one all right?
You: Yes, I'll take that one.

To give students further practice, you can extend **Your Turn 14** to include more situations. On index cards or slips of paper, write the names of places like the following, along with vocabulary that will help pairs of students make up conversations.

Car showroom: sports car, van, pickup truck, interior/exterior color, price range

Coffee shop: espresso, cappuccino, latte, milk, cream, sugar, artificial sweetener

Clothing store: sweater, pants, jeans, blouse, shirt, jacket, hat, scarf, gloves

Fast-food restaurant: hamburger, cheeseburger, fries, milkshake, soda, ice cream

Pharmacy: aspirin, cold tablets, cough syrup, sleeping pills, allergy tablets

Restaurant: salad, steak, fish, baked potato, vegetables, wine, beer, soda, iced tea

When students finish their dialogue, they can either write it down or say it in front of the class.

5e The Definite Article *The*

Student Books 3 and 3A p. 138

Practice

1. The **2.** the **3.** a **4.** an **5.** a **6.** X **7.** X **8.** X **9.** The **10.** a **11.** the **12.** The **13.** the **14.** the **15.** a **16.** a **17.** X **18.** The **19.** a **20.** the **21.** the **22.** The **23.** a **24.** The **25.** a

Practice

1. an **2.** the **3.** the **4.** the **5.** the **6.** the **7.** X **8.** the **9.** The **10.** a **11.** X **12.** the **13.** X **14.** X **15.** the **16.** X **17.** the **18.** the **19.** the **20.** X **21.** X **22.** X **23.** X **24.** X **25.** the

17 ## What Do You Think?

Answers will vary. Sample answers:

1. Madagascar is unique because of the plants and animals.
2. I'd like to visit the capital, with its narrow streets, and the rainforests. I love old cities, and I love nature.
3. It used to be a French colony.

18 | Your Turn

Answers will vary. Sample answer:
The Dominican Republic is a small tropical island with one large city, Santo Domingo, and several smaller ones. The beaches are beautiful and have large hotels and resorts on them. People can go sailing, swimming, snorkeling, or windsurfing. The principal crop is sugar cane, and one of the products is rum. The island also produces coffee and tropical fruit. The Dominicans like to dance, and there are many restaurants and clubs where people can go to listen to music and dance the merengue.

Country Activity

❖ After the students write a short description of their country in **Your Turn 18,** have them exchange papers with someone from a different country, if possible. That person will read their classmate's description and then write five questions that weren't answered. For example, for the description above, they could write:

> *What language do they speak in the Dominican Republic?*
> *What kind of transportation is there on the island?*
> *Are there any other countries on the island?*
> *What are the names of some of the big hotels?*
> *How do you dance the merengue?*

❖ Point out that students should use the tables on pages 000-000 to make sure that articles are used correctly. When they finish the questions, their partner can write the answers and share them.

 # Review

Student Books 3 and 3A p. 142

1 | Review (5a, 5e)

1. X **2.** X **3.** They **4.** X **5.** the **6.** X **7.** Other **8.** the **9.** X **10.** X **11.** The **12.** the **13.** X **14.** It **15.** the **16.** the **17.** the **18.** The **19.** a **20.** X **21.** X **22.** X **23.** X **24.** X **25.** X/the **26.** X **27.** they **28.** the **29.** the **30.** it **31.** X **32.** Their **33.** the **34.** X **35.** a **36.** they **37.** X **38.** X/their **39.** X **40.** they **41.** their/the **42.** another **43.** the **44.** their **45.** they **46.** X **47.** the

2 | Review (5d, 5e)

1. an **2.** the **3.** the **4.** a **5.** X **6.** the **7.** The **8.** X **9.** X **10.** a **11.** The **12.** a **13.** them **14.** the **15.** a **16.** a **17.** the **18.** a **19.** the **20.** X **21.** X **22.** the **23.** a **24.** The **25.** X **26.** X

3 Review (5a–5b, 5d)

1. you **2.** it **3.** X **4.** it **5.** the **6.** a **7.** myself **8.** us **9.** herself **10.** a
11. them **12.** one **13.** X **14.** hers **15.** a **16.** one **17.** it

4 Review (5a, 5c)

1. other **2.** other **3.** other **4.** other **5.** a **6.** me **7.** me **8.** you **9.** one **10.** it
11. The **12.** Another **13.** him **14.** the

5 Review (5d–5e)

1. The word "Olympic" comes from name of the town Olympia in ~~the~~ Greece where ∧ *the*
first games started.

2. The athletes in the first modern Olympic Games in 1896 were only ~~the~~ men, as in
ancient ~~the~~ Greece. In 1900, ~~the~~ women became eligible to participate in ∧ *the* Games.

3. In 1932, ~~the~~ women could not participate in more than ~~the~~ three events.

4. The five rings on ∧ *the* Olympic flag represent five geographic areas of the world: ~~the~~
Europe, Asia, Africa, ~~the~~ Australia, and the Americas.

5. Muhammad Ali won ~~a~~ *an* Olympic gold medal in boxing in 1960. At the time, he called ~~him~~ *himself*
Cassius Clay. In 1996, he returned to ∧ *the* Olympics and lit ∧ *the* Olympic flame at the opening
ceremony.

6. Before ∧ *the* Olympic Games start, runners carry ∧ *a* torch all the way from Greece to the site
of the games. On ∧ *the* first day, the last runner lights a huge torch. This flame burns until
∧ *the* last day.

7. ∧ *The* Olympic Games have taken place every four years since 1896, except for 1916, 1940,
and 1944, during ∧ *the* two World Wars.

8. ∧ *The* Summer Games were seen on ~~the~~ television for the first time in 1936.

9. In ancient Greece, the prize for the winner was not $\overset{a}{\wedge}$ gold medal. It was $\overset{a}{\wedge}$ branch from

$\overset{an}{\cancel{a}}$ olive tree; however, the winners became very famous and were like celebrities

in $\overset{their}{\wedge}$ hometowns.

Writing Expansion

Student Books 3 and 3A p. 146

Several students may have written about the same movie. Have them get together and discuss their reviews, comparing reactions to the movie. If there is time during the course, these groups of students can bring videos to class and show a few scenes. Then they can lead discussions about the movies with the rest of the class.

Unit 5 Student Book Self-Test

Student Books 3 and 3A p. 147

A. **1.** B   **2.** D   **3.** A   **4.** C   **5.** D   **6.** A   **7.** B   **8.** C   **9.** A   **10.** C

B. **1.** A   **2.** B   **3.** D   **4.** C   **5.** D   **6.** B   **7.** C   **8.** C   **9.** B   **10.** B

UNIT 6

MODALS I

Unit 6 introduces the form and function of modal verbs, beginning with a chart illustrating modals and examples. Modals of ability in the present and past are given in both the *can/could* and *be able to* forms and distinctions among them are made, followed by sentence completion and pair-work exercises.

Then, modals of obligation and necessity in the present and past are given in the *must, have to,* and *have got to* forms, with variations noted. These are followed by exercises designed to illustrate and help students practice the forms.

Next, modals expressing regret or admission of mistakes are given in the *should/not* and *ought/not* forms, with helpful charts to illustrate them.

Finally, the modal of expectation is given in the *supposed to* form with useful exercises to help students practice what they have learned.

The writing activity focuses on mealtime customs, and an expansion activity follows, further extending the students' practice of modals.

6a Introduction to Modal Verbs

Student Books 3 and 3A p. 150

❖ Give students a few quick pronunciation pointers for models:

can /kən/ vs. can't /kænt/

I can /kən/ run one mile, but I can't /kænt/ run 10 miles.

The vowel sound in *can* and *can't* is different. The positive is shorter and unstressed, and the negative is longer and stressed. In short answers, however, the vowel in *can* is longer and stressed.

could /kʊd/   should /šʊd/   would /wʊd/

Remember that the *l* in these words is silent.

Aliana could spell her name when she was three.
Marcus should call when he's going to be late.
Gerry would like us to come to dinner tonight.

6b *Can, Could,* and *Be Able To* to Express Ability

Student Books 3 and 3A p. 151

1 Practice

1. wasn't able to swim   **2.** 'm not able to make   **3.** won't be able to attend
4. is able to use   **5.** weren't able to reach   **6.** isn't able to drive
7. Are/Were you able to take   **8.** won't be able to get

2 Practice

1. can't smell   **2.** aren't able to/can't detect   **3.** can help   **4.** can affect
5. are able to get   **6.** will be able to deliver   **7.** 'll be able to smell   **8.** can

3 Your Turn

Answers will vary. Sample answers:

Your partner: Can you ski?
You: No, but it is a sport that you can do in the winter.
Your partner: Can you play hockey?
You: No. It's not a team sport.
Your partner: Can you skate?
You: Yes. But it's a special kind of skating.
Your partner: Can you figure skate?
You: Yes, I can. That's the answer.

❖ To practice the modals in this section, put a contrasting chart like the following on the board and ask students to fill it in with types of exercise or other categories, such as sports. The idea is to represent what students could or could not do 10 years ago and what they can or can't do now:

10 Years Ago	Now
do 20 sit-ups	do 50 sit-ups
run a mile	run two miles
lift 100 pounds	lift 100 pounds
swim four laps	swim eight laps

❖ Either tell students to take turns saying sentences to each other in pairs, or you can go around the classroom and have each student say a sentence in turn. For example:

Ten years ago, I could do 20 sit-ups, but now I can do 50 sit-ups.
Ten years ago, I wasn't able to run a mile, but now I can run two miles.
Ten years ago, I couldn't lift 100 pounds, and I still can't lift 100 pounds.
Ten years ago, I was able to swim four laps, but now I'm able to swim eight laps.

6c *Must, Have To,* and *Have Got To* to Express Obligation and Necessity

Student Books 3 and 3A p. 154

4 Practice

1. You must sit in your assigned seat. OR You have to sit in your assigned seat.
2. You must fasten your seatbelt when the seatbelt sign is on. OR You have to fasten your seatbelt when the seatbelt sign is on.
3. You must stay seated when the seatbelt sign is on. OR You have to stay seated when the seatbelt sign is on.
4. You must turn off your cell phone. OR You have to turn off your cell phone.
5. You must talk quietly—if at all. OR You have to talk quietly—if at all.
6. You must buy your food or drinks at the theater. OR You have to buy your food or drinks at the theater.
7. You must buy a ticket. OR You have to buy a ticket.
8. You must respect the animals. OR You have to respect the animals.
9. You must put your litter into a proper container. OR You have to put your litter into a proper container.

5 Practice

Answers will vary. Sample answers:
1. must **2.** must **3.** have to **4.** have to **5.** have to **6.** have to **7.** have to
8. must **9.** have to **10.** must

6 Your Turn

Answers will vary. Sample answers:

You:	Do I have to pay the fees before I start the class?
Your partner:	Yes, you have to pay them when you register for the class.
You:	Do I have to type the first draft of my assignments?
Your partner:	Yes, you have to type all drafts of the assignments.

Rules Activity

❖ To expand the dialogue in **Your Turn 6,** write the names of other places in and around the school on the board or a flip chart; in small groups, students should make up a few rules for these places. Here are some examples of places you can list with sample rules:

Dormitory:	*You mustn't make noise after midnight.*
Cafeteria:	*You have to pay for the food before you sit down and eat.*
Library:	*You have to pay a fine if your book is overdue.*
Football field:	*You mustn't throw anything onto the field during a game.*
Basketball court:	*You have to wear sneakers on the court.*
Ice rink:	*You mustn't play hockey when the rink is open to the public.*

❖ When the students are finished making up the rules, have them read them aloud to the rest of the class.

6d *Not Have To* and *Must Not* to Express Lack of Necessity and Prohibition

Student Books 3 and 3A p. 157

7 Practice

1.	must	museum, theater, zoo
2.	don't have to	hotel, museum, theater, zoo
3.	don't have to	hotel, restaurant
4.	must	theater
5.	must	hotel
6.	must	airport
7.	must	airplane, theater
8.	must	museum, zoo

8 Practice

1. don't have to wear **2.** had to keep **3.** has to wear **4.** doesn't have to keep
5. must/have to clear **6.** mustn't put **7.** mustn't be **8.** mustn't be **9.** had to get
10. must/have to tell **11.** have to go

9 Your Turn

Answers will vary. Sample answers:

You: At my old job, we didn't have to come in at any specific time. We chose our own hours. But in my new job, we mustn't ever be late or we'll get in trouble.

Your partner: We don't have to come at a specific time either, but we have to work eight hours each day. So we can come in at 8:00 and leave at 4:00, or come in at 10:00 and leave at 6:00. It helps us avoid the rush-hour traffic and be with our families when we want to.

Comparison Activity 2

❖ Continue with comparisons and ask the students to talk about the differences between weekdays and weekends. For example:

> get up early - *On weekdays, I have to get up early, but on weekends I don't.*
> follow a schedule - *On weekends I don't have to follow a schedule, but on weekdays, I do.*
> eat lunch at school/work -
> do homework -
> go to bed early -

❖ Have them say the sentences to each other in pairs.

6e *Should, Ought To,* and *Had Better* to Give Advice

Student Books 3 and 3A p. 159

10 Practice

A. Reading

B. Answers will vary. Sample answers:
   1. She should talk to her supervisor about her workload.
   2. She ought to ask about getting a larger cubicle.
   3. She should get an extra table or bookcase for her papers and files.
   4. She shouldn't suffer in silence.
   5. She should ask her supervisor to turn the heat down.
   6. She should ask if she could eat lunch with her coworkers.

C. Answers will vary. Sample answers:
   Friend: I think you should talk to your supervisor about your workload.
   Lara: I've tried that. She said that she couldn't change it.
   Friend: How about asking for a larger cubicle?
   Lara: That's a good idea. Maybe she'll give me one.

Friend: Talk to her about the heat, too. It's not healthy to work in a hot place.
Lara: I hadn't thought of that.
Friend: About your coworkers—maybe you could make some cookies and bring them in.
Lara: That might work; maybe I'll try that tomorrow.

11 Your Turn

Answers will vary. Sample answers:
You: I don't have anyone to speak English with. What should I do?
Your partner: You should find an English-speaking key pal on the Internet.
You: I don't like the food in the cafeteria. What should I do?
Your partner: You should move to an apartment next semester and cook your own food.
You: My roommate talks on the phone late at night. What should I do?
Your partner: You should ask her to stop talking at midnight and let you sleep.

Problem Activity 1

❖ A variation on **Your Turn 11** is to pass out slips of paper and ask students to write a problem on one side.

❖ Collect the slips and distribute them to students again, making sure no student receives the problem they wrote. Instruct them to read the problems and write a sentence giving advice.

❖ When they finish, have students take turns reading the problems and advice aloud to the rest of the class.

6f *Should Have* and *Ought to Have* to Express Regret or a Mistake

Student Books 3 and 3A p. 161

12 Practice

A. Reading

B. Answers will vary. Sample answers:
  1. They should have booked the trip with a travel company that they knew about.
  2. They should have confirmed their flight ahead of time.
  3. They should have looked up the hotel on the Internet to see where it was.
  4. They should have taken Spanish lessons before going to Spain.
  5. Julia shouldn't have left the phrasebook at the hotel.
  6. They should have asked for a waiter that could speak English.
  7. Gary should have taken his camera and cell phone with him.
  8. They should have complained to the travel agency and reported them to the Better Business Bureau.

13 | **Your Turn**

Answers will vary. Sample answers:

You: I failed my math exam. What should I have done?
Your partner: You should have studied harder. You shouldn't have spent so much time
                watching TV.
You: I spent too much money on my credit card. What should I have done?
Your partner: You should have paid in cash. You shouldn't have bought so many clothes.
You: I got a low score on the TOEFL. What should I have done?
Your partner: You should have taken a TOEFL prep course. You shouldn't have tried to
                study by yourself.

Problem Activity 2

❖ In this activity, instead of having students think of problems, make some up for them
using students' names and writing them on slips of paper. They can be silly or serious;
for example:

Joan colored her hair, and it turned purple. What should she have done?
Misha was playing football, and he made a goal for the other team.
Latoya was driving on the freeway, and she ran out of gas.
Roberto was in a hurry, and he locked his keys in the car.

❖ Give the problems out to different students and after they think of a sentence with
should have, have them read the sentence aloud to the rest of the class.

6g *Be Supposed To* to Express Expectation

Student Books 3 and 3A p. 164

14 | **Practice**

1. d/was supposed to go   **2.** c/Aren't you supposed to be   **3.** d/were supposed to visit
4. e/'m not supposed to tell   **5.** a/'re supposed to take off
6. e/'re not (aren't) supposed to drive   **7.** b/is supposed to tell
8. a/Am I supposed to put

15 | **Your Turn**

Answers will vary. Sample answers:
Putting cold water on a burn is supposed to help it. You're not supposed to put butter on it.
You're supposed to stay home if you have a cold.
You're supposed to take a pain killer if you have a headache. You're not supposed to exercise.
You're not supposed to stay out in the sun if you have a sunburn. It will only get worse.

❖ Bring a newspaper to class and cut out headlines that can be altered to create a sentence with *be supposed to*. Tell students to incorporate the headlines into their sentences; for example:

Headline	**Sentence**
President goes to Camp David	*The president was supposed to go to China, but he went to Camp David instead.*
Stocks plunge on Wall St.	*Stocks were supposed to stay up, but they went down.*
Lawmakers pass tax hike	*Lawmakers weren't supposed to raise taxes, but they did.*

❖ When they finish, have students share their sentences in small groups or write them on the board, and tape the headline above each sentence so students can circulate and read them.

Review

Student Books 3 and 3A p. 166

 Review (6b–6c, 6e, 6g)

1. can   **2.** be able to   **3.** should   **4.** had better   **5.** don't have to   **6.** must   **7.** should
8. don't have to   **9.** aren't supposed   **10.** you've got to   **11.** must   **12.** may not
13. ought to   **14.** should   **15.** might   **16.** had better   **17.** supposed to   **18.** shouldn't
19. must   **20.** shouldn't have   **21.** ought to   **22.** are supposed   **23.** must

 Review (6b–6c, 6e)

1. had to go   **2.** was supposed to go   **3.** had to take   **4.** should have called/ought to have called   **5.** could have taken   **6.** should learn/ought to learn/had better learn
7. can't help   **8.** shouldn't feel   **9.** can   **10.** can you do   **11.** must get/may get/can get/'ll be able to get   **12.** must hurry/have to hurry/should hurry   **13.** can you drive
14. should never have thrown   **15.** could use   **16.** you should always keep/must always keep/ought to always keep   **17.** can drive   **18.** you mustn't go/had better not go
19. should call/ought to call   **20.** can stop/could stop   **21.** was supposed to meet/should have met   **22.** should hurry/ought to hurry/had better hurry/have to hurry

3 **Review (6b–6c, 6e–6f)**

1. Can you find   **2.** have to go/'m supposed go   **3.** don't have to help   **4.** have to know/'m supposed to know   **5.** 'd better leave/should leave/ought to leave   **6.** was supposed to stay   **7.** 'll be able to go/can go   **8.** was supposed to take   **9.** should I do/am I supposed to do   **10.** never should have taken   **11.** should never have gone   **12.** may never have seen/might never have seen   **13.** never should have tried out   **14.** should have known/ought to have known   **15.** could   **16.** should do/ought to do/have to do
17. can come/may be able to come/might be able to come   **18.** should never have agreed

19. should stay/ought to stay/had better stay   **20.** shouldn't cancel/don't have to cancel
21. Have to go/had better go

4 Review (6b)

Do you love to paint? ~~Ought~~ *Should* you have gone to art school? Maybe you didn't have the

opportunity. You ~~should~~ *might* think it's too late for you to start now, but that's not true.

You ~~have to~~ *should* never think it's too late to do something that you love. You don't ~~must~~ *have to* spend

a lot of money, either. And after you finish our six-week course, you'll ~~can~~ *be able to* say that you're

an artist. You ~~cannot~~ *won't be able to* produce masterpieces for a while, but you'll be proud of your work.

Our lessons teach the techniques of watercolor painting. Do you think you can't ~~not~~

do it? Well, ~~may you~~ *can you/are you able to* draw a picture? ~~Might you~~ *Can you/are you able to* brush paper with water? Then you

~~must~~ *can* paint with watercolors. Call us for a free brochure.

Writing Expansion

Student Books 3 and 3A p. 170

Before the students make notes, divide them into groups by country or region (as closely as possible) to discuss mealtime customs. After they finish their essays, have each group give a presentation about mealtime customs to the class. To enhance their presentations, students can bring in special utensils, tableware, or even some food if they are able. The other students should ask questions at the end of each presentation.

◆ Unit 6 Student Book Self-Test

Student Books 3 and 3A p. 171

A. **1.** A **2.** B **3.** C **4.** A **5.** B **6.** C **7.** D **8.** B **9.** A **10.** A

B. **1.** A **2.** D **3.** A **4.** D **5.** D **6.** A **7.** B **8.** A **9.** C **10.** B

UNIT 7

MODALS II

Unit 7 begins with the forms and functions of modals used to give suggestions through responses of agreement and disagreement in statements, negatives, questions, and short answers. These explanations are illustrated by activities that give students the opportunity to put concepts into practice.

The next section presents modals used to express preference, followed by those used to ask permission and express ability. These sections have useful exercises that enable students to see how these auxiliaries are used in different contexts.

Modals for making both polite and informal requests are then reviewed and accompanied, again, by useful practices and activities. Next, modals for expressing possibility are explained in present, past and future, with a reading about Agatha Christie adding interest to the exercises.

Modals for expressing probability and making deductions come next, with an interesting reading about the statues on Easter Island.

Finally, the forms and functions of the progressive and perfect progressive forms of modals are laid out in helpful charts and augmented by exercises designed to clarify their meanings.

The writing activity presents a business letter of complaint that students analyze and follow in order to learn the correct format and practice of modals.

7a *Shall, Let's, How About, What About, Why Don't, Could, and Can* to Make Suggestions
Student Books 3 and 3A p. 174

1 Practice

1. Shall   **2.** How about   **3.** Shall/Why don't   **4.** could/can   **5.** could/can   **6.** Why don't

2 Your Turn

Answers will vary. Sample answers:

You: Let's go bowling on Saturday.
Your partner: Hmm. The bowling alley is always so crowded on Saturdays. How about going dancing?
You: We went dancing last week. Maybe we could do something at the Culture Center.
Your partner: That's a good idea. Shall we try to get tickets for the ballet?
You: Ugh, I hate the ballet. How about going to a baseball game?
Your partner: I think the Red Sox are playing out of town this weekend.
You: Oh, then let's go to a concert on the Esplanade.
Your partner: I think it's going to rain. Maybe we could go to Laura's party.
You: That's a great idea! Shall I pick you up at eight?
Your partner: I can pick *you* up. You drove last time.

Social Activity

❖ Divide the students into small groups of about four each and tell them they are going to plan a social activity for the class. They should use the modals from the first section to make suggestions.

❖ Give them a five-minute time limit and tell them they have to come up with an activity and a day that all members of their group agree on.

- ❖ You can circulate and listen to what the students are saying. When time is up, ask each group to report on the day and type of activity they have chosen.
- ❖ To carry this one step further, you can ask for one volunteer from each group to get together in another group and, in front of the class, try to agree upon an activity from among those they have chosen.

7b *Prefer, Would Prefer,* and *Would Rather* to Express Preference

Student Books 3 and 3A p. 176

3 Practice

Answers will vary. Sample answers:
1. Bob prefers fish to tofu.
2. He would rather play tennis than listen to classical music.
3. He would prefer listening to rock music more than classical music.
4. He prefers playing chess to playing scrabble.
5. He would rather eat out than at home.
6. He would prefer sending email messages to writing letters.
7. He prefers fish and meat to tofu.
8. He would rather play tennis than go jogging.
9. He would prefer having someone cook for him to cooking for himself.
10. He prefers sending e-mail messages to writing letters.

4 Your Turn

Answers will vary. Sample answers:

A.

You:	Do you prefer jogging to tennis?
Your partner:	No, I don't. I like tennis because it is more competitive.
You:	Do you like eating out?
Your partner:	Yes. I would rather eat out than eat at home. It's less work.
You:	Do you prefer tofu to meat?
Your partner:	Yes, I'm a vegetarian so I don't eat meat.
You:	Would you prefer to go to a rock concert or a classical music concert?
Your partner:	I'd prefer to go to a rock concert because it's more exciting.

B. He prefers jogging to tennis because he's not very competitive.
He prefers tofu because he's a vegetarian.
He would rather listen to rock music because it's more exciting.

❖ To expand on the questionnaire activity in **Your Turn 4,** as one student is telling the class about his or her partner, have the next pair compare the preferences being presented with their own. You can put the expressions *Me too, Me neither,* and *Not me* on the board. These expressions are used in informal spoken English.

❖ If a student says, *He prefers jogging to tennis; he's not very competitive,* the next student can say *Me too* if he or she agrees with the statement. Or, if a student says, *She doesn't like fish,* the next student can say, *Me neither.* Students can also say *Not me; I like tennis because I'm competitive,* or *Not me; I like fish because it's good for your health.*

❖ You can continue this activity until all the students have had a chance to comment on another student's preferences.

7c *May, Could,* and *Can* to Ask Permission

Student Books 3 and 3A p. 180

5 Practice

1. can/ability   **2.** can't/permission   **3.** can/permission   **4.** can't/ability
5. can/ability (or permission)   **6.** can't/permission   **7.** can't/ability   **8.** can/permission

6 Practice

A. 1. Could/May Certainly. That's fine.   **2.** Could/May Of course.   **3.** Could/Can Sure! Right away.   **4.** Could Of course. What time should she be there?   **5.** May/Could I'm sorry, but the date can't be changed.   **6.** Could/Can/Would Certainly not! I've already given you your allowance for this week!   **7.** Would No. It's getting cold in here.

B. 1. formal   **2.** formal   **3.** informal   **4.** formal   **5.** formal   **6.** informal   **7.** informal

7 Your Turn

Answers will vary. Sample answers:

One passenger on a train to another
Passenger 1:   May I close the window? It's cold in here.
Passenger 2:   Sure. That's fine. OR I'd rather you didn't.

Husband to wife
Husband: Would you mind if I bought a Porsche?
Wife: I'd rather you didn't. Our Subaru is only five years old.

❖ Write the following role-play situations on index cards or on slips of paper. After students finish **Your Turn 7,** put them in pairs. For variety, pair students who don't usually talk with each other.

❖ *Role-Plays*

Customer to salesperson in store:	Ask if you can try on some clothing.
Brother to sister in car:	Ask if you can listen to a CD.
Friend 1 to friend 2 in workplace:	Ask if you can borrow some money.
Student to staff person in office:	Ask if you can use the office phone.
Student to professor in classroom:	Ask if you can take the exam before the scheduled date.
Children to parents at home:	Ask if you can stay up late to watch TV.
Customer to travel agent in office:	Ask if you can buy a discounted ticket.

❖ Call on pairs randomly and give them a card or a slip; they should be able to do a short impromptu dialogue in front of the class.

7d *Will, Can, Could, Would,* and *Would You Mind* to Make Requests

Student Books 3 and 3A p. 184

8 Practice

Answers will vary. Sample answers:

1. Request A: Would you mind opening the window?
   Reply: I'd be happy to.
   Request B: Could you turn down the heat?
   Reply: Sure. No problem.
   Request C: Would you open the door?
   Reply: I'd be glad to.
2. Request A: I left my train pass at home. Could you let me ride without it for today?
   Reply: Sorry, I can't.
   Request B: Can I pay for a one-way ticket and go both ways?
   Reply: I'm not sure I can do that. I won't be working later today.
   Request C: Could I give you my ID until tomorrow? Then I'll bring my train pass.
   Reply: Well, maybe just this once.
3. Request A: Can you finish your dinner first?
   Reply: I'm not very hungry. But I'll eat a few more bites.
   Request B: Would you clean up your room a bit before you go?
   Reply: OK, but just for five minutes.
   Request C: Could you take your books and do your homework while you're there?
   Reply: Sure. That's why I'm going to Nancy's house.

9 | Your Turn

I was at the copy shop, and I didn't know how to work the machine. I asked the clerk, "Could you show me how to work this machine?" She said, "Sure."

I was at the coffee shop, and I ordered a drink. I said, "Could you give me a large iced coffee with whipped cream?" And he said, "Sure. That'll be $2.50."

Dialogue Activity

❖ After students tell their partners about three requests they have made recently, they should write them down.

❖ When they finish writing, have the students exchange papers with their partners and check each other's papers.

❖ Then, call on one or two students to read their requests aloud to the class.

 ## 7e *May, Might,* and *Could* to Express Possibility
Student Books 3 and 3A p. 187

10 | Practice

Answers will vary. Sample answers:

A. Reading

B. 1. She might have been so sad that she needed to be alone for a while.
  2. She may have lost her memory and thought the hotel was a safe place to be.
  3. She could have forgotten her real name and chosen another one.
  4. She may not have wanted anyone to find her.
  5. They might have checked in all the hotels in the area.
  6. She could have wanted to forget about it.

11 | Your Turn

Answers will vary. Sample answers:

He could have had a dental appointment. He might have been sick, or he could have had a personal appointment of some kind. He may have overslept. He might have wanted to take a day off, or he could have had an accident. I hope not!

❖ Write these facts about Agatha Christie on the board. Then, have students use the facts to write sentences with *may, might,* or *could.*

> At the hotel, Agatha Christie used the name of the woman whom her husband had fallen in love with.
>
> Later, she traveled around the Middle East and wrote in her books about some of the places she visited.
>
> While she was there, she met a young archaeologist and they fell in love.
>
> They got married and had a long and happy life together, making many trips to the Middle East.
>
> After writing more than 50 books, she was given a title of honor by the queen: Dame Agatha Christie.

❖ Have the students read the sentences on the board, correcting any mistakes.

7f *Should* and *Ought To* to Express Probability

Student Books 3 and 3A p. 192

12 Practice

1. Jim should/ought to be at the office by now.
2. He should/ought to have replied to it by now.
3. He should have/ought to have finished it before going home.
4. He shouldn't feel tired by noon.
5. He shouldn't have to borrow money.
6. He should/ought to get a high grade.
7. It shouldn't need repairs yet.
8. He should/ought to be in good physical shape.
9. He should/ought to get an interview soon.
10. He should/ought to get the new job.
11. ...he should/ought to earn a higher salary.

13 Your Turn

Answers will vary. Sample answers:
I should get into a good university because I studied hard for the exams.
I'm a really good soccer player, so I should be able to get on the school team.
I should graduate in four years because I am a good student.
I ought to make it to a professional team after college because I will work very hard.

❖ Bring in headlines from newspapers to help students practice the modals *should* or *shouldn't* and *ought to* or *ought not to*. Here are a few examples you can write on the board before you hand out the headlines:

Fuel Prices Rise	*The government ought to try to lower them.*
President Speaks to Public	*He shouldn't lower taxes.*
Scientist Wins Nobel Prize	*She should continue working on her discovery.*
Fires Continue to Burn	*They shouldn't allow them to burn.*

❖ Either give the students one page of the newspaper and have them choose a few headlines themselves, or hand out an envelope with several cut-out headlines in it. Ask students to each write one headline and sentence on the board.

7g *Must, Must Not,* and *Can't* to Make Deductions

Student Books 3 and 3A p. 194

14 Practice

1. must 2. must 3. must 4. can't 5. must 6. can't 7. can't 8. must

15 Practice

1. must have died 2. must have been 3. can't have gone 4. can't have had 5. must have worked 6. must have worked 7. must have been 8. can't have been

16 Practice

A. Reading

B. Answers will vary. Possible answers:
1. They can't have used machines.
2. They must not have had time to take them to their final destination. They can't have just left them there.
3. They must have represented gods and goddesses.
4. They can't have carved them afterwards if some carved ones are still at the quarry.
5. They can't have carved them just for fun.
6. They must have been killed by a disease.
7. They must not have known how to read and write.
8. They must have collected evidence on the island. They can't have made it up.

17 **Your Turn**

Answers will vary. Sample answers:

She might have had an accident.

He must not be able to telephone.

She might have lost her memory.

He must not be able to call the school.

She could have gotten caught in traffic.

He can't have forgotten it was Monday.

She must be in some kind of trouble.

Picture Activity

❖ You can use the same newspapers that you used in the above activity for this one. Show a picture to the class and write a sentence with *must, must not,* or *can't* on the board as an example. For instance, if there is a picture of a family, you can write:

The family must be looking for a new house.
The family must have found a new house.
The family can't have paid too much for their house.

❖ You can either give the students one page of the newspaper and have them choose a few pictures, or hand out an envelope with several cut-out pictures in it. Working in small groups, have each student write a different sentence about their group's picture.

7h The Progressive and Perfect Progressive Forms of Modals

Student Books 3 and 3A p. 198

18 **Practice**

1. could be waiting
2. must be raining
3. may/might/could have been working
4. must have been reading
5. must have been drinking
6. must be coming
7. might/may/could be coming
8. may/might/could be studying
9. might be getting off
10. must be feeling

19 **Practice**

1. They must have been having an argument.
2. A new neighbor may/might/could/must have been moving in.
3. They may/might/could be expecting a lot of guests.
4. The neighbors may/might/could/must be having a party.

5. They must be cooking on the grill.
6. They may/might/could/must have been planning the party for some time.
7. They may/might/could/must be celebrating a birthday.
8. They must be playing music too loud to hear anything.

20 Your Turn

Answers will vary. Sample answers:
They must be having a party.
They might be celebrating a student's birthday.
They may be showing dances from different countries.
They could be having a cultural demonstration.

Repeat Activity

 Divide students into groups of three. Tell them to repeat **Practice 19,** this time adding a sentence about what the people should have done. For example:

Student 1:	*I heard a man and woman shouting at each other.*
Student 2:	*They must have been having an argument.*
Student 3:	*They shouldn't have shouted so loudly.*
Student 1:	*I heard loud noises coming from the stairs yesterday.*
Student 2:	*Our neighbors may have been moving in.*
Student 3:	*They should have tried to be quieter.*

 You can circulate in case students need help with the sentences.

◆ Review

Student Books 3 and 3A p. 203

1 Review (7b, 7d–7f)

1. may/might/could **2.** could/may/might **3.** would you mind **4.** may not
5. could/might **6.** could/may/might **7.** would prefer **8.** can **9.** may/might/should
10. can/could/shall/should **11.** can/could/may/shall/should **12.** could/may/might
13. couldn't **14.** should **15.** would you mind **16.** must/might/could/may
17. could/may/might **18.** ought to

2 Review (7e, 7g)

1. may **2.** might **3.** might **4.** could **5.** must **6.** prefer **7.** could **8.** may **9.** Could
10. must **11.** might **12.** could **13.** must **14.** can **15.** might **16.** ought to

3 Review (7a–7e)

1. Could/May **2.** may not **3.** couldn't have **4.** should have **5.** must **6.** can't
7. Could/Will **8.** Why don't **9.** Let's not **10.** prefer **11.** could have **12.** rather not
13. could have **14.** Maybe **15.** Would you mind **16.** Could/Will

4 Review (7e–7h)

Brenda: Good morning, Neil. How ~~is~~ about getting a cup of coffee?

Neil: Sorry, I ~~can~~ *can't*. I'm late for a meeting with Foster.

Brenda: Then you'll be happy to hear that Foster isn't in the office today. He ~~can't~~ *may/might/must* be out sick.

Neil: But that can't ~~not~~ be true! I thought I saw him coming into the building an hour ago.
I ~~musn't be~~ *must have been* mistaken.

Brenda: Well, that's lucky for you. Now, I'm going to get some coffee. Can I bring you some?

Neil: Actually, I ~~would rather~~ *'d rather have/prefer* tea.

Brenda: Fine. By the way, has David left for Djakarta yet?

Neil: Yes, he's on the way. He ~~would~~ *should* be there in three hours. No, wait. I forgot about the
time difference. Actually, his plane ought to ~~land~~ *have landed* an hour ago.

Brenda: He ~~can~~ *must* know Djakarta very well by now. He's been there at least a dozen times.

Neil: Yes, he has. Oh, that reminds me. I ~~should~~ *may/might* be going to Mexico City next week. It isn't
certain yet, but ~~may~~ *can/could/will* you check on flight times for me this morning?

Brenda: ~~No.~~ *Sorry, I can't.*

Neil: Oh, no problem. I ~~can~~ *may/might/should* have some time to do it myself this afternoon. By the way, does
everyone know that we're having a group meeting at 3:00 today?

Brenda: I think most people know, although a few ~~could~~ *may/might* not have heard about it yet.

Neil: Then ~~how~~ *why* don't we make an announcement? I'll write it down and give it to Betty.

Brenda: Good idea, but I think Betty ~~should~~ *may/might* have already gone to lunch.

Neil: Lunch! It's 10:00 in the morning! She ~~may~~ *can't* be at lunch!

Brenda: Oh, you're right. It's been such a busy morning that it feels like I've been here
four hours!

Writing Expansion

Student Books 3 and 3A p. 207

After the students write and revise their letters, collect them and then give them out to different students. Tell them to write a response using a business letter format, again typing them on a computer. When they have written and revised the response letters, they should give them back to the original writers.

Unit 7 Student Book Self-Test

Student Books 3 and 3A p. 208

A. **1.** C **2.** A **3.** B **4.** A **5.** D **6.** B **7.** A **8.** C **9.** C **10.** C

B. **1.** A **2.** D **3.** D **4.** C **5.** A **6.** C **7.** B **8.** A **9.** B **10.** C

THE PASSIVE VOICE, CAUSATIVES, AND PHRASAL VERBS

Unit 8 begins with an overview of the passive voice in different tenses, including *yes/no* and *wh*-questions. The difference between transitive and intransitive verbs, as well as between active and stative verbs, is explained, and the different forms and functions are illustrated through re-writing exercises.

Next, the forms of the passive in modals and modal phrases are laid out in charts that clarify different tenses. The functions are explained through examples that students will find helpful in doing the fill-in-the-blank and re-writing exercises.

Then, structures that use the passive *it* + verb + *that* clause are taught with copious explanations and examples. An explanation of present and past participles as adjectives follows, and any confusion that students may have with these forms is cleared up through explanations and practices.

The causative structures with *have, get,* and *make* are taught next in both active and passive with interesting exercises. Finally, the forms and functions of separable and inseparable phrasal verbs are reviewed, followed by a related structure: prepositions with verbs, adjectives, and nouns. Helpful charts in both sections enable students to see and understand how all are used, and exercises help them practice the forms.

The writing activity is a cover letter that would accompany a résumé in the job application process, which students follow in order to learn the format and practice the forms of the verbs taught in this unit.

8a The Passive Voice: Overview

Student Book 3 p. 212, Student Book 3B p. 2

1 Practice

1. Coffee isn't grown in Italy. It is grown in Brazil.
2. The telephone wasn't invented by Picasso. It was invented by Alexander Graham Bell.
3. True
4. True
5. The summit of Mount Everest wasn't reached by Marco Polo. It was reached by Edmund Hillary and Tenzing Norgay.
6. The world's first Olympic Games weren't held in France. They were held in Greece.
7. Blood pressure isn't measured on the Richter scale. Earthquakes are measured on the Richter scale.
8. True
9. Sugar isn't needed for strong bones. Calcium is needed for strong bones.
10. Data on a computer isn't stored on plates. Data on a computer is stored on disks.

2 Practice

1. A movie star has been questioned in a murder case. OR A movie star was questioned in a murder case.
2. Higher wages have been demanded by teachers. OR Higher wages were demanded by teachers.
3. Twelve people have been injured in Friday's earthquake. OR Twelve people were injured in Friday's earthquake.
4. A plane has been captured by hijackers. OR A plane was captured by hijackers.
5. The airport has been closed, and all flights have been cancelled. OR The airport was closed, and all flights were cancelled.
6. Ten people have been hospitalized after a gas explosion. OR Ten people were hospitalized after a gas explosion.

3 Practice

1. Many towns in the north have been cut off by snowstorms. The main highway to the north has been blocked by snow. The road cannot be cleared because the snow is still coming down heavily.

2. A total of two million dollars has been stolen from the National Bank in New York City. Two guards were/have been taken to the hospital. Two men have been/were arrested in connection with the robbery. Another man is being questioned.

3. Two teenage boys were found in a small boat far offshore yesterday by the Coast Guard. The boys and the boat had been missing since last Friday. The two boys were alive but weak. They were taken to the hospital. They are expected to recover soon.

4. Two men are being sought in connection with a robbery at a gas station. The cashier was held up, but he was not injured. While the money was being stolen, the cashier was tied up. A black truck was used to escape, and police think that the truck was used in other robberies in the same area.

---

4 | Your Turn

Answers will vary. Sample answers:

Local Student Chosen for Big Scholarship	A local student was chosen for a big scholarship.
Stock Market Hit by High Interest Rates	The stock market has been hit by high interest rates.
Bank Robber Found	The bank robber has been found.
Cost of Living Down	The cost of living has gone down.

Headline Activity

❖ Bring a newspaper to class and give a page to each pair or small group of students. Ask them to cut out at least five headlines and tape them to the board or wall.

❖ Tell them to write complete sentences from the headlines—in the passive voice if possible—on the board or a big piece of paper that you can tape to the wall.

❖ Tell the students to go around the room and read the headlines that the other groups have written, correcting any mistakes they find.

8b The Passive Voice of Modals and Modal Phrases

Student Book 3 p. 219, Student Book 3B p. 9

5 | Practice

1. can be used 2. may have been mistreated 3. may have been shot 4. may have been forced 5. can be done 6. can more elephants be saved 7. will be moved 8. can be preserved 9. will be established 10. should have been done 11. must not be allowed

6 Your Turn

Answers will vary. Sample answer:
In the past, wolves were found in all of North America, but now, there are very few left.
Although they only attack cattle when they cannot find other food, hunters shoot them.
Now they are an endangered species in the United States and other countries.
Organizations that protect wolves should be supported so that their numbers grow again.

Animal Activity

❖ Tell students about endangered animal species and ask if they know of any in their regions of the world. If they do not, here are a few examples:

Africa	African wild ass, golden bamboo lemur, riverine rabbit
Australia	northern hairy-nosed wombat
Central America	gulf porpoise
China	Yangtze river dolphin, giant panda, dwarf blue sheep
Europe	Iberian lynx, Mediterranean monk seal
India	Assam rabbit, Malabar large spotted civet
Middle East	Arabian oryx
North America	Vancouver Island marmot, gray wolf, red wolf
South America	yellow-tailed woolly monkey, black-faced lion tamarin, muriqui
Southeast Asia	Javan and Sumatran rhinos, Visayan spotted deer, dwarf water buffalo

❖ Ask students to look up the animals on the Internet, if possible, and write short reports about them. Then they can each share their information with the class.

8c The Passive Voice with *Get; Get* + Adjective
Student Book 3 p. 222, Student Book 3B p. 12

7 Practice

A. 1. got involved **2.** got engaged **3.** got married **4.** got depressed **5.** got jealous **6.** got divorced **7.** got involved **8.** got killed **9.** got criticized **10.** got blamed
B. Answers will vary.

8 Practice

A. 1. O **2.** B **3.** O **4.** O **5.** B **6.** O **7.** B **8.** B **9.** O **10.** B **11.** B

B. Answers will vary. Sample answers: **1.** Janice is (a) punctual because she gets up at 8 A.M., (b) not lazy because she always gets her work done by the end of the day, (c) and confident because she would like to get another job next year. **2.** Janice is (a) efficient and (b) hardworking because she always gets her work done by the end of the day, (c) but impatient because she gets irritated when the bus is late. **3.** Janice is (a) energetic because she gets up at 8 A.M., (b) ambitious because she would like to get another job next year, (c) and nervous because she doesn't like it when her boss gets angry.

| 9 | **Your Turn** |

9 **Your Turn**

Answers will vary. Sample answers:

You: When do you get angry?

Your partner: I get angry when my husband forgets important family events. When do you get angry?

You: I get angry when someone lies to me. When do you get bored?

Your partner: I get bored when people talk about politics. How about you?

You: I get bored when I do my math homework. It's too easy for me. When do you get worried?

Your partner: I get worried when I don't hear from my parents for a long time.

You: Me too.

Vocabulary Notes 1

❖ You can tell students about word forms and put the categories on the board in the form of a chart.

❖ Then you can write the forms of *angry* on the board and explain them. Next, you can dictate the other words to the students or send a student to the board for each of the words and have him or her write the forms as the rest of the class copies them.

Adjective	Adverb	Verb	Noun
angry	angrily	anger	anger
bored/-ing	boringly	bore	bore/boredom
depressed/-ing	depressingly	depress	depression
irritated/-ing	irritatingly	irritate	irritation
worried/-ing	worryingly	worry	worry/worrier

❖ For homework or as a class activity, you can tell students to write or say some of the words in sentences.

8d *It* + a Passive Voice Verb + a *That* Clause

Student Book 3 p. 226, Student Book 3B p. 16

10 **Practice**

1. It is believed that calcium builds strong bones and teeth.

2. It is known that fruits and vegetables are important for our health.

3. It is thought that some fruits and grains can help to prevent cancer.

4. It is said that fruit improves your immune system.

5. It is believed that nuts help to lower cholesterol.

6. It is known that eating too much sugar can be bad for our teeth.

11 Practice

Answers will vary. Sample answers:

1. Norah Jones is thought/said/considered to be...   **2.** Mangoes are said to taste...
3. Brazil is expected to win...   **4.** Argentina is reported/expected to have...
5. Prunes are considered/thought to be...

12 Your Turn

Answers will vary. Sample answers:
1. The Japanese are known to have a healthy diet.
2. Hamburgers have been known to transmit Mad Cow Disease (BSE).
3. Computers are reported to be faster, cheaper, and more powerful than ever.
4. The United States has been known to possess high-tech military equipment.
5. My country is reported to have huge petroleum reserves.

Newspaper Activity

❖ Bring in a tabloid-type newspaper that exaggerates the news or tells stories that may not be true, like *Extraterrestrial brings Elvis back.*

❖ Give pairs of students one page each and have them make up sentences using the phrases learned in **8d,** like *It has been reported that an extraterrestrial brought Elvis Presley back to earth.*

❖ Circulate and ask each pair to write one sentence on the board – the funnier, the better!

8e Present and Past Participles Used as Adjectives

Student Book 3 p. 228, Student Book 3B p. 18

13 Practice

1. terrifying   **2.** exhausted   **3.** depressing   **4.** tired   **5.** surprised   **6.** disappointing
7. boring   **8.** relaxed   **9.** frightened   **10.** terrified

14 Your Turn

Answers will vary. Sample answer:
I was camping in the mountains with a group of friends. We had stayed up late telling ghost stories, but finally we got tired and went to bed. In the middle of the night, we heard some strange sounds. We were all scared, so we turned on our flashlights. There was a big bear eating our food! We were so frightened that we jumped out of our sleeping bags and ran to the car. Even though it was uncomfortable, we slept in the car all night long. The next morning, we saw that the bear had eaten all our food. We were really shocked, so we packed up our gear and drove home.

❖ Have students extend the list on Student Book 3 p. 229, Student Book 3B p. 19 #3 to include adverbs, verbs and nouns. Put the categories and the first line on the board and then dictate the other lines to students in their seats or at the board.

Adverb	Verb	Noun
amazingly	amaze	amazement
amusingly	amuse	amusement
confusingly	confuse	confusion
depressingly	depress	depression
embarrassingly	embarrass	embarrassment
exhaustingly	exhaust	exhaustion
frighteningly	frighten	fright
impressively	impress	impression
interestingly	interest	interest
relaxingly	relax	relaxation
shockingly	shock	shock
surprisingly	surprise	surprise

❖ Point out that most adverbs are formed from the present participle of the verb, or the –ing adjective form. Also point out that most verbs are in the base form, and most nouns have a suffix like –ment or –ion, although some are also in the base form.

❖ For further practice, ask students in pairs to write sentences with one set of the word forms and either say them aloud or turn them in for correction.

8f Causative Sentences with *Have, Get,* and *Make:* Active Voice

Student Book 3 p. 231, Student Book 3B p. 21

 ### Practice

1. Please have the front desk call him at 6:00 A.M.

2. Please have the bellhop deliver three daily newspapers first thing in the morning.

3. Please have room service bring (him) fresh fruit and coffee for breakfast at 7:00 A.M.

4. Don't have the florist put fresh flowers in his room.

5. Please have the laundry wash three shirts (for him) every day.

6. Please get the technical staff to install a computer, an Internet connection, a fax machine, and a flat-screen TV in his room as soon as he checks in.

7. Please have the bellhop polish his shoes and leave them outside his door every morning.

8. Please get a chauffeur to meet him in front of the hotel each day at 9:00 A.M.

❖ Tell students to think of some famous people and make up questions about them. For example:

> *Does Queen Elizabeth make her own clothes?*
> *Does Arnold Schwarzenegger iron his own shirts?*
> *Does Penelope Cruz design her own costumes?*
> *Does David Beckham wash his own soccer uniforms?*

❖ Then, have them ask a partner about these people. The partners should answer with *have* + base form or *get* + infinitive. For example:

> *No, she has a dressmaker make them.*
> *No, he gets a dry-cleaner to iron them.*
> *No, she has a costume-designer do them.*
> *No, he gets the team laundry to wash them.*

 ## 8g Causative Sentences with *Have* and *Get:* Passive Voice

Student Book 3 p. 234, Student Book 3B p. 24

16 Practice

Answers will vary. Sample answers:

1. You can get copies made at a copy shop. You can also get them bound.

2. You can have your teeth cleaned at the dentist's. You can also have them pulled.

3. You can have your car repaired at a garage. You can also get the oil or tires changed.

4. You can have your hair cut at a hair salon. You can also have it colored.

5. You can get your clothes washed at a laundromat. You can also get them folded.

6. You can get your suits cleaned at a dry cleaner's. You can also get your shirts pressed.

7. You can have your eyes checked at an optician's. You can also have your glasses made.

8. You can get your trousers altered at a tailor's. You can also have your zippers repaired.

17 Your Turn

Answers will vary. Sample answers:

1. If I were at an expensive hotel, I would get my meals and drinks brought up to my room.

2. If I were the president of a huge company, I would have a limousine pick me up and drop me off every day.

3. If I were in the hospital with a broken leg, I would have my friends bring me good food and my family bring me a good book.

- ❖ Tell students to think of at least five things they have done for them by other people. Then ask them to write down five questions with *have* or *get* to ask a partner. For example:

  > *Where do you get your hair cut?*
  > *Where do you have your clothes dry-cleaned?*
  > *Where do you get the oil in your car changed?*

- ❖ When students finish asking questions and jotting down answers, have one pair join another and make five statements about each member of their group. For example:

  > *Tanya gets her hair cut at Prime Cuts.*
  > *She gets her clothes dry-cleaned at Mr. Clean's.*
  > *She gets the oil in her car changed at the Body Shop.*

◆ 8h Phrasal Verbs

Student Book 3 p. 236, Student Book 3B p. 26

18 Practice

1. They will pick him up at 6:45 P.M.
2. They will drop him off at 7:30 P.M.
3. He will check into it at 7:35 P.M.
4. A tour guide will look after him during his stay.
5. He will call for him at 7:00 A.M.
6. They'll set it up for 9:00 A.M.
7. If he calls it off, they'll call him immediately.
8. They'll pick him up at 10:30 A.M.
9. He'll go over it with him from 11:00 to 12:30 P.M.
10. They'll drop him off at 1:15 P.M.

19 Practice

A. 1. up 2. after 3. over 4. across 5. up 6. down 7. up 8. out 9. up 10. down

B. 1. come across 2. think up 3. write down 4. give up 5. bring up 6. get over
   7. calm down 8. work out 9. look after 10. use up

20 Your Turn

Answers will vary. Sample answers:
1. I was *brought up* in Monterrey.
2. My siblings *looked after* me.
3. One day, when I was 12, I *came across* a watch someone had lost.
4. Yes, I find it easy to *think up* excuses. Once I stayed out too late and my parents were angry. I said that I had run out of gas.
5. I *work out* every other morning.
6. I *work* it *out* while I'm doing other things.
7. I'd like to *give up* fattening foods.
8. Listening to classical music *calms* me *down*.

Story Activity

❖ Divide students into groups of four and tell them that they are going to make up a story using the phrasal verbs in section **8h.** Assign each group one column from the charts on Student Book 3 pp. 237 and 239, Student Book 3B pp. 27 and 29. Give them 10-15 minutes for this activity.

❖ As they work, circulate to check their work and answer any questions they may have. When they finish, they can either write their story on the board or read it to the class. They could also type it on a computer and put it on a bulletin board or website.

8i Prepositions Following Verbs, Adjectives, and Nouns; Other Combinations with Prepositions

Student Book 3 p. 244, Student Book 3B p. 34

21 Practice

A. 1. an increase in **2.** changes in **3.** an impact on **4.** One example of **5.** a threat to
B. 1. essential to **2.** responsible for **3.** opposed to **4.** free of
C. 1. come from **2.** contribute to **3.** account for **4.** results in **5.** recover from

22 **Your Turn**

Answers will vary. Sample answers:
We can make *changes in* how we travel. For example, we can walk or ride short distances and take public transportation instead of driving everywhere. We can be *opposed to* bigger and more powerful cars, like sports utility vehicles (SUVs). We can also *contribute to* organizations that support the environment, either by giving our money or our time as volunteers.

Preposition Activity

❖ Bring a newspaper or some short news articles from the Internet into class. Divide students into pairs and give each pair an article to read. As they are reading, students should underline the preposition combinations they find. Many of them are listed in section **8i.**

❖ After students finish underlining the prepositions, they should try to write a few sentences summarizing the article. Give them 10-15 minutes for this activity. Circulate to check their work and answer any questions they may have.

❖ When they finish, have one pair get together with another and take turns reading their summaries. They could also type them on computers and put them on a bulletin board or website.

Review

Student Book 3 p. 248, Student Book 3B p. 38

1 **Review (8a, 8e, 8i)**

1. get   **2.** get angry   **3.** depressing   **4.** relaxing   **5.** be obeyed   **6.** obeys   **7.** in
8. on   **9.** to   **10.** was worshipped   **11.** in   **12.** amazing   **13.** are heated   **14.** is
15. of   **16.** gets   **17.** are   **18.** move   **19.** would get   **20.** would get   **21.** in
22. around   **23.** are   **24.** on   **25.** going   **26.** in

2 **Review (8a–8b, 8d)**

1. is said/has been said   **2.** is known   **3.** is blocked   **4.** can be taken   **5.** can be carried
6. is provided   **7.** has been provided   **8.** were conquered   **9.** was ruled
10. was taken over   **11.** was seized   **12.** was ignored   **13.** was visited   **14.** can be said
15. was introduced   **16.** was invited

3 **Review (8f–8g)**

1. got, to give   **2.** made, clean   **3.** 've had/'ve gotten, upgraded   **4.** made, paint
5. get, to stay   **6.** have/get, examined   **7.** 'm going to make, finish   **8.** have/make, take
9. get, to help   **10.** make, wear

The Passive Voice, Causatives, and Phrasal Verbs

4 **Review (8h–8i)**

1. dream of   **2.** use up   **3.** solution to   **4.** take off   **5.** pick up   **6.** demand for
7. impact on   **8.** tear up   **9.** trace of

5 **Review (8c, 8h)**

Melinda: Did you hear that Joe and Marian are ~~being~~ *getting* married?

Patrick: No way! They broke ∧ *up* last month.

Melinda: They did, but I guess they decided to start ~~out~~ *over*. Anyway, I don't know how she puts ∧ *up* with him.

Patrick: Him! You're not trying to ~~have~~ *make* me believe that he's the problem, are you?

Melinda: No, you're right. Their problems ~~cause~~ *are caused/must be caused* by both of them. I still can't believe they're engaged. Do you think we can get them ~~change~~ *to change* their minds?

Patrick: I doubt it. Remember what ~~write~~ *was written* by Shakespeare: "Love is blind." Anyway, don't be so ~~worry~~ *worried*. They'll work ~~up~~ *out* their problems. They'll probably end ~~over~~ *up* being very happy.

Writing Expansion

Student Book 3 p. 252, Student Book 3B p. 42

Bring in the classified advertising section of a newspaper and give a page to each student. Tell them to find a job they might be interested in and use the ad as the basis for another cover letter.

 # Unit 8 Student Book Self-Test

Student Book 3 p. 253, Student Book 3B p. 43

A. **1.** C   **2.** A   **3.** C   **4.** D   **5.** B   **6.** A   **7.** C   **8.** B   **9.** B   **10.** B

B. **1.** C   **2.** C   **3.** C   **4.** B   **5.** B   **6.** C   **7.** C   **8.** B   **9.** A   **10.** B

GERUNDS AND INFINITIVES

Unit 9 begins with an overview of the forms and functions of gerunds, first as subjects and objects, then as objects of prepositions. Helpful charts assist students in learning what verbs and prepositions are followed by gerunds, and fill-in-the-blank and rewriting exercises allow students to practice what they learn.

Next, an overview of the forms and functions of infinitives is presented with more charts to help students remember which verbs and prepositions are followed by infinitives. Differences in the uses of gerunds and infinitives are also explained, followed by exercises that help students understand and recognize these differences.

Other constructions that employ infinitives—certain adjectives, nouns, and indefinite pronouns—are then presented, as is the construction too, enough, and in order followed by infinitives. Of course, charts are utilized to clearly identify the relationship between terms, and exercises ask students to demonstrate what they are learning.

The forms and functions of perfect and passive gerunds and infinitives are next explained through useful charts and examples. Finally, the unit concludes with explanations and exercises focused on the use of verbs of perception with gerunds and infinitives, and the person + gerund construction.

The writing activity is an essay of analysis on an academic topic, which the students discuss and then write in order to practice the gerunds and infinitives taught in this unit.

9a Gerunds as Subjects and Objects
Student Book 3 p. 256, Student Book 3B p. 46

1 Practice

(Items 4, 5, and 6 may be in any order.)
1. skiing **2.** camping **3.** climbing **4.** swimming **5.** sailing **6.** diving **7.** jogging **8.** cycling **9.** exercising **10.** sleeping

2 Practice

1. getting heart disease **2.** going on a diet **3.** drinking coffee **4.** drinking coffee when I'm tired **5.** eating ice cream **6.** buying potato chips **7.** counting calories at every meal **8.** cooking a lot of rich food **9.** making new dishes with fewer calories **10.** taking care of my health

3 Your Turn

Answers will vary. Sample answers:
1. mountain climbing   You could fall and not be able to get help quickly.
2. skateboarding   You could fall and break an arm or leg.
3. scuba diving   You could be attacked by a shark.
4. swimming   You could have cramps and drown.
5. jogging   You could injure the joints or muscles of your legs.
6. cycling   You could have an accident or injure your knees.
7. hiking   You could get lost in the woods or be attacked by a bear.

Notes on Vocabulary 1

❖ Although most students at this level are aware of how to form gerunds, give them a quick reminder of the following spelling rules:

- drop final *e* before adding *-ing* — *appreciating, continuing, imagining*
- don't drop *e* if final syllable is stressed — *canoeing, critiquing*
- double final consonant of single or stressed c-v-c syllable* — *admitting, quitting, putting*

❖ If students need more information on these rules, refer them to Student Book 3, p. 440, Student Book 3B p. 230.

* **c**onsonant-**v**owel-**c**onsonant

9b Gerunds as Objects of Prepositions; Gerunds after Certain Expressions

Student Book 3 p. 260, Student Book 3B p. 50

4 Practice

1. h **2.** d **3.** f **4.** c **5.** b **6.** a **7.** g **8.** i **9.** j **10.** e

5 Practice

1. b **2.** b **3.** a **4.** c **5.** a **6.** c

6 Your Turn

Answers will vary. Sample answers:
I'm good at playing the flute and making pottery. I'm interested in kayaking and hiking. I'm tired of getting up early and going to work when it's cold outside.

Dictation Activity

❖ To practice the *prepositions* and *expressions* + *gerund* construction, read the sentences from the charts on Student Book 3 p. 260, Student Book 3B p. 50 and ask the students to repeat after you. Or tell them to practice with a partner to prepare for a dictation activity.

❖ The next day, dictate the sentences in the charts, omitting the prepositions or a word from the expressions. You can either dictate to all the students writing in their seats and then check answers orally, or you can send half of the students to the board to write while those in their seats dictate and check the answers. If using the latter organization, have the students change places and go through the activity again when the first group is finished.

9c Verbs Followed by Infinitives

Student Book 3 p. 263, Student Book 3B p. 53

7 Practice

1. She invited us to come to her house for a barbecue on Saturday.

2. She reminded us to bring the children.

3. She warned us not to knock on the door loudly or we'd wake up the baby.

4. She would like us to bring a salad.

5. She promised to make a big chocolate cake.

6. She wanted us to come at 6:00 P.M.

7. She encouraged us to be on time.

8. She said we'd be allowed to cook our own meat if we want.

9. She said she'd expect us to stay for a game of softball.

10. She'll teach us to play softball if we don't know how to play.

8 | Your Turn

Answers will vary. Sample answers:

1. My teacher expects me to write a composition every week. He wants me to watch the news on TV. He allows me to watch American movies on Friday afternoon.

2. My parents expect me to get good grades in my courses. They want me to get a good education. They allow me to study abroad so I'll learn more about other countries.

3. My boss expects me to be on time every day. She wants me to get all my work done by the end of the week. She allows me to take personal phone calls if they're important.

4. My friend expects me to go out with her every month. She wants me to give her advice if she has problems. She allows me to borrow money if I forget to go to the bank.

Notes on Vocabulary 2

❖ Many of the verbs in this section are examples of legal language used in contracts or pledges. Here are a few examples you can put on the board for students to read.

Affidavit*	*I certify that the above is true to the best of my knowledge.*
Civil Union	*I promise to love and honor you all the days of my life.*
Employment Agreement	*I hereby** agree to serve as _____ under the conditions stated above.*
Rental Contract	*I hereby conform to the terms of this lease.*

* Written testimony that may be used in court
** By signing this

9d Verbs Followed by a Gerund or an Infinitive

Student Book 3 p. 265, Student Book 3B p. 55

9 | Practice

1. climbing **2.** walking **3.** to hike / hiking **4.** to send **5.** to take **6.** to mail
7. going **8.** to travel / traveling **9.** to take **10.** to look / looking **11.** thinking
12. to plan / planning

10 Your Turn

Answers will vary. Sample answer:
I remember going to Madrid last year with you. We loved eating *tapas* at those small restaurants where the food was cheap but *deliciosa*. We also enjoyed visiting the museums. We met some German students at the Prado and started talking to them. We forgot to check the time, and we missed the bus to Sevilla. So we stopped chatting and took the train instead. Let's try to take another trip again this year – how about Greece?

Love, Marianna

E-Mail Activity

❖ After students write e-mail message in **Your Turn 10,** collect and then distribute them to different students to read, check, and answer. In their answers, they should use at least three verbs from the list.

❖ When finished, have the students return the emails to the original writer to read and check.

9e Infinitives after Certain Adjectives, Nouns, and Indefinite Pronouns

Student Book 3 p. 268, Student Book 3B p. 58

11 Practice

1. to hear   **2.** to find out   **3.** to finish   **4.** to travel   **5.** to aim for   **6.** to have
7. to think   **8.** to plan   **9.** to do   **10.** to be

12 Your Turn

Answers will vary. Sample answers:
It's very important to learn about financial matters at a young age.
It's never too late to learn a new sport or hobby.
There is never enough time to spend with family and friends.
It's good to have something to look forward to, like a vacation.

❖ To practice the adjectives that take infinitives, you can do this activity with the class. First, write the words from Chart 9e, 1 across the board.

❖ Then, tell students they have one minute to go to the board and write a phrase under one of the adjectives. For example, they might write phrases like this:

afraid	ashamed	careful
to swim in deep water	*to admit I can't type*	*to hide my jewelry at home*
to drive in this country	*to cook for my friends*	*to put my money in the bank*

❖ Afterward, have each student put his or her phrase in a sentence and say it aloud, e.g., *My little brother is afraid to swim in deep water.*

9f *Too* and *Enough* Followed by Infinitives

Student Book 3 p. 270, Student Book 3B p. 60

13 Practice

1. The tea was too hot for us to drink.
   The tea wasn't cool enough for us to drink.
2. The server spoke too fast for us to understand.
   The server didn't speak slowly enough for us to understand.
3. The words on the menu were too difficult for me to pronounce.
   The words on the menu weren't easy enough for me to pronounce.
4. The room was too dark for me to see the food.
   The room wasn't bright enough for me to see the food.
5. The music was too loud for us to have a conversation.
   The music wasn't soft enough for us to have a conversation.
6. I was too shy to complain.
   I wasn't brave enough to complain.
7. We were too disappointed to leave a tip.
   We weren't satisfied enough to leave a tip.
8. We were too tired to walk home.
   We weren't energetic enough to walk home.

14 Your Turn

Answers will vary. Sample answers:

You: When I was younger, I was so clumsy that I couldn't do any sport I tried. Now I'm much more graceful than I was before, and I participate in several sports.

Your partner: When my partner was younger, he was too clumsy to play a lot of sports. Now he's more athletic and plays many sports.

❖ To practice these structures, divide the students into groups of three or four. Tell each student to take a piece of paper and begin sentences like the ones below using phrases they have learned in this section:

> *Arnold was too busy...*
> *Sofia has enough money...*
> *Edgar was so late that...*

❖ When the beginnings are written, each student should pass his or her paper on to the next person in the group, who writes the endings:

> *...to phone his family.*
> *...to go to Florida for a week.*
> *...he missed the first part of the concert.*

❖ Then each student will pass the paper on again, with the next person beginning three new sentences, and the person after that ending them. Continue until each student has the piece of paper he or she started with.

9g The Infinitive of Purpose

Student Book 3 p. 273, Student Book 3B p. 63

15 Practice

1. She needs matches to start a fire.
2. She needs a tent to sleep in.
3. She needs insect repellent to keep mosquitoes away.
4. She needs an ice chest to keep food cold.
5. She needs a kettle to boil water.
6. She needs a flashlight to see in the dark.
7. She needs a backpack to carry things.
8. She needs a compass to find her way.

16 Your Turn

Answers will vary. Sample answer:
I usually go to a travel agent to pick up plane tickets and hotel and car reservations.
I sometimes go to a clothing store to get a few new clothes.

❖ To give students more practice with this form, divide them into groups and put a few situations like the following on the board. There should be one situation for each group.

take the TOEFL	apply to a university	get a driver's license
get married	take the GRE	open a business

❖ Ask students to generate a list of tasks that are necessary in order to accomplish these things:

You have to go to the language center to get a TOEFL application.
You have to go to the post office to mail the application.
You have to go to the bookstore to buy a TOEFL practice book.
You have to meet with your friends to practice every day.
You have to go to the testing center to take the test.
You have to look in your mailbox to see if the score report is there.

❖ When they finish, ask them to read their lists to the rest of the class.

9h Perfect Infinitives and Perfect Gerunds; Passive Voice of Infinitives and Gerunds

Student Book 3 p. 275, Student Book 3B p. 65

17 Practice

1. to have heard **2.** to have been chosen **3.** Having received **4.** to be
5. to have spent **6.** not having seen **7.** Having been told **8.** to be recognized

18 Practice

1. Having spent **2.** having found **3.** having made **4.** having been warned
5. having been told **6.** having been treated **7.** having lost **8.** Having heard

19 Practice

1. They need cleaning.   They need to be cleaned.
2. It needs repairing.   It needs to be repaired.
3. It needs cutting.   It needs to be cut.
4. They need sweeping.   They need to be swept.
5. They need painting.   They need to be painted.
6. They need washing.   They need to be washed.
7. It needs replacing.   It needs to be replaced.
8. They need doing.   They need to be done.

20 Your Turn

Answers will vary. Sample answers:
My car needs to be washed. My bedroom needs to be vacuumed. My bathroom needs to be scrubbed. My kitchen floor needs to be mopped. My living room furniture needs to be dusted.

Speaking Activity

❖ You can do a response exercise with **Practice 19** so that students have further reinforcement of this structure. For example, say *The windows are dirty,* then ask one student to respond with *They need cleaning,* and another with *They need to be cleaned;* make sure they answer without looking at their books.

❖ Continue around the classroom until all the students have responded to at least one sentence.

9i Gerunds and Infinitives with Verbs of Perception

Student Book 3 p. 279, Student Book 3B p. 69

21 Practice

1. stealing (in progress) **2.** leave (completed action) **3.** breaking (in progress)
4. shouting (in progress) **5.** scream / fall (completed action) **6.** crawling (in progress)
7. sitting (in progress)

22 Your Turn

Answers will vary. Sample answers:
1. I'd call the police.
2. I'd tell them their car lights were on.
3. I'd call the police and then wake everyone up.
4. I wouldn't interfere.
5. I'd run to help and then call an ambulance if the person were hurt.
6. I'd get away fast.
7. I'd brush it off.

❖ Students have probably seen a lot of films about the supernatural or alien beings, so you can put some unusual situations on the board and have students ask a partner what he or she would do. Here are some examples:

What would you do if you...?

...*saw a ghost walking around your house?*
...*noticed objects moving in your room?*
...*heard strange noises at night?*
...*saw an alien or extraterrestrial walking in your yard?*
...*noticed a UFO hovering over your apartment?*
...*heard someone speaking a strange language, but didn't see anyone?*

❖ Have students speculate about the answers with their partners and report back to the class.

9j Person + Gerund

Student Book 3 p. 281, Student Book 3B p. 71

23 Practice

(Informal nouns and pronouns are shown first.)

1. I was surprised at David/David's forgetting to call me on my birthday.
2. I don't like him/his phoning me at work when I'm busy.
3. I don't mind him/his phoning me in the evening before 9:00.
4. My parents don't approve of him/his taking me dancing every Saturday night.
5. I can't stand his friends/friends' talking on their cell phones all the time.
6. He doesn't like me/my going out with other friends.
7. I don't listen to my parents/parents' telling me that David isn't good enough for me.
8. I'm tired of my parents/parents' always telling me what to do.

24 Your Turn

Answers will vary. Sample answers:

1. I can't stand people telling me to clean up my dorm room.
2. I don't mind people telling me to take a break.
3. My friends criticize me for studying too much.

❖ To practice this structure, put a list of verbs on the board that can be used in sentences as gerunds. For example:

approve	finish	eat	drive
arrive	listen	drink	think
dance	phone	buy	send
forget	talk	travel	follow
go	tell	have fun	invite

❖ Tell students to go to the board and write one sentence about a classmate containing a gerund. For example, *Roberto's eating in class bothers the teacher* or *I saw Anita dancing at the party; she's a good dancer.* After they are finished with their sentences, have them read them aloud to the class.

❖ If you have limited board space, you can tell students to write five sentences about classmates containing gerunds. When they are finished, tell them to exchange papers with a partner and check the sentences.

Review

Student Book 3 p. 283, Student Book 3B p. 73

1 Review (9a–9d, 9f–9g, 9i)

1. camping **2.** doing/to do **3.** shopping/to shop **4.** shopping **5.** to sleep **6.** saying
7. going **8.** to stay **9.** to hear **10.** talk **11.** to get **12.** to get **13.** to do
14. to bring **15.** hiking **16.** to go **17.** to stay **18.** to stay **19.** to pick **20.** growing
21. itching **22.** to bring **23.** eating **24.** to eat **25.** swimming **26.** to argue
27. to do **28.** cooking **29.** to start **30.** to light **31.** to rain **32.** thinking
33. to go **34.** sleeping

2 Review (9b–9c, 9e, 9g–9h)

1. competing **2.** worrying **3.** to be **4.** (to) win **5.** sleeping **6.** to rest **7.** meeting
8. swimming **9.** to cycle **10.** running **11.** doing **12.** Having worked **13.** to prepare
14. to see

3 Review (9c–9e, 9g, 9j)

1. to hear **2.** going **3.** to do **4.** joining **5.** to pay **6.** to think **7.** reminding
8. to pack **9.** snowing **10.** reading **11.** to learn **12.** to write

4 Review (9a–9e, 9g)

1. traveling **2.** to understand **3.** meeting **4.** riding **5.** cycling **6.** to be **7.** thinking
8. to get **9.** starting **10.** to get **11.** to prepare **12.** training **13.** to ride
14. to do **15.** cross-training **16.** cycling **17.** running **18.** hiking **19.** swimming
20. To get **21.** building **22.** to know **23.** committing **24.** to have **25.** losing
26. to cycle **27.** cycling/to cycle **28.** to love **29.** to be **30.** to participate
31. being **32.** seeing **33.** having **34.** riding

Writing Expansion

Student Book 3 p. 287, Student Book 3B p. 77

Bring in some articles from print or online newspapers so that students can read them and choose a topic based on their reading. If several students are going to write about one of the topics, have them sit in a group and make an outline together before writing the essay. When they finish, the students in the group can read each other's essays and suggest areas for revision. When the essays are done, they can be put into a publication like a print or online newsletter.

Unit 9 Student Book Self-Test

Student Book 3 p. 288, Student Book 3B p. 78

A. **1.** B **2.** A **3.** C **4.** C **5.** C **6.** A **7.** B **8.** C **9.** C **10.** D

B. **1.** D **2.** C **3.** A **4.** C **5.** D **6.** A **7.** B **8.** B **9.** B **10.** A

AGREEMENT AND PARALLEL STRUCTURE

Unit Sections	Notes/Activities	Student Book 3 page	Student Book 3B page	Teacher's Manual page
10a Subject-Verb Agreement: General Rules Part 1	Vocabulary Activity	292	82	90
10b Subject-Verb Agreement: General Rules Part 2	Sentence Activity	295	85	90
10c Subject-Verb Agreement with Quantity Words	Survey Activity	297	87	91
10d Parallel Structure	Parallel Activity	301	91	92
10e Coordinating Conjunctions	Notes on Culture 1	304	94	93
10f Correlative Conjunctions: *Both...And; Not Only...But Also; Either...Or; Neither...Nor*	Notes on Culture 2	307	97	95
❖ Review	Review Answer Key	310	100	96
❖ Writing	Writing Expansion	314	104	98
❖ Unit 10 Student Book Self-Test	Unit 10 Self-Test Answer Key	315	105	98

Unit 10 begins with an overview of subject-verb agreement by presenting general rules for compound subjects, indefinite adjectives and pronouns, and singular and plural subjects. Next, subjects followed by prepositional phrases and the existential *there* are reviewed and practiced. Finally, subject-verb agreement with quantity words expressing time, money, distance, weight, and measurement are presented along with useful exercises. Included in these sections are fill-in-the-blank and personal opinion questions that allow students to practice what they've learned.

In the next section, parallel structure in different grammatical forms is reviewed with exercises to help students not only distinguish the structures but also practice using them.

Finally, the forms and functions of coordinating conjunctions and then correlative conjunctions are reviewed. Punctuation, personal opinion, and word choice exercises give students the opportunity to work with and better understand the functions of conjunctions.

The writing activity is an essay of definition on an abstract concept, which the students discuss and then write in order to practice the agreement and parallel structure taught in this unit.

10a Subject-Verb Agreement: General Rules Part 1

Student Book 3 p. 292, Student Book 3B p. 82

1 Practice

1. has **2.** is **3.** is **4.** are **5.** applies **6.** is **7.** is **8.** receives **9.** require **10.** is

2 Your Turn

Answers will vary. Sample answers:
Every student has to write an essay.
Most students have to go to an interview.
All students have to take a national exam. Depending on their scores, they can be accepted into universities of different levels. If students do well, they can get into the best universities. If they don't, they have to go to universities that are not so good. Many times these universities are far away or in small towns rather than in a city.

Vocabulary Activity

 Major areas of study, or majors, often end with the suffix *–ics,* which means *study of.* Write these words on the board and ask students to define or explain them. For example:

Economics is the study of the economy, or the production and distribution of goods and services and ways of managing them.

economics	electronics	genetics	genomics	linguistics
mathematics	pharmaceutics	physics	politics	statistics

10b Subject-Verb Agreement: General Rules Part II

Student Book 3 p. 295, Student Book 3B p. 85

3 Practice

1. are **2.** is **3.** is **4.** are **5.** are **6.** is **7.** are **8.** is **9.** are **10.** is

4 Your Turn

Answers will vary. Sample answers:
The people are standing in line at an ATM. All of them want to use the ATM. One woman is using it. One man is talking on the phone. The others aren't. One man is carrying an umbrella. Another is carrying a briefcase. One woman has an envelope. The other people don't.

❖ Write a list of words on the board and have students see how many prepositional phrases they can make with the words. Use and add to this partial list:

accountants	directions	graduation	machinery	space shuttle
architect	enterprises	hospital	operations	stock market
astronauts	fortune	investments	orthopedics	structures

Prepositional Phrases: *the accountants at the hospital*
the graduation of the astronauts
the structures of the architect

❖ After they make the phrases, have the students write sentences, either at the board or in their seats, using the phrases. Tell them to check that the verb agrees with the subject in each sentence.

Sentences: *The accountants at the hospital send paychecks to the employees.*
The graduation of the astronauts was attended by their families.
The structures of that architect have won many prizes.

10c Subject-Verb Agreement with Quantity Words

Student Book 3 p. 297, Student Book 3B p. 87

5 Practice

1. The number of   **2.** A number of   **3.** One of the   **4.** Each of the   **5.** None of the
6. The number of

6 Practice

1. are   **2.** spends   **3.** spends   **4.** does-formal / do-informal   **5.** spend   **6.** watches
7. watches   **8.** talks   **9.** talks   **10.** don't talk

7 What Do You Think?

Answers will vary. Sample answers:
1. Yes, 40 minutes is too long to talk on the phone.
2. No, 20 minutes isn't enough time to finish my homework.
3. Yes, more that an hour is too much time to spend eating dinner.
4. Yes, two hours is enough time to spend watching TV.

8 Your Turn

Answers will vary. Sample answers:
A. You: How much time do you spend exercising every day?
   Your classmate: I exercise for about an hour each day.
   You: How much time do you spend sleeping each day?
   Your classmate: I sleep 8 to 10 hours a day.
B. All the students sleep for at least 8 hours a day.
C. Answers will vary.

- ❖ Have students make a bar graph or pie chart for each survey question in **Practice 6.** They can do this either by drawing it or creating it on a computer.

- ❖ Divide the students into groups and assign one question to each group. You can make up more questions if there are not enough to go around. Group A will have question 1, Group B, question 2, and so on.

- ❖ First, students should write headings for incremental time measurements on a piece of paper, like every 20, 40, 60 minutes. Then, they will tally up the number of students for each increment and express the totals as a bar in a bar graph or section of a circle in a pie chart.

- ❖ When the students finish their graphs, one idea is to make transparencies and have each group stand up and report on their findings.

10d Parallel Structure

Student Book 3 p. 301, Student Book 3B p. 91

9 Practice

1. home, office, car—nouns   **2.** to ease, to fill, to reduce—infinitives   **3.** quickly, carelessly—adverbs   **4.** calming, relaxing, peaceful—adjectives   **5.** excites, stimulates, warms—verbs   **6.** energizes, stimulates—verbs   **7.** remembering, relieving—gerunds
8. sleeping, eating—verbs

10 Practice

1. humid / adjectives   **2.** self-confident / adjectives   **3.** stimulating / gerunds   **4.** pain / nouns   **5.** correct / nouns   **6.** correct / verbs   **7.** health / nouns

11 Practice

1. health / nutrition   **2.** psychology   **3.** lowers   **4.** anxiety/illnesses
5. elevates / anxiety   **6.** length   **7.** correct

12 Your Turn

Answers will vary. Sample answers:
1. The night before a test, it is important to study a lot, relax a little, and go to bed early.
2. On the day of the test, you must be cool, calm, and collected.
3. During the test, you must concentrate on the test, watch the time, and work as quickly as possible.
4. After the test, you can relax, hang out with your friends, and celebrate!

❖ Write categories on the board and tell students to look at chart 10d.

Categories: sports   transportation   communication   music
             majors   hobbies   vacations   food

❖ In pairs or small groups, have the students choose a category (or assign one to each group) and write five sentences, one for each of the forms. For example:

Nouns: *Apples and oranges are good for your health.*
Adjectives: *I like steamed or stir-fried broccoli.*
Verbs: *He buys and cooks only organic food.*
Adverbs: *She ate the noodles quickly and quietly.*
Gerunds: *The pastry chef enjoyed slicing fruit and chopping nuts.*

❖ You can circulate and check the sentences or collect them when students finish.

10e Coordinating Conjunctions

Student Book 3 p. 304, Student Book 3B p. 94

13 Practice

                                              He
Terry Fox was born in 1958 in Canada. ~~he~~ played soccer and basketball in high school, for

                 When
he loved sports. ~~when~~ he was eighteen, he had problems with his knee, so he went to the

        The   *This*
doctor. ~~the~~ doctor told him he had bone cancer and would lose his leg. ~~this~~ was a terrible

                              He   *His*
shock, yet Terry had an idea. ~~he~~ decided he could help people even with one leg. ~~his~~ idea

                                                        He
was to run across Canada to collect money to fight cancer. ~~he~~ wore an artificial leg and

                      His   *In*
started to prepare for the run. ~~his~~ progress was very slow, but he did not give up. ~~in~~ 1980,

                                                    He
he started his run and called it the "Marathon of Hope." ~~he~~ ran 26 miles a day, seven days

        This   *Later*
a week. ~~this~~ was amazing, but it was more amazing because he had only one leg. ~~later~~

                                            He
that year, Terry got sick again and had to stop running. ~~he~~ received letters from all over

                                                            The
the world, and Canadian television showed a program about him. ~~the~~ program collected

$10 million dollars for the Canadian Cancer Society. Terry Fox collected almost $24 million

                 He
for cancer. ~~he~~ died in 1981, but his story did not end with his death. Terry Fox events

started all over the world and collected millions of dollars to help fight cancer.

14 Practice

                                        They
A.   Dolphins live in the sea, yet they are mammals. ~~they~~ breathe air and give live birth

              Young   *Their*
to their young. ~~young~~ dolphins are intelligent and sensitive animals. ~~their~~ brains are

almost as large as ours, and they have a language of more than 30 sounds for

                           They
communicating with each other. ~~they~~ live in groups of several hundred and always help

any dolphins that may be in danger.

     Dolphins
     ~~dolphins~~ are friendly to humans, and there are many reports of dolphins helping

people in danger. In one case, in 1983, a helicopter crashed into the Java Sea, and it was

                                 The
a dolphin that saved the pilot's life. ~~the~~ dolphin pushed the rubber raft for nine days until

it reached the coast.

                                                                                                             This
B.   Family names usually go from father to son, but some family names have the

phrase "son of" to make the connection clear. ~~this~~ happens in Scottish and Irish names,

such as MacDonald or O'Connor. *Mac* and *O'* mean "son of," so *MacDonald* means "son of

Donald," and *O'Connor* means "son of Connor."

15 Your Turn

Answers will vary. Sample answer:
Our classroom has a blackboard, desks, and chairs, but it doesn't have computers. There is
an overhead projector, but the teacher doesn't use it very often. There are large windows,
and we can see the street below and the people passing by.

❖ Expand on the topic of family names by pointing out English names that also mean "son of," like *Johnson, Peterson,* and *Thomson.* In Scandinavian countries, you hear *Jensen, Petersen,* and *Sørensen,* which mean "son of," and *Jensdottir, Petersdottir,* and *Sørensdottir,* which mean "daughter of."

❖ In Russian, *Illyich* and *Illyovna* mean "son of" and "daughter of," respectively. Family names also have masculine and feminine endings, as in *Petrovsky* and *Petrovskaya.*

❖ In Arabic, you hear the prefixes *Abu* for "father of," as in *Abu-Nasser,* and *Bin* for "son of," as in *Bin-Yusef.* This is similar to *Ben* in Hebrew, as in *Judah Ben-Hur.*

❖ Ask students to add to the list with examples from their own languages.

10f Correlative Conjunctions: *Both…And; Not Only…But Also; Either…Or; Neither…Nor*

Student Book 3 p. 307, Student Book 3B p. 97

16 Practice
1. are **2.** need **3.** contain **4.** require **5.** has **6.** contain **7.** makes **8.** gives

17 Practice
1. Both fruits and vegetables have vitamin C. OR Not only fruits but also vegetables…
2. Both heat and exposure to air destroy vitamin C. OR Not only heat but also exposure to air…
3. You can take vitamin C either naturally in food or in tablet supplements. OR You can take vitamin C both naturally in food and… OR You can take vitamin C not only naturally in food but also …
4. Neither rice nor pasta have vitamin C.
5. Both oranges and lemons have a lot of vitamin C. OR Not only oranges but also lemons…
6. They say vitamin C prevents both heat disease and colds. OR They say vitamin C not only prevents heart disease but also prevents colds.
7. Vitamin C prevents neither cancer nor infection.
8. Both natural and synthetic vitamins are good for the body. OR Not only natural but also synthetic vitamins… OR Either natural or synthetic vitamins are good…

18 Your Turn
Answers will vary. Sample answers:
A. 1. Neither my partner nor I am wearing watches.
2. Not only I but also my partner likes jazz.
3. Both my partner and I are from Russia.

Notes on Culture 2

❖ Talk to the students about the custom of taking vitamin supplements in North America and other regions of the world. Here, many children and adults take a daily multi-vitamin in case they do not get enough nutrients in their diet.

❖ People also take other supplements like calcium, iron, and herbal products to stay healthy. Some of these products actually improve health, but others don't.

❖ Supplements are a multi-million dollar industry, and through advertising, manufacturers induce consumers to believe that they need to take them to stay healthy.

❖ Ask students what the customs are in their countries concerning dietary supplements and have them share information during a class discussion.

Review

Student Book 3 p. 310, Student Book 3B p. 100

1 ## Review (10a–10c)

1. are **2.** the lightest **3.** is **4.** width **5.** are **6.** measures **7.** is **8.** weighs
9. weigh **10.** has **11.** are **12.** is **13.** nor **14.** have **15.** lacks **16.** is **17.** is
18. wants **19.** is **20.** are **21.** exploring **22.** say **23.** demonstrates **24.** animals
25. remain

2 ## Review (10a–10b, 10d, 10f)

1. is **2.** makes **3.** Each **4.** are **5.** is **6.** is **7.** is **8.** humid **9.** is **10.** rainy
11. is **12.** are **13.** beautiful **14.** are **15.** is **16.** is **17.** sell **18.** are **19.** is
20. have **21.** hit **22.** lost **23.** desperately **24.** neither **25.** rebuild **26.** learning
27. writing **28.** was **29.** were **30.** charts **31.** nor **32.** was **33.** is

3 ## Review (10a–10d)

We measure things to find out how wide, ~~taller~~ *tall*, hot, cold, or ~~heavily~~ *heavy* they are. We ~~needs~~ *need*

accurate measurements in science and everyday activities such as cooking and ~~when we sew~~ *sewing*.

There ~~is~~ *are* different types of instruments for measuring, and different instruments ~~is~~ *are*

used to measure ~~long~~ *length*, ~~wide~~ *width*, volume, mass, and temperature.

In the old days, people used objects along with their hands and feet for measuring.
Having systems for measuring ~~have~~ *has* always been important. Some cultures still ~~uses~~ *use* ancient
methods for measuring. One of these methods ~~are~~ *is* the abacus. The abacus ~~have~~ *has* been
used in China since ancient times. With the abacus, you can add, ~~subtraction~~ *subtract*, ~~multiplying~~ *multiply*,
and ~~do division~~ *divide*. Most people ~~uses~~ *use* calculators to do that today. Each method ~~have~~ *has* its
own advantages.

There ~~is~~ *are* many measuring tools. Every one of them ~~are~~ *is* useful. We can measure ~~long~~ *length* and
width by using a ruler or a tape measure, and we ∧ *can* measure weight by using a scale.

The metric system originated in France in 1795. It uses meters to measure length and
grams ~~for measuring~~ *to measure* weight. Most countries and scientists ~~uses~~ *use* this system. The United
States ~~use~~ *uses* the U.S. customary system. This system ~~utilize~~ *utilizes* feet and inches to measure
length and pounds and ounces ~~measures~~ *to measure* weight.

Two methods of measuring temperature ~~is~~ *are* Fahrenheit and Celsius. Americans ~~measures~~ *measure*
temperature by using the Fahrenheit scale. Fahrenheit ~~register~~ *registers* the freezing point of water
as 32° and the boiling point as 212°. Most other countries ~~uses~~ *use* Celsius. Celsius ~~register~~ *registers*
the freezing point as 0° and the boiling point as 100°.

Which measuring systems ~~do~~ *does* your country use?

4 Review (10a, 10c–10f)

Neil Armstrong and Buzz Aldrin walked on the moon on July 21, 1969. Neither
of them ~~are~~ *is* still there, of course, ~~and~~ *but* one of their experiments ~~are~~ *is*. Armstrong and Aldrin
~~wasn't~~ *weren't* only walking and ~~jumped~~ *jumping* around on the moon. They ~~was~~ *were* busy placing instruments
on the surface and ~~conducted~~ *conducting* experiments. About an hour before the end of their final
moonwalk, they set up a science experiment, a two-foot wide panel with 100 mirrors. This
panel, along with many other objects, is still on the moon today, for no one ~~have~~ *has* gone
back to get them. Neither the U.S. ~~or~~ *nor* any other country ~~have~~ *has* gone back to the moon. The

Agreement and Parallel Structure

exact number of objects on the moon ~~are~~ *is* unknown. However, astronauts landing on the

moon today would find only one piece of equipment that ~~are~~ *is* still working—the panel. None

of the other experiments are still running. The panel, called a "lunar laser ranging retro-

reflector array," is small and ~~simplicity, or~~ *simple yet* it ~~give~~ *gives* scientists lots of important information.

The operation of the panel is simple. The mirrors on the panel ~~points~~ *point* at Earth. A laser

pulse shoots out of a telescope on Earth, crossing the Earth-moon space, ~~so~~ *and* hits the mirrors.

The mirrors ~~sends~~ *send* the pulse straight back. On Earth, scientists measure the travel time and

~~determining~~ *determine* the moon's distance, not only quickly but very ~~accurate~~ *accurately*. For decades, scientists,

along with an occasional researcher, ~~has~~ *have* traced the moon's orbit and learned many remark-

able things.

Everyone ~~seem~~ *seems* to have something to gain. The lunar laser ranging retroreflector array

has provided information to many fields of science. Physics ~~are~~ *is* a good example.

Physicists ~~has~~ *have* used the laser results to check Einstein's theories of gravity and relativity.

So far, Einstein ~~are~~ *is* still considered correct, ~~so~~ *but* who ~~know~~ *knows* whether the lunar laser ranging

retroreflector array will someday tell us something different!

Writing Expansion

Student Book 3 p. 314, Student Book 3B p. 104

Bring in some magazines with pictures and ask the students to make a collage illustrating
their essay. Have them look through the magazines and cut out pictures that represent the
term they defined. On a blank piece of paper, have them glue or tape the pictures together
in an artistic fashion, allowing some of the pictures to hang over the edges of the paper.
After they write their essay neatly or type it on a computer, have them cut the margins
from the paper and glue or tape it on top of the collage of pictures. Then they can display
it on a bulletin board. This activity can also be done on a webpage using public domain
picture files, or by copying and pasting images from the web.

Unit 10 Student Book Self-Test

Student Book 3 p. 315, Student Book 3B p. 105

A. 1. A 2. B 3. A 4. C 5. D 6. C 7. A 8. D 9. C 10. B

B. 1. C 2. D 3. C 4. A 5. D 6. B 7. C 8. A 9. D 10. B

NOUN CLAUSES AND REPORTED SPEECH

Unit Sections	Notes/Activities	Student Book 3 page	Student Book 3B page	Teacher's Manual page
11a Noun Clauses Beginning with *That*	Future Activity	318	108	100
11b Noun Clauses Beginning with Wh- Words (Indirect Wh- Questions)	Interview Activity	321	111	101
11c Noun Clauses Beginning with *If* or *Whether* (Indirect Yes/No Questions)	Wondering Activity	324	114	102
11d Quoted Speech	Quotation Activity 1	327	117	104
11e Reported Speech: Statements	Quotation Activity 2	328	118	105
11f Reported Speech: Questions	Newspaper Activity	334	124	106
11g Reported Commands, Requests, Offers, Advice, Invitations, and Warnings	Function Activity	336	126	108
11h The Subjunctive in Noun Clauses	Case Activity	338	128	109
❖ Review	Review Answer Key	342	132	110
❖ Writing	Writing Expansion	346	136	113
❖ Unit 11 Student Book Self-Test	Unit 11 Self-Test Answer Key	347	137	113

Unit 11 introduces the forms and functions of noun clauses beginning with *that* and gives a list of verbs that are usually followed by these structures. Short responses with *so* and *not* are also given, followed by matching and personal opinion exercises.

Noun clauses beginning with wh- words come next, and in this section students learn the correct word order for indirect questions. Questions and answers that might be asked at an interview are practiced through sentence completion and personal opinion activities.

Indirect yes/no questions beginning with *if* or *whether* are then introduced, and the correct word order for these queries is compared with that of direct questions. Students will practice these different word orders in sentence completion exercises.

Punctuation for quoted speech is demonstrated in section 11d, and students practice by reading stories and adding correct punctuation.

Next, statements in reported speech are presented, along with a chart that gives a clear comparison between quoted and reported speech so that students understand the differences. Interesting exercises that involve making excuses and taking messages follow.

Questions in reported speech are taught in section 11f, starting with a comparison between direct questions, indirect questions, and reported questions.

Finally, functional language that includes commands, requests, offers, advice, invitation and warnings is given, followed by the subjunctive in noun clauses and the verbs that precede it. Both sections include exercises allowing students to implement what they learn.

The writing activity is a fable or a legend, which the students discuss to find a moral and then write in order to practice the noun clauses and reported speech taught in this unit.

11a Noun Clauses Beginning with *That*

Student Book 3 p. 318, Student Book 3B p. 108

1 Practice

1. d **2.** f **3.** a **4.** c **5.** b **6.** e

2 What Do You Think?

Answers will vary. Sample answers:
1. I'm afraid so.
2. I hope so.
3. I don't think so.
4. I guess so.
5. I don't think so.

3 Your Turn

Answers will vary. Sample answers:
1. I predict that the world's population will increase.
2. I expect that hunger will grow as population increases.
3. I believe that science will prove there is life on other planets.
4. I guess that scientists will discover new sources of energy.
5. I don't think that everyone should speak the same language.

Future Activity

❖ Divide the students into six groups, if possible, and have them discuss the changes predicted in **Practice 1.** They should try to use the verbs in the chart on Student Book 3 p. 318, Student Book 3B p. 108 to express their feelings, thoughts, and opinions.

❖ After about ten minutes of discussion, ask the students to write sentences on the topic below using a row of verbs from the chart; circulate and help with the sentences.

Group 1	Population	verbs in first row
Group 2	Food	verbs in second row
Group 3	Energy	verbs in third row
Group 4	Astronauts	verbs in fourth row
Group 5	Robots	verbs in fifth row
Group 6	Language	verbs in sixth row

❖ When they finish, ask a student from each group to read their sentences to the class or have them hand the sentences in to be corrected.

11b Noun Clauses Beginning with Wh- Words (Indirect Wh- Questions)

Student Book 3 p. 321, Student Book 3B p. 111

4 Practice

1. how many people the company employs?
2. when the company first got started.
3. where the head office is?
4. what the job benefits are?
5. how many vacation days people get?
6. what the salary is?
7. who my manager will be.
8. when the job starts?
9. how many people you are going to interview for this job?
10. when you can tell me the results of this interview.

5 Practice

1. what your current job title is.
2. what your job duties are.
3. what qualifications you have.
4. who your previous employer was.
5. how long you worked in your last job.
6. why you left your last job.
7. what your salary was.
8. why you want this job.
9. how you found out about the job.
10. when you can start work.

6 Your Turn

Answers will vary. Sample answers:
(The unusual job was a lion tamer.)
They asked (me) why I was interested in lions.
(The unusual job was a parachutist.)
They asked (me) how many times I had jumped from a plane.
(The unusual job was a trainer of marine animals.)
They asked me what kind of whales I was familiar with.

Interview Activity

❖ Use the jobs in **Your Turn 6** for a paired interview activity. Divide the students into pairs and give each student an unusual job. Here are some suggestions:

sushi maker	parachutist	marine animal trainer	skyscraper window washer
food taster	traffic cop	parakeet breeder	underwater trash collector
lion tamer	clown	trapeze artist	helicopter traffic reporter

❖ Each person will write five interview questions and exchange them with their partner to write answers. When the students finish writing the answers, have them exchange papers again and do the interviews orally, trying not to look at their papers.

11c Noun Clauses Beginning with *If* or *Whether* (Indirect Yes/No Questions)

Student Book 3 p. 324, Student Book 3B p. 114

7 Practice

The noun clauses can start with *if* or *whether*.
1. if we ate lunch there together last year.
2. if we liked the food.
3. if they're open for lunch on Saturday.
4. if there is a fixed price lunch menu.
5. if there are enough tables for fifty guests.
6. if they have live music.
7. if they can order a special birthday cake.
8. if they have a vegetarian meal option.
9. if they have high chairs for children.
10. if it's a good idea to go there or not.

8 | Your Turn

Answers will vary. Sample answers:

You: I wonder if they have a sports center.

Your partner: Of course. They have a huge sports center with an Olympic-sized pool.

You: Do you know if they have a nightclub?

Your partner: Yes, they have three clubs with different kinds of music.

You: Do you think they have a restaurant?

Your partner: They have at least six restaurants, from casual to very formal.

You: I wonder if they have a children's program.

Your partner: Yes, they have childcare, a playground, and a wading pool.

You: Do you know if they have a spa?

Your partner: Of course. You can get a massage, a facial, or a haircut.

Wondering Activity

❖ You can get students to practice clauses with *if* and *whether* by putting them in pairs, giving them situations and asking them to make up five sentences about each scenario. Here are a few situations you might use:

New people are moving in next door. You're watching through a window and wondering what kind of neighbors they'll be.

Your parents have decided to buy a new car. You're waiting for them to come home and wondering what kind of car they've bought.

You see someone in the cafeteria you'd like to get to know. You're shy about introducing yourself, so you just sit there and wonder what kind of a person he/she is.

You've just had some lab tests done at the doctor's office. You're waiting to speak to the doctor, and you're wondering what the results of the tests are.

You're in the mall looking for a birthday present for your husband/wife. You're wondering what to get and how much to spend.

❖ When they have finished making up the sentences, ask the students to read them aloud to the class. Collect the papers and save them for **Quotation Activity 1** at the end of the next section.

Noun Clauses and Reported Speech

11d Quoted Speech

Student Book 3 p. 327, Student Book 3B p. 117

9 Practice

"Look," said one. "There is a big ship coming from far away with gold and riches on it."

"No," said the other. "That is not a treasure ship. It's a fisherman's boat with the day's catch of good fish."

"It's a chest of gold lost from a shipwreck," they both said.

The first quotation can be punctuated in two additional ways:
"Look!" said one. "There is a big ship..." OR "Look," said one, "there is a big ship..."

10 Practice

"How lucky I am," he said. "I've found a purse. Judging by its weight, it must be full of gold."

"Don't say *I* have found a purse," said his companion. "Instead, say *we* have found a purse and how lucky *we* are. Travelers should share the fortunes and misfortunes of the road."

"No, no," replied the other angrily. "*I* found it and *I* am going to keep it!"

"We'll be in trouble if they find the purse on us," he said.

"No, no," replied the other. "You would not say *we* before, so now stick to your *I*. Say *I* am in trouble."

11 Your Turn

Answers will vary. Sample answers:
My teacher said, "I want you to do all the exercises on quoted speech by the next lesson."
She asked us, "Would you prefer to take the exam on Monday or on Friday?"
He said, "Study the list of vocabulary words for a quiz tomorrow."

Quotation Activity 1

❖ Take the papers you collected after the **Wondering Activity** in the previous section and pass them around to different pairs of students.

❖ Tell them to re-write the sentences as quoted speech using correct punctuation marks. They will have to add speakers. For example:

> *I wonder whether our new neighbors have children.*
> *"Do our new neighbors have children?" wondered the little boy.*

> *I wonder if my parents bought a sports utility vehicle (SUV).*
> *Michelle asked her brother, "Did Mom and Dad buy an SUV?"*

❖ When they finish, have students return the papers to the pair that wrote the **Wondering Activity** sentences to check.

11e Reported Speech: Statements

Student Book 3 p. 328, Student Book 3B p. 118

12 Practice

1. Susan said that she couldn't work on Saturday because she was having her car fixed and she wouldn't be able to get there.
2. Mary Ann said that she had made other arrangements and couldn't change them then.
3. Ted explained that he would be out of town taking his children to see their grandparents.
4. Stanley complained that he was too tired and needed Saturday and Sunday to relax.
5. Steve insisted that he would work on Saturday morning only if he got paid double.
6. Kate wondered why she had to come in if the others didn't / weren't.
7. I said I would work if I could take off the next Monday. (Answers will vary.)

13 Practice

Answers will vary.
1. Cindy called from the dentist's office. She was calling to remind you that you had a dental appointment the next day at 10:00.
2. Janet called to say hello. She said she'd call you later.
3. Ken Stevens called. He said he'd been trying to reach you about a new work schedule. He said that his number was 678-9542. He'd like you to call him back.
4. Tony from the Travel Shop called to say your tickets would be ready the next day. He said that if you'd like them mailed, they could send them by regular or express mail. He wants you to let him know.
5. Jim called. He said that his boss had given him two tickets for the Wild Rockers concert the following week. He asked if you wanted to go with him.
6. Your mother called. She said that she'd called you at work, but you weren't there. She said she'd been calling you at home, but there was no answer. She said she wanted to know where you were and that she was worried. She asked you to please call her.
7. Your mother called again. She said that it'd been twenty-four hours and she still hadn't heard from you. She said that something had to be wrong. She asked you once again to please call her.

14 Your Turn

Answers will vary. Sample answers:
My friend told me that he saw Ben Affleck in the street yesterday.
My sister said that she had hoped to watch the parade, but it rained so she stayed home.
My father said that he wanted me to study at a state university because it would be less expensive than a private university.

Noun Clauses and Reported Speech

❖ Here are quotations by famous people you can put on the board. Have students go to the board in pairs to write them as indirect speech. Then ask them to take turns reading the sentences they created.

Carl Sagan	Somewhere, something incredible is waiting to be known. *Carl Sagan said that somewhere, something incredible was waiting to be known.*
Chinese Proverb	Deal with the faults of others as gently as with your own.
Ernest Hemingway	Never mistake motion for action.
Fred Dehner	The best helping hand that you will ever receive is the one at the end of your own arm.
Henry Ford	Obstacles are those frightful things you see when you take your eyes off your goal.
Julius Caesar	I came, I saw, I conquered.
Mark Twain	It's not the size of the dog in the fight; it's the size of the fight in the dog.
René Descartes	I think, therefore, I am.
Thomas Edison	I have not failed. I've just found 10,000 ways that won't work.
Victor Borge	Laughter is the shortest distance between two people.

❖ If you don't have enough board space, you can make a photocopy and do the activity orally. Have one student read the direct quotation and another make it indirect.

11f Reported Speech: Questions

Student Book 3 p. 334, Student Book 3B p. 124

15 Practice

The verbs in the main clauses will vary.
1. He asked me how I was.
2. He asked me when I had gotten back.
3. He wanted to know if I had liked Los Angeles.
4. He wondered why I hadn't stayed longer.
5. He asked me if I was living in my old neighborhood.
6. He asked me if I was still living alone.
7. He wondered what I was doing for a living now.
8. He asked me if I'd like to play tennis with him again, like old times.
9. He wanted to know if I had the same cell phone number.
10. He asked if he could call me that night.

Newspaper Activity

❖   Bring in a newspaper and give a page to pairs of students. Have them look at the headlines of the stories and guess what the stories are about. Then, have one person in each pair formulate indirect questions while the other creates reported questions about the stories; ask them to switch roles. Here are some examples:

Headline   *Auto sales slow*

Indirect Question   *I wonder why auto sales are slow.*

Reported Question   *Alicia wonders(ed) why auto sales are (were) slow.*

Headline   *Gas prices up*

Indirect Question   *I want to know when gas prices will go down.*

Reported Question   *Hiro wants(ed) to know when gas prices will (would) go down.*

Headline   *Awards night for stars*

Indirect Question   *I'd like to find out if my favorite actor is getting an award.*

Reported Question   *Nasser would like to find out if his favorite actor is getting an award.*

11g Reported Commands, Requests, Offers, Advice, Invitations, and Warnings

Student Book 3 p. 336, Student Book 3B p. 126

17 Practice

1. He told us to listen carefully.

2. He told us not to talk.

3. He asked us to put all our books and papers away.

4. He asked us not to try to copy our neighbor's work.

5. He threatened to tell the principal if we tried to copy answers from our neighbor.

6. He warned us that cheating would be severely punished.

7. He advised us to check the answers carefully before handing in our papers.

8. He promised that we would get a prize if we finished all the questions.

9. He invited someone to help him give out the papers.

10. He offered to repeat the instructions.

18 Your Turn

Answers will vary. Sample answers:
I'll help you with your homework, if you do the dishes. (promise)
I'll let you know about my party. (invite)
I'll never speak to you again if you tell them my secret. (threaten)
I'll walk your dog for you. (offer)
I'll tell you which courses to take next semester. (advise)

Function Activity

❖ To practice the functions presented in the chart in section **11g,** give students the following situations and ask them to write three reported commands with a partner or in small groups. Examples are given for the first situation.

> At a Girl or Boy Scout Camp, the counselors are giving orders to the children.

She told them to gather wood for the fire.
He ordered them to pile it near the lodge.
She ordered them to pick up trash around the campsite.

> A director of a movie on a set is asking the actors and extras to do the scene again.

> An advisor in high school is giving advice to students about to graduate.

> A couple that is going to get married is inviting the people they work with to their wedding.

The weather forecaster is warning people of a hurricane that is about to strike land.

Parents are threatening their son at college not to send any more money because of bad grades.

A parent is promising to take a junior soccer team out for ice cream if they win the game.

A teenager is offering to help an older neighbor with her chores.

❖ When they finish, have the students join another group or pair and read their sentences.

11h The Subjunctive in Noun Clauses

Student Book 3 p. 338, Student Book 3B p. 128

19 Practice

1. that he go to jail for two months.
2. that he get another trial.
3. that he do community service.
4. that he repay the money to the store owner.
5. that he return the CDs.
6. that he do all of the above except go to jail. (Answers will vary.)

20 Practice

Answers will vary. Sample answers:
1. that the government pass laws to protect them.
2. that we create new technology that will use alternate sources of energy.
3. that we develop low-cost housing in suburban areas.
4. that we restrict the use of cars and encourage the use of public transportation.
5. that factories stop emitting pollutants that destroy the ozone layer.
6. that we reduce our waste through stricter recycling regulations.
7. that we improve agricultural production in poorer areas of the world.
8. that we try diplomatic means before military force.

21 Your Turn

Answers will vary. Sample answers:
1. The train conductor insisted that the boy get off at the next station.
   The boy asked that he be let off at a station near his house.
   The passengers proposed that they take up a collection and pay for his ticket.
2. One friend suggested that she return the items that still had price tags on them.
   Another friend recommended that she sell them to other students.
   I advised that she tell her parents what she did and ask for help.
3. The insurance company demanded that he tell the truth.
   His wife insisted that he sell the car for parts and use public transportation.
   His lawyer urged him to tell the truth and accept the consequences.

Continue the activity started in **Your Turn 21** with the following cases. Have the students imagine the opinions of different people involved in each case.

❖ A child lets his dog run into the street and a car going very fast hits it. The dog is taken to the animal hospital and treated. The bill is $250. (child, parents, driver, veterinarian)

❖ A student leaves her backpack in the lounge near the secretary's desk. She goes to lunch with her classmates. When she comes back, one of her books is missing. (student, secretary, teacher, classmates)

❖ At a party, people hang their coats in a closet. When the party is over, a set of car keys is missing, and the car is gone from the driveway. Later the friends of the host's son bring the car back safely. (owner, host, son, friends)

Review

Student Book 3 p. 342, Student Book 3B p. 132

1 │ Review (11a–11c, 11e–11g)

1. Cindy told Matthew to get out of bed or he'd be late for his interview.
2. Matthew wanted to know why Cindy didn't get him up earlier.
3. Cindy said that she had gone to the gym.
4. Matthew couldn't remember if he had set his alarm clock or not.
5. Cindy suggested that Matthew hurry if he wanted to get that job.
6. The interviewer had insisted that he be there on time.
7. Cindy said she didn't understand why he had slept so late.
8. Matthew explained that he had been preparing for the interview until 2:00 A.M.
9. Cindy asked Matthew how he expected to get there.
10. Matthew wondered if she could drive him there.
11. Cindy wanted to know how far it was to the office.
12. Matthew explained that it was about 20 miles.

2 │ Review (11a–11c, 11e–11g)

1. Michael asked Susan if they were going to the museum that day.
2. Susan asked that he get her umbrella./Susan asked him to get her umbrella.
3. Michael wanted to know if it was raining then.
4. Michael wanted to know if the museum was open on Mondays.
5. Susan said she was really excited about seeing the new abstract art exhibit.
6. Michael said that his car wasn't running.
7. Susan told him not to worry because her mother could take them.
8. Michael suggested that they go by bus.
9. Susan wanted to know what time the next bus came.
10. Michael told Susan that it would be there in five minutes.
11. Michael couldn't remember if he had given her the discount tickets.
12. Susan recommended that he not look for them then.
13. Susan warned Michael that they would miss the bus.

3 | Review (11a–11e)

Ananse lived with his family. One year there was no rain, so the crops did not grow. Ananse ~~that~~ knew ⋀*that* there would not be enough food to feed everyone. One day his wife asked, "Will it rain at all this summer?"

"I don't believe so," he replied. "You know, I prefer to die than to see my children starve. Therefore, I will allow myself to die so that there will be enough food for the family." Ananse then told ~~to~~ his wife that he ~~wants~~*wanted* the family to bury ~~me~~*him* on the farm and to put into ~~my~~*his* coffin all the things ~~I will~~*he would* need for ~~my~~*his* journey into the next world. He said, "It's critical that you ~~left~~*leave* my grave open. I want my soul to be free to wander. And I insist that no one ~~visits~~*visit* visit the farm for three months after my death."

The next morning, Ananse's family found him dead. But Ananse was only pretending. At night he would lift the lid of his coffin and take food from the farm. One day his son, Ntikuma, realized that there wasn't much food in the house and that he must visit the farm to get some. He said he needed to go that day and get what little food the farm had to feed the family. "Where is all the corn and millet?" he said to himself when he got to the farm. His mother told him the food was disappearing at night. "It's a thief!" exclaimed Ntikuma. "I want to know who ~~is he~~*he is*."

Ntikuma carved a statue from wood and covered it with tar*. Then he placed the figure in the field. That evening, Ananse came out of his coffin and saw the figure. "Good evening," he said. "I don't know you. Please tell me who ~~are you~~*you are*?" The figure did not reply. Ananse got angry, so he slapped the figure. His hand stuck fast. Ananse shouted, "If ~~I~~*you* don't let go of ~~his~~*my* right hand, ~~he'll~~*I'll* hit you with ~~his~~*my* left!" He hit the statue with his left hand. He hit with his right leg, then the left. Ananse struggled as the figure fell. ~~He~~*That he* was stuck was very clear.

The next day Ntikuma and others went to the field. "I wonder ∧*if* Ntikuma caught the thief?" someone asked. Then they found Ananse. He was so ashamed he didn't know what to do, so he turned into a spider and climbed up a tree where he could not be seen.

4 | Review (11c–11e, 11h)

"I want more excitement," said one traveler.

"I want different things to do," said another.

When asked, many travelers have insisted that ~~we~~ *they* don't want to do just one thing while ~~we~~ *they*'re on vacation. In response, many tour operators now offer combination packages, or "combos." David Rose of High Roads Traveled says, "We now offer combo packages that mix several activities in one outing." Mr. Rose recommends that a traveler ~~takes~~ *take* a combo if he or she likes fun and adventure. "∧*That* people love these trips is very clear," he adds.

Combo packages mix hiking, cycling, biking, climbing, rafting, horseback riding, or other activities. Ron Clair of Ways Traveled says, "Combos are ~~his~~ *my* most popular trips."

"Sunbathing at the beach all week is a thing of the past," says Margaret Erikson, author of *Your Adventure*. "Can I tell you why are combos so popular?" she asks. She continues, "Today travelers demand tour operators that will give them a variety of adventures. Will this trend continue? I believe so. Sometimes I wonder ∧*if* the old car trip will eventually fade away."

Some people wonder ~~if~~ *whether* or not they must be a superior athlete to take a combo adventure. "Top athletes do things on their own," says Mary Miller of High Mountain Bike Tours. She adds that ~~my~~ *her* company is oriented toward vacations for the average person. She does say that ~~I talk~~ *she talks* to a client first and advises ~~he or her~~ *him or her/them* ∧*to* prepare. She says, "It's important that you ~~are doing~~ *do* some cycling or hiking before you go on any adventure vacation. But I urge that every client ~~remembers~~ *remember* that our tours are designed to be enjoyed at your own pace and in your own style."

Do you know where ~~are you~~ *you are* going on your next vacation? If you're into major thrills, a combo adventure may be just what ~~are you~~ *you are* looking for.

Writing Expansion

Student Book 3 p. 346, Student Book 3B p. 136

After the students finish their fable or legend, have them illustrate it, either by drawing a picture or using a graphic from a magazine or the Internet. The fables and legends can then be put on a bulletin board or on the class website.

❖ Unit 11 Student Book Self-Test

Student Book 3 p. 347, Student Book 3B p. 137

A. **1.** A **2.** D **3.** C **4.** C **5.** B **6.** C **7.** C **8.** C **9.** A **10.** C

B. **1.** C **2.** B **3.** B **4.** A **5.** B **6.** C **7.** C **8.** D **9.** B **10.** C

ADJECTIVE CLAUSES

Unit 12 first introduces the forms and functions of adjective clauses with the subject relative pronouns *who, that,* and *which*. Charts illustrate the use of these pronouns, and are followed by sentence completion and description exercises.

Next, adjective clauses are introduced with the object relative pronouns *who, whom, that,* and *which;* a distinction is made between formal and informal usage. The optional omission of the object relative pronoun is also presented, and matching, writing, and conversation exercises give students the opportunity to practice what they learn.

Adjective clauses with *whose* are presented and practiced in 12c, and the difference between *who's* and *whose* is made clear; exercises allow students to practice recognizing this difference.

Then, *when, where, why,* and *that* as relative pronouns are explained and exercises are provided to clarify when each is used.

Defining and non-defining adjective clauses are presented in 12e with numerous explanations, examples, and exercises.

The use of *which* to refer to an entire clause is explained in section 12f and is made clear through sentence-combining exercises.

Finally, reduced adjective clauses are explained and exercises provide students with an illustration of their function.

The writing activity is an essay that describes a process. The students determine the steps of the process through discussion and then write their essays, in which they can practice the adjective clauses taught in this unit.

12a Adjective Clauses with Subject Relative Pronouns

Student Book 3 p. 350, Student Book 3B p. 140

1 Practice

1. a. who invented the windshield wiper.
   b. that made streetcars safer in the rain.
2. a. who invented contact lenses for animals.
   b. that helped people see things at a distance.
3. a. who made tents.
   b. who went to California to look for gold
   c. that were made from tent material.

2 Your Turn

Answers will vary. Sample answers:

You: I'm thinking of a black and white bird that can swim but can't fly.
Your partner: Is it a penguin?
You: Yes, it is.
Your partner: I'm thinking of an animal that has a long neck and four legs.
You: Is it a giraffe?
Your partner: Yes, it is.
You: I'm thinking of an animal that eats nuts and lives in trees.
Your partner: Is it a squirrel?
You: Yes, it is.

Description Activity

❖ Continue the activity in **Your Turn 2** by writing different categories on the board, like *Fruits, Vegetables, Vehicles, Cities, Countries,* and so forth. Elicit additional ideas from the students.

❖ Tell the students they have one minute to take turns asking a partner as many questions as possible about a category. They should write down the number of questions they ask and receive an answer for within the time limit. Look at your watch and say, "Go!" When a minute is up, say, "Stop!" Then continue with the next category until you've done them all.

❖ The pair that completes the most questions in all the categories is the winner.

12b Adjective Clauses with Object Relative Pronouns

Student Book 3 p. 353, Student Book 3B p. 143

3 Practice

A. 1. h **2.** e **3.** i **4.** d **5.** f **6.** j **7.** b **8.** g **9.** c **10.** a

B. 1. A refrigerator is a machine that we use to keep food cold.

    2. Ketchup is a sauce that we eat with burgers and French fries.

    3. A telephone is a device that we use to speak over long distances.

    4. A firefighter is a person that we ask for help when we see a fire.

    5. A library is the place that we go to when we need to borrow a book.

    6. A telescope is a device that we use to see objects far away.

    7. A dictionary is a book that we look in when we need to know the meaning of a word.

    8. A light bulb is a thing that we use to see in the dark.

    9. A doctor is a person that we ask for help when we are sick.

    10. A bank is a place that we go to when we need to borrow some money.

4 Your Turn

Answers will vary. Sample answers:

You: What is a book that you always like to look at?

Your partner: *A China Journey* is a book that I always like to look at. It has beautiful photos.

Your partner: What is something that you can't live without?

You: I can't live without my cell phone. I need to stay in touch with my friends.

You: What is a food that you always think about?

Your partner: I always think about the *miso* soup my mother makes. It reminds me of home.

Your partner: What is a television show that you always like to watch.

You: A show that I like to watch is "Food Fight." Three chefs have a race to see who can make a dish the best.

You: Who is someone you look up to?

Your partner: I look up to my father because he's always honest and kind.

5 Your Turn

Answers will vary. Sample answers:

You: It's a machine that you use for storing and working with information.

Your partner: It's a computer.

Your partner: It's a vehicle that flies in the air from city to city or country to country.

You: It's an airplane.

You: It's a small device with earphones that you use to play music on discs.

Your partner: It's a CD player.

❖ If students can't think of many inventions for **Your Turn 5,** give them slips of paper with some inventions written on them. Here are two lists that you can add ideas to:

airplane	automobile
blender	cassette player
cell phone	computer
dryer	electric mixer
electron microscope	helicopter
jet engine	jet skis
pacemaker	parachute
printer	racing car
refrigerator	speedboat
toaster	typewriter
vaccine	videotape recorder
washing machine	x-ray machine

12c Adjective Clauses with *Whose*

Student Book 3 p. 356, Student Book 3B p. 146

6 Practice

1. Martin Luther King, Jr., was a civil rights leader whose most famous speech contains the words "I have a dream."
2. Abraham Lincoln was a president of the United States whose most famous achievement was freeing African-Americans from slavery.
3. Benjamin Franklin was an American statesman and inventor whose most famous invention was the lightning rod.
4. Wilbur and Orville Wright were brothers whose aircraft was the first wooden, piloted, heavier-than-air, self-propelled craft to fly.
5. Dorothea Lange was a photographer whose photos made people realize the poverty of workers during the Great Depression.
6. Alice Walker is an African-American writer whose novel *The Color Purple* received the Pulitzer Prize in 1983.
7. Elizabeth Cady Stanton was a leader of the American women's rights movement whose lifetime of work helped women gain the right to vote in the United States.
8. Neil Armstrong was an astronaut whose most famous achievement was walking on the moon.

7 Your Turn

Answers will vary. Sample answers:
Simon Bolívar was a South American leader whose armies fought for independence from Spain.
Mao Zedong was a Chinese leader whose revolution led to the People's Republic of China.
Napoleon Bonaparte was a French general whose bravery brought him victory and made him emperor of France.

❖ Continue **Your Turn 7** by writing some of these names on the board. Tell students that if they know who any of the people are, they should write a sentence about that person with an adjective clause containing *whose*.

Charlemagne	Ché Guevarra	Mao Zedong
Christopher Columbus	Cleopatra	Emiliano Zapata
George Washington	Golda Meir	Jacqueline Kennedy
Indira Ghandi	Joan of Arc	Kemal Atatürk
Nelson Mandela	Queen Victoria	Tutankamen

12d *When, Where, Why,* and *That* as Relative Pronouns

Student Book 3 p. 358, Student Book 3B p. 148

8 Practice

A. 1. where **2.** why/that **3.** that **4.** that **5.** when
B. 1. who/that **2.** when **3.** where **4.** that **5.** that
C. 1. that **2.** that **3.** when **4.** where **5.** that/who

9 Your Turn

Answers will vary. Sample answers:

A place where I feel peaceful is in my kitchen. It's especially nice at times when I am cooking dinner for my family.

A reason why I feel anxious is because I have only a year to study English. Then I have to be accepted into a university to keep my scholarship.

A time when I feel happiest is on Friday afternoon after class. The week is over, and I have two whole days to relax and hang out with my friends.

❖ Write these words on the board so that students can continue the **Your Turn 9** activity, talking further about their feelings:

amused	calm	confident	frightened
nervous	relaxed	sleepy	smart
stressed	tired	troubled	worried

12e Defining and Nondefining Adjective Clauses

Student Book 3 p. 361, Student Book 3B p. 151

 Practice

D	that have animals in them
ND	, which seem to be about animals,
D	that people do
D	that can get us into trouble
ND	, which is the lesson people should learn
ND	, whose fables are world famous
D	who wrote them
ND	, who lived a long time ago in Greece,
ND	, of which he wrote about 350,
ND	, which give us lessons about life,

11 Practice

1. most of which   **2.** none of which   **3.** all of which   **4.** both of whom
5. neither of whom   **6.** a little of which

12 Your Turn

Answers will vary. Sample answers:
My classmate, whose name is Ariella, is from Italy. She has a large family that is composed of a mother, a father, and four brothers. She plays a lot of tennis, which is a fast sport that keeps her in shape. She likes speaking in front of the class, which all of the students enjoy. The presentations that we have to give every week are easy for her.

Paragraph Activity

❖ To continue **Your Turn 12**, have students write about each other in pairs. Tell them to work with someone they don't usually work with.

❖ When the students finish the paragraphs, collect them and read some aloud to the class, omitting the names. See if students can guess who is being described in the paragraph.

12f Using *Which* to Refer to an Entire Clause

Student Book 3 p. 364, Student Book 3B p. 154

 Practice

A. 1. c **2.** h **3.** a **4.** b **5.** f **6.** e **7.** d **8.** g

B. 1. The teacher encouraged me, which motivated me to work harder.

2. The teacher corrected my paper in red ink, which helped me find my mistakes.

3. She let us use the Internet to do our research, which was easier than finding books from the library.

4. We didn't have tests every week in this class, which made us feel less pressure.

5. We wrote about the news of the day, which made me read newspapers and listen to the news.

6. We worked with other students in class, which helped me make new friends.

7. The teacher always paid a lot of attention to us, which made us feel like she cared about us.

8. We lost points when we handed in homework late, which meant I had to do my homework on time.

14 | Your Turn

Answers will vary. Sample answers:
1. I heard the news about the principal of the school, which was a shock to me.
2. Our principal let us say goodbye to her, which was a nice surprise.
3. The principal had tears in her eyes, which made it more difficult.
4. She gave us the next Friday off, which was very kind of her.
5. Her taxi to the airport was late, which irritated me.
6. She said she had found a position at another school, which disappointed me.

Bad Day/Good Day Activity

❖ Tell students about a bad day that you had when your flight was cancelled, your car broke down, your dog ran away, or something else bad happened. Ask them if they've ever had a bad day and make a list on the board of the reasons why: *credit card was stolen, lost a cell phone, failed an exam.*

❖ Write down expressions we use to reply to these situations: *Sorry to hear that, That's a shame, Too bad.*

❖ Go around the class by having a student say a sentence, adding a non-defining clause. Have the next person respond appropriately. For example:

A: My credit card was stolen, which made it difficult to buy books for class.
B: Sorry to hear that!
B: I lost my cell phone, which made my parents mad.
C: That's a shame!
C: We failed the exam, which disappointed our teacher.
D: Too bad!

- ❖ Then, tell the students about a good day you had when you won a prize, finished a project, got a pay raise, or experienced some other positive event. Elicit good days from them and make a list on the board of the reasons why, just as you did above with bad days.
- ❖ Write down expressions we use to reply to these good situations: *Glad to hear that, That's great, Awesome.*
- ❖ Go around the class by having a student say a sentence, adding a non-defining clause. Have the next person respond appropriately, and so forth. For example:

> A: *I won first prize in the essay contest, which was a nice surprise.*
> B: *Glad to hear that!*
> B: *We finished our project early, which was such a relief!*
> C: *That's great!*
> C: *I just got a pay raise, which will help me save for my vacation!*
> D: *Awesome!*

12g Reduced Adjective Clauses
Student Book 3 p. 367, Student Book 3B p. 157

15 Practice

~~who is~~ famous for his fairy tales

~~that are~~ well known all over the world

~~who was~~ born in Denmark in 1805

~~who was~~ growing up in poverty

~~who was~~ a shoemaker

~~who was~~ unable to read or write

~~who was~~ dreaming of becoming an actor

~~which was~~ the capital city of Denmark

~~who wanted~~ wanting his dream to come true

~~who saw~~ seeing him act

~~who was~~ feeling very disappointed

~~who was~~ studying hard

~~which is~~ a fairy tale about a baby duck

~~who was~~ like a child

~~who was~~ getting disappointed

~~which were~~ thought to be too adult at first

16 Practice

1. grown **2.** drunk **3.** sold **4.** eaten **5.** served **6.** taken **7.** mashed, fried **8.** ripened

17 Your Turn

Answers will vary. Sample answers:
Once upon a time, there was a little girl living in a forest...
A long, long time ago, there lived a princess locked in a high tower...
In a faraway land lived a sultan with a magic carpet...

Fairy Tale Activity

❖ To make **Your Turn 17** more fun, divide the students into groups representing different regions of the world and have them write a fairy tale from their region. If the class is from one country, divide them into groups and ask each to choose a different fairy tale.

❖ When the groups finish writing and checking their work, tell them they have to act out their fairy tales. One student in each group will be the reader; the others will be the actors, miming the actions and possibly playing different parts.

❖ Give them time to practice in separate corners of the classroom. When they are ready, let the plays begin!

◆ Review

Student Book 3 p. 371, Student Book 3B p. 161

 Review (12a–12b, 12e–12f)

1. who, who **2.** which **3.** that **4.** which **5.** whom **6.** which, which **7.** that/which **8.** whom **9.** who **10.** who **11.** which **12.** why, that

 Review (12a, 12e)

1. that **2.** who/that **3.** in which/where **4.** which **5.** which **6.** why **7.** which **8.** who **9.** who/that **10.** whom **11.** that/which **12.** who **13.** which **14.** whose **15.** who/that **16.** which **17.** whose

 Review (12a–12f)

1. where **2.** where **3.** who **4.** whose **5.** who/that **6.** that/which **7.** which **8.** which **9.** which **10.** whose **11.** who/that **12.** which **13.** who/that **14.** who **15.** that/which **16.** who **17.** who/that **18.** that/which **19.** which **20.** that/no pronoun **21.** who/that **22.** that/no pronoun

4 Review (12a, 12c–12e, 12g)

On the morning of November 4, 1966, ~~that~~ *which* was a terrible day for art lovers, it was raining very hard in Italy. For many days, terrible rains had fallen on Italy, ~~which~~ *whose* cities are filled with the world's greatest works of art. The Arno River, ~~fill~~ *filling* quickly, threatened to flood. Just before dawn, the river, ~~that~~ *which* flows through Florence, overflowed its banks, sending water into the countryside. The citizens of Florence, ~~which~~ *who* had been sleeping, awakened to find their city under water. Florence, ~~who~~ *which* is a famous art center, was under 14 feet of water and mud in some places. Thousands of art works, many of ~~whom~~ *which* were priceless masterpieces, were also under water. Suddenly Florence was a city ~~who~~ *that* was a graveyard of the world's finest art.

The Florentines, ~~that~~ *who* survived by climbing to their rooftops, faced a terrible disaster. The city that they loved was flooded. The greatest art works in the world, many *of* ∧ which had survived for hundreds of years, were buried in water and mud. But Florence is a city in ~~whom~~ *which* there are many art lovers.

On the morning after the flood, art students formed a human chain and pulled the art works out of the water. Within 24 hours, people ~~which~~ *who/that* restored paintings began arriving in the city. It was a time ~~that~~ *when* many people came together for a common cause—to save the art work. This disaster, from ~~who~~ *which* the Florentines never expected to recover, caught the interest of people around the world. Donations came from everywhere. Experts worked tirelessly and much was saved. To be sure, many books and manuscripts ~~who~~ *that/which* were very valuable were lost to the flood, but many were rescued. Perhaps most important, the flood of 1966 taught lessons *that* ∧ will not be forgotten. Experts developed new methods ~~whom~~ *that/which* protect artworks from natural disasters. People ~~which~~ *who/that* worked on the art also developed new techniques *that/which* ∧ will help keep art safe for future generations.

Writing Expansion

Student Book 3 p. 375, Student Book 3B p. 165

After the students finish their process essay, have them illustrate it, either by drawing a picture, or by cutting one out of a magazine or finding one on the Internet. The process essay can then be put on a bulletin board or on the class website.

Unit 12 Student Book Self-Test

Student Book 3 p. 376, Student Book 3B p. 166

A. **1.** D **2.** B **3.** C **4.** B **5.** C **6.** A **7.** C **8.** A **9.** B **10.** B

B. **1.** B **2.** B **3.** D **4.** B **5.** B **6.** A **7.** B **8.** C **9.** A **10.** B

ADVERB CLAUSES

Unit 13 first introduces the forms and functions of adverb clauses of time through a helpful chart showing uses and examples. Students will practice these uses and examples in the matching and personal opinion exercises that follow.

Next, adverb clauses of reason and result are introduced and distinctions are made between the two functions. Fill-in-the-blank and rewriting exercises test what the students have learned.

Then, in 13c, adverb clauses of purpose with *so that* are presented to answer questions that include the phrases *what for?* or *for what purpose?*

Adverb clauses of contrast—including clauses of condition—are explained in sections 13d and e to show relationships. Students will practice learning these relationships through a variety of exercises.

Finally, reduced adverb clauses are explained, using numerous examples, and exercises are provided to expand the students' understanding.

The writing activity is an essay of comparison or contrast. Students will first discuss the essay to find similarities and differences between situations, and then they will write in order to practice the adverb clauses taught in this unit.

13a Adverb Clauses of Time

Student Book 3 p. 380, Student Book 3B p. 170

 Practice

A. Reading

B. 1. b **2.** e **3.** a **4.** d **5.** c

C. 1. When she was attacked by polar bears, her dog Charlie protected her.
   2. While she was resting at night, she talked to Charlie about her thoughts and plans.
   3. She knew she would not give up until she achieved her goal.
   4. As soon as she returned home, she wrote a book, *Polar Dreams,* about her amazing adventures.
   5. Since she returned from her trip, she has traveled all over the world, giving talks about her amazing experiences.

2 What Do You Think?

Answers will vary. Sample answers:

Helen Thayer was a strong woman. The fact that she tried to walk to the North Pole at 50 is surprising. The fact that she actually succeeded is even more surprising, and her adventures are very interesting.

3 Your Turn

Answers will vary. Sample answers:

I decided to come to the United States to get a degree in computer engineering. Before I came, I studied for the TOEFL and got a high score. After I arrived, I took courses and got good grades. When I graduated, I felt very proud and happy.

Race Activity

❖ The Iditarod is a 1,100-mile race from Anchorage to Nome, Alaska, that takes place every March. "Mushers" ride on sleds pulled by teams of dogs—huskies, malamutes, or Samoyeds—hoping to be the first to cross the finish line. When the race first started in 1967, it lasted 20 days, but now it only lasts 10 days. In 1985, Libby Riddles became the first woman to win the long, difficult, and dangerous race.

❖ Tell students about the race and put a few facts about Libby Riddles on the board:

> Moved to Alaska as a teenager
> Lived near Anchorage
> Loved to watch dogsled races
> Won her first race in 1978
> Entered the Iditarod in 1980
> Didn't have good dogs
> Finished 18th in the race
> Started breeding sled dogs
> Entered the Iditarod in 1985
> Won despite windstorm

❖ Tell students to go to the board in pairs and have each make up a sentence about Libby Riddles using adverb clause markers from the charts in Section 13a. You can put a few examples on the board:

> _When_ Libby was a teenager, she moved to Alaska.
> She wanted to be a "musher" _as soon as_ she saw her first dogsled race.
> _The first time_ she entered a race, she won.

❖ After students finish writing their sentences, have them read them aloud.

13b Adverb Clauses of Reason and Result

Student Book 3 p. 383, Student Book 3B p. 173

4 Practice

1. because **2.** , so **3.** , so **4.** because **5.** , so **6.** because **7.** , so **8.** because **9.** because **10.** , so

5 Practice

1. The house was so small that she had to stoop down to go in.
It was such a small house that she...

2. The chairs and table were so delicate she was afraid to touch them.
They were such delicate chairs and tables that she...

3. A cake on the kitchen table was so delicious that she ate three slices.
It was such a delicious cake on the kitchen table that she...

4. The house was so beautiful that she felt like she wanted to stay there forever.
It was such a beautiful house that she...

5. The bed was so soft that she couldn't help lying down.
It was such a soft bed that she...

6. She heard music so soft that she fell asleep immediately.
It was such soft music that she...

7. She had a dream that was so peaceful that she didn't want to wake up.
It was such a peaceful dream that she...

8. She heard a noise so loud that she woke up suddenly.
It was such a loud noise that she...

9. The moon was so bright that she could see outside as though it were day.
It was such a bright moon that she could see outside as though it were day.

6 What Do You Think?

Answers will vary. Sample answers:
The loud noise was a car door slamming. Esmeralda had fallen asleep in her family's car while they were driving through a forest. It was dark when they finally reached their house in the country, but the moon was shining brightly. Esmeralda woke up and realized that the tiny house in her dream was really their house in the country.

7 Your Turn

Answers will vary. Sample answers:
I once ate *meze** in Turkey that were so good I couldn't stop eating. When my dinner came, I wasn't hungry any more. I was so embarrassed that I continued eating and could hardly walk out of the restaurant.

*In Turkey, *meze* are foods, usually eaten in small quantities, to begin a meal.

Blackboard Story

❖ Tell students to look at the clause markers of reason and result in chart 3b. You are going to start a story on the board and everyone is going to write a sentence containing one of these markers. Each sentence must be logical and continuous, so the students have to pay attention to what the other students write.

❖ Write the first sentence on the board and underline the clause marker, for example:

> *I was waiting for the bus, and a strange old woman came and stood beside me. She looked <u>so strange that</u> I felt a little afraid.*

❖ The students, in turn, should continue the story to by writing sentences like these, using different clause markers:

> *<u>Because</u> the bus was crowded, she stood beside me.*
> *<u>As a result</u>, I could hear her singing.*
> *<u>As</u> she sang louder and louder, people began to stare at her.*

❖ Tell the last few students that they have to end the story. After they are finished, have each student read his or her sentence aloud.

13c Adverb Clauses of Purpose

Student Book 3 p. 387, Student Book 3B p. 177

8 | Practice

1. so that   **2.** so that   **3.** ; therefore, / . Therefore,   **4.** Therefore,   **5.** so that
6. ; therefore, / . Therefore,   **7.** Therefore,   **8.** so that   **9.** so that

9 | Your Turn

Answers will vary. Sample answers:
It's fun to travel a lot so that you learn about other countries and cultures.
I've traveled through most of Latin America; therefore, I know about different customs.
I try to speak with the local people so that I can practice Spanish.
Many international companies have branches in Latin America; therefore, they hire people who can speak Spanish.

Question-Answer Activity

- ❖ Tell the students to write down three questions to ask their partners beginning with "Why...? Their partners will answer with "So that..." For example:

    Q: Why do you eat a salad every day for lunch?
    A: So that I'll lose some weight.
    Q: Why did you get a cell phone?
    A: So that I could keep in touch with my friends.

- ❖ When the students finish asking their questions, have them switch partners and repeat the activity a few more times.

13d Adverb Clauses of Contrast

Student Book 3 p. 389, Student Book 3B p. 179

10 | Practice

A. 1. f   **2.** c   **3.** b   **4.** a   **5.** e   **6.** d
B. Clause markers will vary.
   1. Although Samuel is rich, he isn't happy.
   2. While Samuel has a lot of "friends," none of them would help him if he were in trouble.
   3. While Samuel works very hard, he doesn't like his job.
   4. Although Samuel has a lot of money, he doesn't know what to spend it on.
   5. While a lot of people want to meet him, he doesn't want to meet them.
   6. Even though Samuel has several houses, none of them feels like home.

11 Practice

Answers will vary. Sample answers:
1. Samuel is rich; however, he is unhappy.
2. Samuel has a lot of "friends;" nevertheless, none of them would help him if he were in trouble.
3. Samuel works very hard; however, he doesn't like his job.
4. Samuel has a lot of money; however, he doesn't know what to spend it on.
5. A lot of people want to meet him; nevertheless, he doesn't want to meet them.
6. Samuel has several houses; however, none of them feels like home.

Rich-Poor Activity

❖ Tell students to look at the sentences about Samuel and make up similar ones about Paul, who doesn't have any money. They can write the sentences in the book beside the ones from **Practice 11.**

❖ Write the first sentence about Paul on the board as an example:

Although Paul is poor, he's happy.

❖ After the students write the sentences, have them take turns reading them aloud.

13e Adverb Clauses of Condition

Student Book 3 p. 391, Student Book 3B p. 181

12 Practice

A. 1. a **2.** c **3.** f **4.** b **5.** e **6.** d

B. 1. You may not use the computer unless you have already registered with the library.
2. Children under six may use the computer only if they are accompanied by an adult.
3. You need to get a new password if you forget your old one.
4. Ask a librarian for assistance in case you can't log on to the Internet.
5. The maximum time per person is one hour whether other students are waiting or not.
6. You may use the computer for the maximum time even if another student is waiting.

13 Your Turn

Answers will vary. Sample answers:
You should wash pots and pans if you've used them.
You may not eat other students' food unless you ask them.
Even if you don't cook much, you have to take turns cleaning the kitchen.
In case you notice a funny smell in the refrigerator, check for spoiled food.

❖ Ask the students to think of classroom rules at the language center and classroom rules in other schools they attended in their home countries. In pairs, have them write a few that may be different from their current class. For example:

Here, absence isn't excused <u>unless</u> you have a note from the health center.
In my country, <u>even if</u> you don't have a note, you can be excused for absence.

❖ After they finish writing, have the students read their rules and discuss the reasons for the differences.

13f Reduced Adverb Clauses

Student Book 3 p. 394, Student Book 3B p. 184

14 Practice

1. before beginning   **2.** While running   **3.** After coming back   **4.** When/While setting
5. Once completed   **6.** Hoping   **7.** while studying   **8.** After eating   **9.** Since starting
10. After being checked   **11.** Filed

15 Practice

Y   **1.** After finishing an assignment, Julia checks her work carefully.
N   **2.**
Y   **3.** Since starting her new schedule, Julia has been much happier.
N   **4.**
N   **5.**
Y   **6.** Knowing that she must stay healthy, Julia runs every day and eats lots of fruit.
Y   **7.** Before returning home, she goes to the coffee shop with her friends.
N   **8.**

16 Your Turn

Answers will vary. Sample answers:
While working or studying, I listen to soft music on the radio. That relaxes me and helps me concentrate on what I'm doing.
After finishing work or study, I go home and turn on the TV. Usually I watch half an hour of news and then the educational channel. I like programs about history, science, and nature.

❖ Put students into groups of four and tell them to look at Julia's schedule in **Practice 15.** Write a few discussion questions on the board like the following:

Why does Julia   - think about her day while running?
                     - set goals for each part of the day?
                     - keep track of her progress?
                     - follow a strict schedule?
                     - organize her assignments?

❖ When they finish discussing the questions, ask the students to make up a schedule for themselves like Julia's. If possible, the groups should meet for a few minutes every day for the next week or two so members can ask each other how their schedules are going.

Review

Student Book 3 p. 398, Student Book 3B p. 188

1   Review (13a–13b, 13d–13e)

1. but   **2.** While   **3.** however   **4.** While   **5.** As   **6.** After   **7.** unless   **8.** When   **9.** however
10. Even though   **11.** so   **12.** Although   **13.** Because   **14.** nevertheless   **15.** whereas
16. but   **17.** consequently   **18.** so   **19.** After   **20.** however   **21.** nevertheless

2   Review (13a–13b, 13d–13e)

1. so   **2.** Even though/Although   **3.** Because/Since/As   **4.** However,   **5.** so
6. Although/Even though   **7.** Because/As/Since   **8.** After   **9.** unless   **10.** , but
11. After/As soon as   **12.** When   **13.** If only   **14.** Because/Since/As
15. When/As soon as/As   **16.** When/By the time   **17.** Consequently,/Therefore,
18. ; consequently,/; therefore,   **19.** Since

3   Review (13b–13e)

A. 1. i   **2.** c   **3.** d   **4.** j   **5.** a   **6.** g   **7.** h   **8.** e   **9.** f   **10.** b
B.

1. Jeff is starting a new job today, so he's a little nervous.

2. He set his alarm clock so that he would wake up on time.

3. He changed his clothes three times before leaving home although/even though he had chosen a suit the night before.

4. He wanted to drive his car today; however, it is in the shop for repairs. OR ...today, but it is...

5. He's going to take the bus although/even though a friend offered to drive him.

6. He will usually take the bus because he wants to save money on gas.

7. He thinks he's well-prepared for his work as a computer programmer; nevertheless, he's afraid they'll ask him something he doesn't know. OR ...programmer, but he's afraid...

8. He had several jobs while he was in school, but he has never worked in an office.

9. Jeff has met his new boss, but he hasn't met any of his coworkers. OR ...new boss; however he...

10. He is determined to succeed in this job even if it is difficult at first.

4 Review (13a, 13c–13f)

~~As soon as~~ *As* more and more people try cross-country, or Nordic, skiing, it is becoming more popular than ever. There are several reasons why. In order ∧ *to* ski downhill or snowboard, you must have deep snow, ~~where~~ *while/whereas/but* to do cross-country skiing, you need only a few inches of snow on the ground. ~~While~~ *When* you downhill ski, you need to go to a special area and take lifts to the top of the mountain, ~~nevertheless,~~ *, but* when you cross-country ski, you can use any field or forest. You don't need to buy lift tickets to ski along a forest trail ~~because~~ *, so/; therefore,* cross-country skiing doesn't cost very much to do.

Because ~~of~~ you're not rushing down a hill at a high speed, cross-country skiing is safe and easy to learn. It's good for you, too. ~~Since~~ *As/While* you're enjoying your winter surroundings, you're also getting a complete physical workout. ~~While~~ *When* you're ready to go cross-country skiing, it's easy to find good cross-country routes. Even ∧ *if* there's no snow where you live, most mountain ski areas have miles and miles of trails.

~~Since~~ *Before* it became a popular sport, cross-country skiing was often the only way to travel for people in snow country. In cold areas of the north, people couldn't go anywhere ~~though~~ *unless* they strapped on their skis. ~~Because~~ *Although/Whereas* some people still cross-country ski out of necessity, most people do it for fun. Before ~~go~~ *going* cross-country skiing, you probably should take a lesson. It may seem hard at first, ~~since~~ *but* most instructors say that people are usually gliding along after only a few hours.

Writing Expansion

Student Book 3 p. 402, Student Book 3B p. 192

After the students finish their comparison/contrast essay, ask them to do oral presentations on their topics. If several students have written on the same topic, they can organize a debate or panel discussion. The other students should listen and ask questions when they are finished. If appropriate, write a short evaluation of each student or group presentation and give feedback.

Unit 13 Student Book Self-Test

Student Book 3 p. 403, Student Book 3B p. 193

A. **1.** A **2.** D **3.** B **4.** C **5.** A **6.** C **7.** A **8.** B **9.** C **10.** A

B. **1.** A **2.** A **3.** C **4.** B **5.** C **6.** A **7.** A **8.** D **9.** B **10.** C

CONDITIONAL SENTENCES

Unit Sections	Notes/Activities	Student Book 3 page	Student Book 3B page	Teacher's Manual page
14a Real Conditional Sentences in the Present and Future	Verb Activity	406	196	136
14b Unreal Conditional Sentences in the Present or Future	*If I were...* Activity	409	199	137
14c Unreal Conditional Sentences in the Past; Mixed Conditional Sentences	Chant Activity	412	202	138
14d Conditional Sentences with *As If* and *As Though*	Picture Activity	416	206	139
14e Conditional Sentences Without *If*	Changing Activity	418	208	140
14f Wishes About the Present, Future, and Past; *Hope*	Advice Activity	422	212	142
14g Conditional Sentences with *If Only*	*If only...* Activity	425	215	143
❖ Review	Review Answer Key	427	217	143
❖ Writing	Writing Expansion	431	221	145
❖ Unit 14 Student Book Self-Test	Unit 14 Self-Test Answer Key	432	222	145

Unit 14 first introduces the forms and functions of real conditional sentences. These are followed by rewriting, matching, and personal knowledge exercises.

Next, unreal conditional sentences in the present and future are explained and practiced. Careful attention is paid to verb tenses.

Then, unreal conditional sentences in the past and mixed conditional sentences are introduced. A series of exercises based on Romeo and Juliet help students understand these concepts more fully.

Conditional sentences with *as if* and *as though* are explained and practiced in section 14d.

Next, expressions used in conditional sentences without *if* are taught and practiced.

The difference between the verbs *wish* and *hope* is explained in section 14f, and practice is provided in the form of writing and personal opinion exercises.

Finally, conditional sentences with *if only* are presented and examples are given.

The writing activity is an essay of argumentation. Students discuss a position to find reasons for and against it and then write an essay that gives them the opportunity to practice the conditionals taught in this unit.

14a Real Conditional Sentences in the Present and Future

Student Book 3 p. 406, Student Book 3B p. 196

1 Practice

Answers will vary. Sample answers:

1. If you make a mistake, there's no point in crying about it.
2. When you make a decision, consider it carefully.
3. If many people help with a job, it'll be done quickly and easily.
4. If something appears to be true, it probably is.
5. If you eat an apple every day, you'll be healthy.
6. When one bad thing happens, lots of bad things happen.
7. If guests stay at your house for more than three days, you'll probably get tired of them.
8. If you have several things to do, do the most important one first.
9. If you don't take risks in life, you won't gain anything.
10. If you don't act at the opportune moment, you may not succeed.
11. If you have money, you decide what to do with it, not other people.
12. If you succeed despite what other people say, you will have more satisfaction in the end than they will.

2 Practice

1. d **2.** e **3.** a **4.** b **5.** c

3 Your Turn

Answers will vary. Sample answers:
If you close the plastic bag tightly, the bread will stay fresh.
If you chop the onion in a food processor, you won't cry.
If you cook rice in the microwave for 20 minutes, it comes out just right.
If you make coffee or tea with filtered water, it tastes better.

- ❖ Write different verbs on slips of paper and give two to each student. Tell them to make real conditional sentences with them, one in the present tense and one in the future.
- ❖ Here are a few examples you can put on the board:

  sit/see   *If you sit too close to the TV, you can't see the picture very well.*
  If we sit too far from the screen, we won't be able to see the details of the movie.

  sing/play   *Don't sing along if a pianist is playing at a concert.*
  We'll sing if the accompanist will play a little faster.

- ❖ When the students finish, have them check their sentences with a partner.

14b Unreal Conditional Sentences in the Present or Future

Student Book 3 p. 409, Student Book 3B p. 199

4 Practice

Answers will vary. Sample answers:

1. If I found a wallet with $500 in it, I would give it to the driver. Maybe the person who lost it would call the taxi company.
   If I found a wallet with $500 in it, I wouldn't keep it. I don't think that's honest.
2. If a burglar broke into my house at night and I was alone, I'd call the police on my cell phone.
   If a burglar broke into my house at night and I was alone, I wouldn't try to catch him by myself because he could hurt or kill me.
3. If I saw someone stealing cans of soup in the supermarket, I'd give him or her some money.
   If I saw someone stealing cans of soup in the supermarket, I wouldn't report him or her to the manager because maybe he or she is poor and can't afford to buy them.
4. If a car hit a cyclist, the driver didn't stop, and the cyclist was left lying injured in the road, I'd copy down the car's license number and call 911 on my cell phone.
   If a car hit a cyclist, the driver didn't stop, and the cyclist was left lying injured in the road, I wouldn't try to move the cyclist because I might injure him or her more.

5 Your Turn

Answers will vary. Sample answer:
Once I saw a candy bar lying on the floor of a convenience store. I bent down to tie my shoe and put the candy in my pocket. I left the store without paying for it. I still feel bad about it because it only cost a dollar, and I could have paid for it. What would you do in that situation?

❖ Tell students to think of three public figures, like politicians, movie stars, musicians, or artists. Have them make up sentences starting with *If I were...* like these examples:

> *If I were Arnold Schwarzenegger, I'd spend more money on education.*
> *If I were the Queen of England, I'd turn Buckingham Palace into a museum.*

❖ When they are finished, have students work with a partner and take turns saying their sentences.

14c Unreal Conditional Sentences in the Past; Mixed Conditional Sentences

Student Book 3 p. 412, Student Book 3B p. 202

6 Practice

A. Reading

B. Answers will vary. Sample answers:
1. If they hadn't fallen in love, this story wouldn't have happened.
2. If he hadn't married them, they would have never been able to be together.
3. If he hadn't given her the drink, she would have had to marry another man.
4. If he had received the friar's message, he wouldn't have drunk poison and died.
5. If Romeo hadn't taken the poison, Juliet wouldn't have killed herself.
6. If Juliet hadn't killed herself, she would probably have had to marry the other man.

C. Answers will vary. Sample answers:
1. If Romeo hadn't met Juliet, he could have married someone else.
2. If Romeo and Juliet's families hadn't hated each other, the two could have been able to get married.
3. If Romeo's friends hadn't been in a fight, he might not have killed Juliet's cousin.
4. If Juliet hadn't taken the sleeping potion, she might have had to marry another man.
5. If Juliet hadn't found Romeo's dagger, she might not have killed herself.
6. If Juliet had woken up a little sooner, Romeo might not have drunk the poison.

D. Answers will vary. Sample answers:
1. If I were Juliet, I would have run away with Romeo when he was sent away from the city.
2. If I were Romeo, I would have taken Juliet with me.
3. If I were the friar, I would have hidden the couple until they could figure out what to do.
4. If I were Juliet's father, I would have allowed her to marry Romeo.

7 **Your Turn**

Answers will vary. Sample answers:
If I hadn't come to Canada to study English,
>   ...I wouldn't have been able to speak English very well.
>   ...I wouldn't have met classmates from all over the world.
>   ...I would have stayed in my country and gone to college there.

Chant Activity

❖ Tell the students that in past unreal conditional sentences, the auxiliary verb + *have* in the main clause is pronounced differently in slow formal speech than in rapid informal speech:

could have	=	coulda
should have	=	shoulda
would have	=	woulda
might have	=	mighta

❖ Put this chant on the board to practice the two forms. You can clap or tap out the rhythm as you say it for the students:

Could **you** have **climbed** Mt. **E**verest?   I **could**a, I **could**a, I **could**a, but I **did**n't.

Should **you** have **eat**en an**oth**er piece of **cake**?   I **should**a, I **should**a, I **should**a, and I **did**!

Would **you** have **passed** the **dri**ving **test**?   I **would**a, I **would**a, I **would**a, but I **did**n't.

Might **you** have **j**umped in**to** the **lake**?   I **might**a, I **might**a, I **might**a, and I **did**!

❖ Say the questions and have the students say the answers. Or you can have one side of the class say the questions and the other side the answers, and then switch sides for more practice.

14d Conditional Sentences with *As If* and *As Though*

Student Book 3 p. 416, Student Book 3B p. 206

8 **Practice**

Answers will vary. Sample answers:
1. It looks as if it's going to rain.
2. He feels as though he's catching a cold / coming down with the flu.
3. It sounds like they're having a fight.
4. It looks as if he's moving to Taiwan.
5. She looks as though she did well on it.
6. It sounds like they all got raises.
7. It looks as if there was a party in here.
8. It sounds as though he's having a hard time getting over his divorce.

9 Your Turn

Answers will vary. Sample answers:

It looks as if she's taken a lot of books off the shelves

She looks as though she can't hold them all.

It looks as if she's going to drop them all.

Picture Activity

❖ Bring in pictures of current events from magazines or newspapers and continue with **Your Turn 9.** Give one to each student and have them make up sentences using *as if, as though,* and *like.*

❖ When they are finished, tell them to give their pictures to their partners to look at and have them read their sentences to each other.

14e Conditional Sentences Without *If*

Student Book 3 p. 418, Student Book 3B p. 208

10 Practice

A. Reading

B. **1.** If I had known that the mixer was faulty, I would never have bought it.

2. (I'm sure that) If I hadn't bought your mixer, we would have enjoyed her birthday better.

3. If the mixer hadn't been faulty, we wouldn't have spent two hours that morning cleaning up the mess.

4. If you don't give me a complete refund, I will take the matter to my lawyer.

5. If our home weren't so far away, I'd bring the mixer back personally.

6. If I need any kitchen appliances in the future, I won't purchase them at your store.

11 What Do You Think?

Answers will vary. Sample answers:

I don't think that the letter is effective because Ms. Winters gives too many details, and she isn't polite.

Note: A business letter is concise and polite. It states what the writer wants very clearly. This letter has effective and ineffective elements.

Effective Elements	Ineffective Elements
It states the problem clearly.	It is not polite—it threatens the recipient with legal action. This would normally be a last resort.
It states what the writer wants.	It gives many details that are not necessary to make the point.
	It is longer than necessary.

12 Practice

A. Reading

B. 1. Had we known that the mixer was faulty, we would never have sold this model in our store.

  2. Had he tried out the machine before selling it to you, the sales assistant would have identified the fault.

  3. Without this information from you, we would have continued selling faulty mixers to other customers.

  4. Should you wish to have a replacement mixer, we will send one out to you immediately.

  5. Should you not wish to have a replacement, we can offer you a complete refund.

  6. Were you to have any further problems with the replacement mixer, please let us know immediately.

  7. Should you have any other questions, please do not hesitate to get in touch.

13 Your Turn

Answers will vary. Sample answers:

If I'd known about downloading songs from the Internet for a dollar, I wouldn't have bought so many CDs. OR Had I known about downloading songs...

If hadn't bought so many CDs, I'd have enough money to buy an iPod.™ OR Had I not bought so many CD's, ...

If I'd bought an iPod™, I'd be able to listen to music anytime and anyplace. OR Had I bought an iPod™, ...

Changing Activity

❖ Continue with **Your Turn 13** and have students read the sentences with *if* to their partners; the partner will then say—not read—sentences without *if*.

❖ Tell the students to switch roles. If there is time, they can switch partners and go through the same procedure again.

14f Wishes about the Present, Future, and Past; *Hope*

Student Book 3 p. 422, Student Book 3B p. 212

14 Practice

A. 1. He wishes he was/were rich.
   2. He wishes his life was/were exciting.
   3. He wishes his apartment wasn't/weren't small.
   4. He wishes he didn't feel tired.
   5. He wishes he had (some) friends.
   6. He wishes he could play the guitar.

B. 1. He wishes his car hadn't broken down.
   2. He wishes he hadn't eaten all the food in the refrigerator.
   3. He wishes he had paid his phone bill last month.
   4. He wishes he hadn't spent all the money on his credit card.
   5. He wishes he hadn't been late for work and gotten fired.
   6. He wishes he could find another job.

15 Your Turn

Answers will vary. Sample answers:
1. I wish I didn't have to do so much homework. I wish I were on vacation. I wish I could take a semester off. I wish my parents sent me more money every month. I wish it were warmer and sunnier here.
2. I wish I hadn't spent so much time at my computer. I wish I had gone out with my friends last weekend. I wish I had done my laundry. I wish I had bought some food at the supermarket. I wish I had cleaned my apartment.

Advice Activity

❖ Have students sit in groups of three or four and take turns reading one of their sentences from **Your Turn 15.** First, one student should read a sentence, then the next student should respond with some advice. The exercise continues in this manner. For example:

> A: *I wish I didn't have to do so much homework.*
> B: *Why don't you ask your teacher to give you less?*
> A: *Good idea.*
> B: *I wish I had done my laundry last weekend.*
> C: *How about doing it today?*
> B: *Yes, I think I will.*

❖ Students should keep going around the group several times, trying not to repeat the same sentences as their partners.

14g Conditional Sentences with *If Only*

Student Book 3 p. 425, Student Book 3B p. 215

16 Practice

1. If only I were athletic.
2. If only I were rich.
3. If only I had more free time.
4. If only I didn't have to work so hard.
5. If only I could sing or dance.
6. If only I could drive a car.
7. If only I had a boyfriend.
8. If only I didn't worry about my life.

17 Your Turn

Answers will vary. Sample answers:

You: If only I had bought a Toyota!
Your partner: Is that because your Chevy just broke down?
You: If only I weren't so short!
Your partner: Is that because you can't reach the top shelf?
You: If only I had studied science instead of languages!
Your partner: Is that because scientists earn more than linguists do?

If only... Activity

❖ Working in pairs, tell students to think about current events and say three sentences to their partners beginning with *If only...* For example:

> *If only people didn't eat so much fast food...*
> *If only wealth were shared among nations...*
> *If only workers earned a living wage...*

❖ Then, tell the partners to try to finish the sentences. For example:

> *If only people didn't eat so much fast food, obesity wouldn't be a problem.*
> *If only wealth were shared among nations, there wouldn't be so much poverty.*
> *If only workers earned a living wage, they could support their families.*

Review

Student Book 3 p. 427, Student Book 3B p. 217

1 Review (14a–14c, 14e–14f)

1. f **2.** g **3.** j **4.** h **5.** i **6.** a **7.** d **8.** c **9.** b **10.** e

2 Review (14b–14d, 14f)

1. as if   2. If (only)   3. as if/as though   4. wish   5. If/Even if   6. as though/as if
7. wish   8. wish   9. wish   10. If (only)   11. as if/as though   12. If (only)   13. If
14. If (only)   15. if   16. as if/as though   17. as if/as though   18. if   19. wish
20. wish

3 Review (14a–14c, 14f)

1. had never come   2. were walking   3. wouldn't have come   4. had researched
5. were   6. 'd love 7. were   8. 'd die   9. wouldn't be   10. have   11. melts
12. had/had had   13. eat   14. wouldn't bring   15. were   16. could leave
17. would have come   18. would stop   19. don't hear   20. send

4 Review (14a, 14c, 14f–14g)

Anita: I wish you hadn't ~~take~~ *taken* me to this party. It's boring. I wish we could ~~have left~~ *leave* right now.

Louis: Well, I wish you ~~stopped~~ *'d stop* telling me that. I wish we ~~go~~ *had gone* to the movies instead. But there's nothing we can do about it now.

Anita: If only you ~~listen~~ *'d listened* to me earlier.

Louis: If only I ~~know~~ *'d known* you would be so difficult! You're acting as if this ~~be~~ *were* all my fault!

Anita: Well, without your invitation, I ~~won't~~ *wouldn't* be here.

Louis: OK. OK. If more people come, we ∧ *'ll* leave, all right?

Anita: Then I wish a hundred people ∧ *would* come through that door right now.

Louis: I wish I ~~not tell~~ *hadn't told* Mark that I had the night off. If only I ~~keep~~ *had kept* it to myself. I usually work on Fridays. The truth is that when Mark first invited me to this party, I said no. Then I felt as though ~~I~~ *I'd* hurt his feelings. "I know you're working," he said. "But I sure wish you ∧ *would/could* come to my party." That's when I broke down. I wish ~~I'm not~~ *I weren't* so softhearted. If someone ~~ask~~ *asks* me a favor, I can't refuse.

Anita: Well, that's what makes you such a nice person. If I ~~don't~~ *didn't* like you so much, I ~~won't~~ *wouldn't* have come.

Louis: Thanks, Anita. If I see Mark, I ∧ *'ll* tell him that we need to leave. If only we ~~have~~ *had* a good excuse. If we had a reason to leave, I ∧ *'d* feel so much better.

Anita: Never mind. He's your friend. Let's stay. If we're lucky more people ~~come~~ *will come* soon.

Louis: Yes, that's right. And if it ~~were~~ *'s* early enough, we can go see a movie. And if you're hungry, I $\wedge$ *'ll* buy you some popcorn.

Anita: That sounds great. I wish I ~~don't say~~ *hadn't said* those things to you earlier. I'm sorry. Without your friendship, my life ~~is not~~ *wouldn't be* the same.

Louis: Thank you, Anita. I feel the same way. Well, it ~~look~~ *looks* as though we ~~were~~ *are* about to get our wish. More people are starting to arrive. Let's say goodbye to Mark.

Writing Expansion

Student Book 3 p. 431, Student Book 3B p. 221

After the students finish their persuasive essay, ask them to give an oral presentation on their topic. If several students have written on the same topic, they can organize a debate or panel discussion. The other students should listen and ask questions when they are finished. If appropriate, you can write a short evaluation of each student or group presentation.

Unit 14 Student Book Self-Test

Student Book 3 p. 432, Student Book 3B p. 222

A. **1.** A **2.** D **3.** C **4.** B **5.** C **6.** B **7.** B **8.** A **9.** A **10.** B

B. **1.** C **2.** A **3.** D **4.** C **5.** D **6.** B **7.** B **8.** B **9.** A **10.** D

Grammar Form and Function

Unit I Quiz

Name: _____ Date: _____

A. **Choose the best answer, A, B, C, or D, to complete each sentence. Mark your answer by darkening the oval with the same letter.**

1. What do you _____ on weekends?

   A. do   Ⓐ Ⓑ Ⓒ Ⓓ
   B. does
   C. doing
   D. done

2. Which computer isn't _____?

   A. works   Ⓐ Ⓑ Ⓒ Ⓓ
   B. working
   C. worked
   D. to work

3. The instructor _____ late for class.

   A. seldom is   Ⓐ Ⓑ Ⓒ Ⓓ
   B. is seldom being
   C. is being seldom
   D. is seldom

4. Many people _____ for jobs these days.

   A. looks   Ⓐ Ⓑ Ⓒ Ⓓ
   B. looked
   C. are looking
   D. looking

5. I _____ my keys at least once a week.

   A. forgets   Ⓐ Ⓑ Ⓒ Ⓓ
   B. forgetting
   C. forget
   D. 'm forgetting

6. That sports car _____ more than I make each year.

   A. costing   Ⓐ Ⓑ Ⓒ Ⓓ
   B. costs
   C. is costing
   D. cost

7. The carpenter _____ the wood now to see if it's long enough.

   A. measure   Ⓐ Ⓑ Ⓒ Ⓓ
   B. measures
   C. measuring
   D. is measuring

8. Roses _____ lovely in June.

   A. smell   Ⓐ Ⓑ Ⓒ Ⓓ
   B. smells
   C. smelling
   D. are smelling

9. I _____ how tall I'll be next year.

   A. prefer   Ⓐ Ⓑ Ⓒ Ⓓ
   B. doubt
   C. wonder
   D. deserve

10. _____ Southeast Asia?

    A. She has ever visited   Ⓐ Ⓑ Ⓒ Ⓓ
    B. Has she ever visited
    C. Ever she has visited
    D. Has ever visited she

11. Yes, she has _____ been there three times.

    A. rarely   Ⓐ Ⓑ Ⓒ Ⓓ
    B. ever
    C. still
    D. already

12. How long _____ parachuting?

    A. have they been   Ⓐ Ⓑ Ⓒ Ⓓ
    B. they have been
    C. has they been
    D. they has been

13. Dimitri has _____ been out on a boat. He's afraid of the water.

    A. so far   Ⓐ Ⓑ Ⓒ Ⓓ
    B. yet
    C. never
    D. still

14. Women _____ in the Olympics for over 100 years.

    A. have been   Ⓐ Ⓑ Ⓒ Ⓓ
        participating
    B. has participated
    C. have participating
    D. have been participated

15. The newest Harry Potter film _____.

    A. has come just out   Ⓐ Ⓑ Ⓒ Ⓓ
    B. has just come out
    C. has out just come
    D. just has come out

(3 points each) _____ / 45

B. **Complete the sentences with the simple present or present progressive tense.**

1. Desirée (try) _____ to do the math problems now.

2. Sam (drive) _____ a taxi on weekends.

3. Actors (memorize) _____ their lines before doing a scene.

4. Although it (rain) _____ here today, it (snow) _____ in the mountains.

5. Which movie (you/watch) _____ ?

(2 points each) _____ / 10

C. **Write the verbs and adverbs in the correct order and the verbs in the correct tense.**

1. Lara (study/never) _____ in the public library.

2. I have no privacy! Fans (stop/always) _____ me to ask for my autograph.

3. The store (be/now) _____ open on Sundays.

4. The twins (dress/sometimes) _____ in the same kind of clothing.

5. The temperature (go/rarely) _____ below zero in New York.

(2 points each) _____ / 10

D. Give short answers to these questions.

1. Have you ever climbed a mountain?   —Yes, _____

2. Do they often play soccer?   —No, _____

3. Does he like orange soda?   —Yes, _____

4. Has it ever snowed in summer?   —Yes, _____

5. Don't they believe in Santa Claus?   —No, _____

(3 points each) _____ / 15

E. Write questions for these answers. Use *who, what, when, where,* and *why*. Look at the words in italics for clues.

1. _____
    JK Rowling *writes* for a few hours every day.

2. _____
    The *Williams sisters* have played tennis for more than 10 years.

3. _____
    Jacob's traveled to *twenty-two* countries so far.

4. _____
    They've been saving money *to buy a house.*

5. _____
    The weather gets warmer *in May.*

(4 points each) _____ / 20

SCORE _____ / 100

Name: _____ Date: _____

A. Choose the best answer, A, B, C, or D, to complete each sentence. Mark your answer by darkening the oval with the same letter.

1. Who gave you that backpack?

 A. He did.   Ⓐ Ⓑ Ⓒ Ⓓ
 B. He does.
 C. He has.
 D. He had.

2. Where did you see the concert?

         Ⓐ Ⓑ Ⓒ Ⓓ
 A. We go to the Opera House.
 B. We had gone to the Opera House.
 C. We went to the Opera House.
 D. We going to the Opera House.

3. Yesterday Amelia _____ for eight hours.

 A. driving   Ⓐ Ⓑ Ⓒ Ⓓ
 B. is driving
 C. has driving
 D. drove

4. As I _____ on the train, I _____ a shout.

 A. am getting/heard Ⓐ Ⓑ Ⓒ Ⓓ
 B. was getting/was hearing
 C. was getting/heard
 D. got/was hearing

5. While the students _____ the test, the teacher _____ their essays.

         Ⓐ Ⓑ Ⓒ Ⓓ
 A. were taking/was correcting
 B. taking/correcting
 C. was taking/were taking
 D. are taking/was correcting

6. Hamid _____ his notes when the teacher _____ in.

 A. reviews/comes Ⓐ Ⓑ Ⓒ Ⓓ
 B. was reviewing/is coming
 C. is reviewing/came
 D. was reviewing/came

7. The composers _____ the competition after they _____ their songs.

         Ⓐ Ⓑ Ⓒ Ⓓ
 A. had entered/had composed
 B. entered/had composed
 C. entered/composing
 D. entering/composed

8. The pastry chef _____ on the wedding cake all day long.

 A. had been working Ⓐ Ⓑ Ⓒ Ⓓ
 B. had working
 C. has working
 D. had been worked

9. Which computer _____ when the power went off?

 A. was you using Ⓐ Ⓑ Ⓒ Ⓓ
 B. are you using
 C. have you been using
 D. had you been using

10. When I _____ at the White House, I _____ the president many times.

 A. worked/was seeing Ⓐ Ⓑ Ⓒ Ⓓ
 B. was working/was seeing
 C. worked/saw
 D. working/seeing

11. Even though they _____ an astronomy course last semester, they _____ Mars until last night.

                        Ⓐ Ⓑ Ⓒ Ⓓ

  A. are taking/haven't been seeing
  B. took/hadn't seen
  C. take/didn't
  D. are taken/aren't seen

12. My grandparents _____ horses to school.

  A. using to ride   Ⓐ Ⓑ Ⓒ Ⓓ
  B. use to ride
  C. used to ride
  D. had used to ride

13. Where _____ Sasha _____ in Russia?

  A. is/used to live   Ⓐ Ⓑ Ⓒ Ⓓ
  B. was/used to live
  C. did/used to live
  D. did/use to live

14. There _____ color television in the 1950s.

  A. didn't use to be   Ⓐ Ⓑ Ⓒ Ⓓ
  B. did used to be
  C. wasn't use to be
  D. hadn't used to be

15. What kind of clothes _____ people _____ in the 1900s?

  A. were/use to wear   Ⓐ Ⓑ Ⓒ Ⓓ
  B. did/use to wear
  C. had/used to wear
  D. did/used to wear

(3 points each) _____ / 45

B. **Complete the sentences with the simple past or past progressive tense.**

1. Raya (iron) _____ all the shirts last night.

2. The birds (fly) _____ above the fishing boat all day.

3. Where (play) _____ the children _____ when it started to rain?

4. Six months ago, I (not/know) _____ you.

5. The band (play) _____ while the team (march)

_____.

(2 points each) _____ / 10

C. **Complete the sentences with the past or past perfect tense and the verbs and adverbs in parentheses.**

1. They (finish/already) _____ their homework when their friends

   (come) _____ to visit.

2. When I was a child, I (walk/sometimes) _____ in my sleep.

3. Pete (see) _____ the movie two times before, so he didn't want to
   see it again.

4. By noon, I was really hungry. I (not/eat) _____ all day.

5. Before he was ten years old, the boy (take/never) _____ care of the
   sheep alone.

(2 points each) _____ / 10

D. **Give short answers to these questions.**

1. Was Leonard Bernstein a famous conductor?   Yes, _____

2. Did George Gershwin write *Porgy & Bess?*   Yes, _____

3. Was Duke Ellington a classical composer?   No, _____

4. Had Aaron Copeland visited Appalachia?   Yes, _____

5. Did Cole Porter tour with the Beatles?   No, _____

(3 points each) _____ / 15

E. **Write questions for these answers. Use** *who, what, when, where,* **and** *why.* **The underlined words are the clues to the questions.**

1. _____

    The boy had shouted <u>"Wolf!"</u> several times before.

2. _____

    <u>Beethoven</u> still conducted an orchestra although he was deaf.

3. _____

    The thieves had stolen the limousine <u>before the police arrived</u>.

4. _____

    The Beatles broke up <u>because they wanted to do different kinds of music.</u>

5. _____

    Bruno used to live <u>in Brazil</u> before he moved to Canada.

(4 points each) _____ / 20

SCORE _____ / 100

Grammar Form and Function   Unit 2 Quiz

Name: _____ Date: _____

A. Choose the best answer, A, B, C, or D, to complete each sentence. Mark your answer by darkening the oval with the same letter.

1. Are you going to invite all your friends to the party?

    A. Yes, I will.   Ⓐ Ⓑ Ⓒ Ⓓ
    B. Yes, he is going to.
    C. Yes, I am.
    D. Yes, I was.

2. I'm afraid Ling _____ lost on the way.

    A. isn't going to get   Ⓐ Ⓑ Ⓒ Ⓓ
    B. won't get
    C. didn't to get
    D. will get

3. I forgot to call Juan yesterday; I _____ him now.

    A. 'll call   Ⓐ Ⓑ Ⓒ Ⓓ
    B. called
    C. call
    D. calling

4. The new pyramid in Tokyo _____ very high.

    A. was   Ⓐ Ⓑ Ⓒ Ⓓ
    B. will be
    C. be
    D. going to be

5. In the future, people _____ in flying saucers.

    A. travel   Ⓐ Ⓑ Ⓒ Ⓓ
    B. is going to travel
    C. will be travel
    D. will travel

6. As soon as I _____ Lorena, I _____ her your message.

    A. am seeing/will give   Ⓐ Ⓑ Ⓒ Ⓓ
    B. 'll see/give
    C. see/'ll give
    D. am going to see/am going to give

7. If Marco _____ on the soccer team, he _____ the star player.

    A. gets/'ll be   Ⓐ Ⓑ Ⓒ Ⓓ
    B. will get/be
    C. gets/is
    D. will get/will be

8. The president _____ the bill into law after the senators _____.

    A. signs/votes   Ⓐ Ⓑ Ⓒ Ⓓ
    B. sign/vote
    C. signs/will vote
    D. will sign/vote

9. By the time I graduate from law school, I _____ for seven years.

    A. will study   Ⓐ Ⓑ Ⓒ Ⓓ
    B. will have been studying
    C. will been studying
    D. will have study

10. New Year's Day _____ on January 1st.

    A. will be   Ⓐ Ⓑ Ⓒ Ⓓ
    B. was
    C. is
    D. has been

11. What _____ tomorrow afternoon at 4:00?

    A. will you doing   Ⓐ Ⓑ Ⓒ Ⓓ
    B. will you be doing
    C. are you do
    D. will you be

12. Susan_____ with Isabel's family in Barcelona.

    A. going to be staying   Ⓐ Ⓑ Ⓒ Ⓓ
    B. is going to be staying
    C. to be staying
    D. will to be staying

13. The ministers _____ on a plan next week.

    A. are to decide   Ⓐ Ⓑ Ⓒ Ⓓ
    B. to decide
    C. are to deciding
    D. are decide

14. Princess Diana _____ a kindergarten teacher.

    A. is going to be   Ⓐ Ⓑ Ⓒ Ⓓ
    B. was to be
    C. was going to be
    D. will to be

15. By the time winter is over, it _____ 42 inches.

    A. is going to snowing   Ⓐ Ⓑ Ⓒ Ⓓ
    B. is going to snow
    C. will snowed
    D. will have snowed

(3 points each) _____ / 45

B. **Complete the sentences with *will* or *going to*.**

1. Sue: Look! There's been an accident. Do you have your cell phone?

    Tom: Yes. I (call) _____ 911.

2. It's very cloudy outside; it (rain) _____ tonight.

3. There's a lot of traffic, so maybe Alfonso (be) _____ late.

4. Anita has been in medical school for four years; now she (become)

    _____ a surgeon.

5. I'm invited to my nephew's birthday this weekend; he (be) _____ two.

(2 points each) _____ / 10

C. **Write the verbs in the present progressive or simple present tense.**

1. The students (go) _____ to Jamaica for spring break.

2. Their plane (leave) _____ at 7:00 in the morning.

3. They (stay) _____ at a hotel on the beach this week.

4. The reggae party (begin) _____ at 9:00 every night.

5. They (come) _____ back after a week.

(2 points each) _____ / 10

D. **Give short answers to these questions.**

1. Are you going to Beijing? —Yes, _____

2. Will you go sightseeing? —Yes, _____

3. Are you renting a car? —No, _____

4. Will you go to Shanghai? —No, _____

5. Are you seeing any of your friends? —Yes, _____

(3 points each) _____ / 15

E. **Write questions for these answers. Use *who, what, when,* and *how*. The underlined words are the clues.**

1. _____
   Scientists are planning to send another rover to Mars.

2. _____
   The new rover will collect more specimens.

3. _____
   Scientists will control the rover by computers at NASA.

4. _____
   This space mission will cost millions of dollars.

5. _____
   Scientists are hoping to send a manned spacecraft to Mars by 2040.

(4 points each) _____ / 20

SCORE _____ / 100

Name: _____ Date: _____

A. Choose the best answer, A, B, C, or D, to complete each sentence. Mark your answer by darkening the oval with the same letter.

1. Look at the animals! My favorites are the _____ and the _____.

   A. mouse/goose   Ⓐ Ⓑ Ⓒ Ⓓ
   B. mouse/geese
   C. mice/goose
   D. mice/geese

2. In biology, we studied about _____.

   A. fungus and bacteria   Ⓐ Ⓑ Ⓒ Ⓓ
   B. fungi and bacteria
   C. fungi and bacterium
   D. fungus and bacterium

3. _____ jeans too tight for me?

   A. Are these   Ⓐ Ⓑ Ⓒ Ⓓ
   B. Is these
   C. Are this
   D. Is this

4. The instructor graded all the _____.

   Ⓐ Ⓑ Ⓒ Ⓓ
   A. student vocabulary test
   B. student's vocabulary's tests
   C. students' vocabulary tests
   D. student vocabulary's tests

5. The president took a _____ at Camp David.

   A. week vacations   Ⓐ Ⓑ Ⓒ Ⓓ
   B. weeks vacation
   C. week vacation
   D. week's vacation

6. The _____ is "Wheel of Fortune."

   A. games' name   Ⓐ Ⓑ Ⓒ Ⓓ
   B. name of the game
   C. name of game
   D. games names

7. Ronaldo will be right back; he went to the _____.

   A. men room   Ⓐ Ⓑ Ⓒ Ⓓ
   B. mens room
   C. men's room
   D. man's room

8. The _____ was Audra MacDonald.

   A. opera singer   Ⓐ Ⓑ Ⓒ Ⓓ
   B. opera's singer
   C. singer of the opera
   D. opera singer's

9. The candidate for president is a _____ senator.

   A. 52-years-old   Ⓐ Ⓑ Ⓒ Ⓓ
   B. 52-year-old
   C. 52-year-olds
   D. 52-years-olds

10. I finally sold my _____ for $25!

    A. racket tennis   Ⓐ Ⓑ Ⓒ Ⓓ
    B. tennis racket
    C. racket's tennis
    D. tennis' racket

11. Is there any _____ in the fridge? Only a _____.

   A. yogurts/few   Ⓐ Ⓑ Ⓒ Ⓓ
   B. yogurt/few
   C. yogurts/little
   D. yogurt/little

12. I'm so thirsty! I could drink a whole _____.

   A. bottle of water   Ⓐ Ⓑ Ⓒ Ⓓ
   B. bottle water
   C. water bottle
   D. water bottles

13. I just saw an old friend, and he's bald— all of his _____ gone!

   A. hairs are   Ⓐ Ⓑ Ⓒ Ⓓ
   B. hair are
   C. hair is
   D. hairs is

14. After the fire, _____ remained in the orchard.

   A. few apple tree   Ⓐ Ⓑ Ⓒ Ⓓ
   B. little apples trees
   C. little apple tree
   D. few apple trees

15. _____ to pay taxes in this country.

   A. Every citizen have   Ⓐ Ⓑ Ⓒ Ⓓ
   B. Every citizens has
   C. Every citizen has
   D. Every citizens have

(3 points each) _____ / 45

B. **Complete the sentences with one of the following words in the plural:** *aircraft, child, knife, medium, thesis.*

1. Please don't leave the sharp _____ on the table.

2. All the _____ flying overhead belong to the military.

3. Selena wants to have six _____.

4. The professor explained both his _____ to the class.

5. Recently, the news on the _____ has been about the election.

(2 points each) _____ / 10

C. Write the possessive of the nouns in the sentences.

1. (Arlene) _____ dress for the dance is from Fifth Avenue.

2. Her (friends) _____ dresses are from a designer boutique.

3. Her (boyfriend) _____ tuxedo is from Rent-a-Tux.

4. Her (hairdresser) _____ salon is on Newbury Street.

5. Her (limousine driver) _____ name is Pierre.

(2 points each) _____ / 10

D. Answer with a compound expression.

1. Was your vacation three weeks?   Yes, it was a _____

2. Does he have a son who is five years old?   Yes, he has a _____

3. Is the TOEFL test two hours?   Yes, it's a _____

4. Are they in a program for four years?   Yes, they're in a _____

5. Was she in a course for six months?   Yes, she was in a _____

(3 points each) _____ / 15

E. Complete the sentences with *one, each, every, both,* or *all*.

1. In this photo, the boys are wearing uniforms; they _____have the
same outfit on.

2. _____of the boys is giving a speech on the stage.

3. Another boy is waiting for his turn; _____ of them look very serious.

4. _____boy in the room is listening carefully to the speech.

5. _____one must give a speech when his turn comes.

(4 points each) _____ / 20

SCORE _____ / 100

Name: _____   Date: _____

A. **Choose the best answer, A, B, C, or D, to complete each sentence. Mark your answer by darkening the oval with the same letter. In the answer choices, "X" means no article.**

1. Did you see Alicia and Bethia at the party?

   A. No, I didn't see she.   Ⓐ Ⓑ Ⓒ Ⓓ
   B. No, I didn't see her.
   C. No, I didn't see they.
   D. No, I didn't see them.

2. Why is the Samir in the hospital?

   A. He broke him leg.   Ⓐ Ⓑ Ⓒ Ⓓ
   B. He broke his leg.
   C. He broke the leg.
   D. He himself broke leg.

3. How do you buy a car?

   Ⓐ Ⓑ Ⓒ Ⓓ
   A. You go to a car showroom.
   B. They go to a car showroom.
   C. One goes to a car showroom.
   D. Somebody goes to a car showroom.

4. The black sweater is _____, and the blue one is _____.

   A. mine/her   Ⓐ Ⓑ Ⓒ Ⓓ
   B. my/hers
   C. mine/hers
   D. my/her

5. A good teacher prepares _____ lessons.

   A. his or her   Ⓐ Ⓑ Ⓒ Ⓓ
   B. theirs
   C. his
   D. her

6. _____ can sing like Rosella; she's so talented!

   A. Everything   Ⓐ Ⓑ Ⓒ Ⓓ
   B. Anybody
   C. Somebody
   D. Nobody

7. The female lemur carries _____ baby from tree to tree.

   A. their   Ⓐ Ⓑ Ⓒ Ⓓ
   B. the
   C. its
   D. it's

8. Juan doesn't have a roommate; he lives _____.

   A. himself   Ⓐ Ⓑ Ⓒ Ⓓ
   B. by himself
   C. his self
   D. by his self

9. Please help _____ to some popcorn.

   A. yourselves   Ⓐ Ⓑ Ⓒ Ⓓ
   B. ourselves
   C. themselves
   D. myself

10. And have _____ soda if you want.

   A. other   Ⓐ Ⓑ Ⓒ Ⓓ
   B. another
   C. others
   D. anothers

11. Some senators came to the ceremony, but _____ stayed home.

   A. other   Ⓐ Ⓑ Ⓒ Ⓓ
   B. another
   C. others
   D. anothers

12. Has anybody seen _____ gold pen? I think I lost mine.

   A. X   Ⓐ Ⓑ Ⓒ Ⓓ
   B. one
   C. an
   D. a

13. Everyone should go to the doctor at least once _____ year.

   A. X   Ⓐ Ⓑ Ⓒ Ⓓ
   B. a
   C. an
   D. one

14. This classroom is smaller than that _____.

   A. one   Ⓐ Ⓑ Ⓒ Ⓓ
   B. ones
   C. X
   D. an

15. _____ Philippines is in Southeast Asia.

   A. An   Ⓐ Ⓑ Ⓒ Ⓓ
   B. A
   C. X
   D. The

(3 points each) _____ / 45

B. **Complete the sentences with *the* if necessary. If not, put X.**

1. _____ Canada has ten provinces and several territories.

2. _____ Sahara is the largest desert in Africa.

3. I don't work on _____ Sunday, but I do work _____ Saturday.

4. We took pictures of _____ Statue of Liberty in New York.

5. _____ Central Park is the largest green area in the city.

(2 points each) _____ / 10

C. **Complete the sentences with *a* or *an* if necessary. If not, put 0**

1. We saw _____ woman in front of the store who looked familiar.

2. Roberto got a ticket for driving 80 miles _____ hour.

3. Babies like _____ soft music and _____ smiling faces.

4. Be sure to bring _____ umbrella; it might rain.

5. Is _____ petroleum plentiful in the Middle East?

(2 points each) _____ / 10

D. **Use *one* or *ones* in short answers to these questions.**

1. What size coffee do you want? Small, medium, or large? _____

2. Which donuts do you want? Jelly or sugar? _____

3. Which bagels do you want? Sesame or onion? _____

4. Which restaurant do you want to go to? Thai or Korean? _____

5. Which camera do you want to use? Digital or regular? _____

(3 points each) _____ / 15

E. **Write *other*, *others*, *the other*, *the others*, or *another* in the blank in each sentence.**

1. I've tried on four of these five pairs of shoes. If _____ one doesn't fit, I'll have to go to another store.

2. _____ people don't mind the cold, but Nuria doesn't like it.

3. The man gave the little girl _____ ice cream cone after hers fell on the floor.

4. Some enjoy the beach when they go on vacation; _____ prefer the mountains.

5. Most of the children came back, but _____ are still in the water.

(4 points each) _____ / 20

SCORE _____ / 100

Grammar Form and Function

Name: _____ Date: _____

A. **Choose the best answer, A, B, C, or D, to complete each sentence. Mark your answer by darkening the oval with the same letter.**

1. The dog _____ up and roll over.

   A. can to sit   Ⓐ Ⓑ Ⓒ Ⓓ
   B. is able sit
   C. able sit
   D. can sit

2. Teenagers _____ a driver's license at age 16.

   A. is able to get   Ⓐ Ⓑ Ⓒ Ⓓ
   B. are able to get
   C. can to get
   D. are can get

3. When Chelsea was younger, she _____ a horse every day.

   A. was able to ride   Ⓐ Ⓑ Ⓒ Ⓓ
   B. could to ride
   C. could riding
   D. able to riding

4. For acceptance to a university, you _____ a high TOEFL score.

   A. had have   Ⓐ Ⓑ Ⓒ Ⓓ
   B. had to have
   C. must have
   D. must to have

5. Marlon _____ to acting school before he got a job.

   A. had go   Ⓐ Ⓑ Ⓒ Ⓓ
   B. had to go
   C. must go
   D. must to go

6. My favorite band is coming to town. I _____ tickets for that concert!

   A. must got   Ⓐ Ⓑ Ⓒ Ⓓ
   B. must to get
   C. had got to get
   D. have got to get

7. _____ we _____ now? It's still early.

   A. Must/to go   Ⓐ Ⓑ Ⓒ Ⓓ
   B. Have/to go
   C. Do/have to go
   D. Are/must go

8. Tell the painter he _____ today.

   A. doesn't have to finish   Ⓐ Ⓑ Ⓒ Ⓓ
   B. don't have to finish
   C. mustn't to finish
   D. mustn't finishing

9. People _____ over 70 on the Interstate.

   A. must drive   Ⓐ Ⓑ Ⓒ Ⓓ
   B. mustn't drive
   C. don't have drive
   D. didn't have drive

10. Children _____ their rooms neat and clean.

   A. have keep   Ⓐ Ⓑ Ⓒ Ⓓ
   B. must to keep
   C. ought to keep
   D. ought keep

11. There's a hole in this shirt. That store _____ me my money back.

    A. had better give   Ⓐ Ⓑ Ⓒ Ⓓ
    B. better give
    C. had given
    D. had better gave

12. Are you sick? I think you _____ home and rest.

    A. shouldn't go   Ⓐ Ⓑ Ⓒ Ⓓ
    B. should go
    C. should to go
    D. should gone

13. Maybe Carla _____ college before she got married.

    A. ought finish   Ⓐ Ⓑ Ⓒ Ⓓ
    B. ought finished
    C. ought to finish
    D. ought to have finished

14. The plants are dying. George _____ them, but he forgot.

    A. should water   Ⓐ Ⓑ Ⓒ Ⓓ
    B. should watered
    C. should have watered
    D. should had watered

15. The microwave is really dirty. Who _____ it this week?

    A. is supposed to clean   Ⓐ Ⓑ Ⓒ Ⓓ
    B. supposed to clean
    C. suppose to cleaned
    D. is suppose cleaned

(3 points each) _____ / 45

B.   **Complete the sentences with a modal of ability: *can, could,* or *be able to.***

1. Lemurs (climb) _____ trees very fast.

2. When he was little, Marco (speak) _____ Italian, but now he isn't.

3. The chameleon (change) _____ color according to its mood.

4. _____ you (ride) _____ a bike when you were five?

5. Who (reach) _____ the light to change the bulb?

(2 points each) _____ / 10

C. Complete the sentences with a modal of necessity: *must, have to,* or *have got to.*

1. Maria (go) _____ home for her sister's wedding before the course is over.

2. Drivers (stop)_____ at intersections and look both ways.

3. How many photos _____ I (have) _____ for a passport?

4. _____ Leonardo (finish) _____ the painting last week?

5. The children (take) _____ an extra bath last night because they were playing in the mud.

(2 points each) _____ / 10

D. Give short answers to these questions.

1. Do they have to go now?   Yes, _____

2. Should Mike do the laundry today?   No, _____

3. Must Clara register by tomorrow?   Yes, _____

4. Was I supposed to pay the bill?   No, _____

5. Should I have told the teacher?   Yes, _____

(3 points each) _____ / 15

E. Write questions for the answers. Use *who, what, when, where,* and *why.* Look at the words in italics for clues.

1. _____
   Yasmine ought to study acting. She loves to show off in front of a crowd.

2. _____
   They could have gone *to the beach*. It's so hot today.

3. _____
   Venus isn't able to play tennis *because she sprained her ankle.*

4. _____
   Thomas has got to *send his application in* before the deadline.

5. _____
   The tourists had better go home *before the hurricane hits.*

(4 points each) _____ / 20

SCORE _____ / 100

Name: _____   Date: _____

A. **Choose the best answer, A, B, C, or D, to complete each sentence. Mark your answer by darkening the oval with the same letter.**

1. _____ we dance? They're playing our song.

   A. Shall   Ⓐ Ⓑ Ⓒ Ⓓ
   B. May
   C. Let's
   D. Why not

2. I'm thirsty. _____ get a soda from the machine.

   A. Shall   Ⓐ Ⓑ Ⓒ Ⓓ
   B. May
   C. Let's
   D. Why not

3. Lawrence hasn't come yet. _____ he got delayed in traffic.

   A. Must be   Ⓐ Ⓑ Ⓒ Ⓓ
   B. Should be
   C. Might be
   D. Maybe

4. Unlike his wife, Perry _____ playing golf _____ tennis.

   A. prefers/than   Ⓐ Ⓑ Ⓒ Ⓓ
   B. prefers/to
   C. would rather/to
   D. would rather/than

5. Merry _____ drink hot tea _____ iced tea, even in summer.

   A. would rather/than   Ⓐ Ⓑ Ⓒ Ⓓ
   B. would rather/to
   C. prefers/than
   D. prefers/to

6. Ms. Killian isn't here. _____ I take a message?

   A. Maybe   Ⓐ Ⓑ Ⓒ Ⓓ
   B. Must
   C. May
   D. Might

7. I forgot my dictionary. _____ I borrow yours?

   A. Can't   Ⓐ Ⓑ Ⓒ Ⓓ
   B. Could
   C. Couldn't
   D. Mayn't

8. _____ you mind if I look at your newspaper?

   A. Do   Ⓐ Ⓑ Ⓒ Ⓓ
   B. Can
   C. Must
   D. May

9. _____ not. Here you are.

   A. Sure   Ⓐ Ⓑ Ⓒ Ⓓ
   B. Go ahead
   C. Of course
   D. No problem

10. Bill: Can you drive me home?
    Betty: _____ happy to.

    A. I   Ⓐ Ⓑ Ⓒ Ⓓ
    B. I've be
    C. I'm be
    D. I'd be

11. Would you mind _____ a package for me?

   A. mail   Ⓐ Ⓑ Ⓒ Ⓓ
   B. mailing
   C. mailed
   D. having mailed

12. Someone's at the door. I'm not expecting anyone, but it _____ the letter carrier.

   A. mayn't be   Ⓐ Ⓑ Ⓒ Ⓓ
   B. should be
   C. might be
   D. has to be

13. A: Where is Samantha?
   B: She _____ at the diner.

   A. may be   Ⓐ Ⓑ Ⓒ Ⓓ
   B. isn't be
   C. could never be

   D. shouldn't be

14. They finally rescued the lost skiers. They _____ for days.

   A. could have lost   Ⓐ Ⓑ Ⓒ Ⓓ
   B. could have been lost
   C. could be lost
   D. could been lost

15. I haven't seen Harry for a week. He _____ a vacation.

   A. could taken   Ⓐ Ⓑ Ⓒ Ⓓ
   B. could take
   C. could taking
   D. could be taking

(3 points each) _____ / 45

B. Complete the sentences with expressions that make suggestions. Use *shall, let's, how about, what about,* or *why don't.*

1. _____ we go for a drive in the country?

2. _____ call our friends on the farm.

3. _____ we take a picnic lunch?

4. _____ bringing our bathing suits so we can swim in the pond?

5. And _____ bringing our kayak, too?

(2 points each) _____ / 10

C. Complete the sentences with *prefer* or *would rather* and the verb in parentheses.

1. Aziz (study) _____ in the dorm to studying in her room.

2. Belinda (drive) _____ a van than a truck.

3. Children usually (eat) _____ fruits to vegetables.

4. I (live) _____ in the country than in a city.

5. The president (have) _____ private press conferences to public ones.

(2 points each) _____ / 10

166

D. **Give appropriate short answers to these requests.**

1. May I come in? Yes, _____

2. Can I smoke in the building? No, _____

3. Would you like a free sample? Yes, _____

4. Could you do me a favor? Yes, _____

5. Would you mind closing the door? No, _____

(3 points each) _____ */ 15*

E. **Write a sentence for each situation using *may, might, could,* and *must* and the verb in parentheses. You can use different tenses.**

1. The sky looks dark, and it's getting windy. (rain)

   _____

2. Raul and Rosa look hot and tired. (just play tennis)

   _____

3. My co-worker, Alan, is looking for another job. (leave the company)

   _____

4. Marina isn't working these days. (stay home with her baby)

   _____

5. There is a moving van in front of our neighbors' house. (buy another house)

   _____

(4 points each) _____ */ 20*

SCORE _____ */ 100*

Name: _____ Date: _____

A. **Choose the best answer, A, B, C, or D, to complete each sentence. Mark your answer by darkening the oval with the same letter.**

1. The Eiffel Tower _____ in 1889.

   A. completed   Ⓐ Ⓑ Ⓒ Ⓓ
   B. was completed
   C. is completed
   D. was completing

2. The last few days of the week _____ for Scandinavian gods.

   A. name   Ⓐ Ⓑ Ⓒ Ⓓ
   B. is named
   C. are named
   D. are naming

3. Gold _____ a precious metal for centuries.

   A. considered   Ⓐ Ⓑ Ⓒ Ⓓ
   B. has been considering
   C. has considered
   D. has been considered

4. A new type of helicopter _____ by the military.

   A. is being developed   Ⓐ Ⓑ Ⓒ Ⓓ
   B. is developing
   C. is been developed
   D. is developed

5. Low cost health care _____ to all citizens.

   A. ought to be   Ⓐ Ⓑ Ⓒ Ⓓ
   B. ought to offer
   C. ought to be offered
   D. ought to be offering

6. The apartment for rent _____ by now.

   A. should be cleaned   Ⓐ Ⓑ Ⓒ Ⓓ
   B. should have been cleaned
   C. should been cleaned
   D. should be cleaning

7. Endangered species _____ by governments.

      Ⓐ Ⓑ Ⓒ Ⓓ
   A. are suppose to be protect
   B. are supposed to protect
   C. are supposed to protected
   D. are supposed to be protected

8. The snow _____ by city snowplows.

   A. gets removed   Ⓐ Ⓑ Ⓒ Ⓓ
   B. getting removed
   C. get removing
   D. is getting remove

9. Princes William and Harry _____ by the royal tailor.

      Ⓐ Ⓑ Ⓒ Ⓓ
   A. have their made clothes
   B. have their clothes made
   C. have clothes to make
   D. have been making clothes

10. _____ that Atlantis really existed.

    A. It believes   Ⓐ Ⓑ Ⓒ Ⓓ
    B. It is believing
    C. It is believed
    D. It be believed

11. Maria Callas _____ one of the finest opera singers of the 20th century.

    A. was thinking   Ⓐ Ⓑ Ⓒ Ⓓ
    B. was thinking to be
    C. was thought be
    D. was thought to be

12. The First Lady _____ her hair _____ by a stylist.

    A. has/done   Ⓐ Ⓑ Ⓒ Ⓓ
    B. has/do
    C. had/do
    D. having/done

13. The tourist _____ his shoes _____ by a shoeshine boy.

    A. having/shined   Ⓐ Ⓑ Ⓒ Ⓓ
    B. having/shining
    C. had/shining
    D. had/shined

14. The aging actress _____ her face _____ next week.

    A. get/lift   Ⓐ Ⓑ Ⓒ Ⓓ
    B. will getting/lifted
    C. will be getting/lifted
    D. will get/lifting

15. The CEO _____ the same chauffeur _____ for 10 years now.

    A. has/picked him up   Ⓐ Ⓑ Ⓒ Ⓓ
    B. has had/pick him up
    C. has having/pick him up
    D. is having/pick him up

(3 points each) _____ / 45

B. Complete the sentences with the present participle or past participle as an adjective. Use the words in parentheses.

1. I'm (exhaust) _____. I've been working for 10 hours!

2. The film was so (bore) _____ that we left before it was over.

3. The assassination of the leader was (shock) _____ to the world.

4. The test was so (confuse) _____ that half the students failed it.

5. Her boss was (impress) _____ by her work, and he gave her a raise.

(2 points each) _____ / 10

C. **Complete the phrasal verbs (fill in the blanks) so that the sentences make sense.**

1. The old man fell _____ and injured his hip.

2. When the couple broke _____, they had to cancel their wedding.

3. The war went _____ for many years.

4. The plane was supposed to leave at 2:45, but it hasn't taken _____ yet.

5. Because he made a mistake, the violinist had to start _____.

(2 points each) _____ / 10

D. **Complete the sentences with the correct prepositions.**

1. I'm not sure what to do. I have to think _____ it some more.

2. The student started crying when the teacher shouted _____ her.

3. They voted for that candidate because they believed _____ him.

4. Who does this bicycle belong _____? It's been here for days.

5. Please try to concentrate _____ the lesson because it's important.

(3 points each) _____ / 15

E. Use pronouns in giving short answers to these questions.

1. Did you take out the garbage?   No, _____

2. Does she dress up her little girl?   Yes, _____

3. Have they worked out the problem?   No, _____

4. Did he hang up the phone?   Yes, _____

5. Have you taken off your shoes?   No, _____

(4 points each) _____ / 20

SCORE _____ / 100

Name: _____ Date: _____

A. Choose the best answer, A, B, C, or D, to complete each sentence. Mark your answer by darkening the oval with the same letter.

1. That man is very generous. Imagine _____ a million dollars to the zoo!

A. give   Ⓐ Ⓑ Ⓒ Ⓓ
B. giving
C. is giving
D. have given

2. The bridge is closed because they put off _____ the repairs.

A. do   Ⓐ Ⓑ Ⓒ Ⓓ
B. to do
C. doing
D. have doing

3. I've just bought a new tent. Let's go _____.

A. camped   Ⓐ Ⓑ Ⓒ Ⓓ
B. camp
C. to camping
D. camping

4. If you eat fatty foods, you risk _____ high cholesterol.

A. having   Ⓐ Ⓑ Ⓒ Ⓓ
B. to have
C. having had
D. being had

5. What do they like about _____ in the country?

A. to live   Ⓐ Ⓑ Ⓒ Ⓓ
B. have lived
C. having lived
D. living

6. My parents are looking forward to _____.

A. be retiring   Ⓐ Ⓑ Ⓒ Ⓓ
B. being retire
C. retiring
D. retired

7. It's not worth _____ so much money for concert tickets. Let's just buy the CD.

A. to pay   Ⓐ Ⓑ Ⓒ Ⓓ
B. paying
C. to paying
D. to be paid

8. Our teacher will be busy _____ our exams this weekend.

A. correcting   Ⓐ Ⓑ Ⓒ Ⓓ
B. corrected
C. having corrected
D. being correct

9. Her husband promised _____ the children while she was away.

A. been taken care of   Ⓐ Ⓑ Ⓒ Ⓓ
B. being taken care of
C. taking care of
D. to take care of

10. The senators have threatened _____ long speeches about the bill.

A. making   Ⓐ Ⓑ Ⓒ Ⓓ
B. to make
C. to made
D. to be making

11. The counselor advised _____ the TOEFL several times.

   A. we take   Ⓐ Ⓑ Ⓒ Ⓓ
   B. we taking
   C. us to take
   D. us taking

12. The travelers were disappointed _____ about the delayed flight.

   A. to hear   Ⓐ Ⓑ Ⓒ Ⓓ
   B. hearing
   C. heard
   D. having heard

13. There is never enough time _____ life.

   A. enjoy   Ⓐ Ⓑ Ⓒ Ⓓ
   B. enjoyed
   C. enjoying
   D. to enjoy

14. I heard the girls' chorus _____ before the concert.

   A. to practice   Ⓐ Ⓑ Ⓒ Ⓓ
   B. practiced
   C. practicing
   D. having practiced

15. His _____ during class annoys the professors.

   A. sleep   Ⓐ Ⓑ Ⓒ Ⓓ
   B. sleeping
   C. slept
   D being slept

(3 points each) _____ / 45

B. **Complete the sentences with a gerund or an infinitive of the verbs in parentheses.**

1. I can't mail this letter. I forgot (buy) _____ stamps at the post office.

2. The old woman remembers (take) _____ money out of the bank, but now she can't find it.

3. The little boy stopped (watch) _____ the fire trucks go by on his way to school.

4. She tried (throw) _____ water on the fire, but it didn't work.

5. I regret (tell) _____ her I had a cell phone. She always wants to borrow it.

(2 points each) _____ / 10

C. Complete the sentences with *too, enough,* or *so.*

1. The snow is _____ deep to walk in; we have to stay home.

2. The runner was _____ tired that she fell down after finishing the race.

3. Their son is old _____ to join the armed forces.

4. The soup was _____ salty that we couldn't eat it.

5. The water in the pool is warm _____ to swim in now.

(2 points each) _____ / 10

D. Complete the sentences with perfect infinitives or gerunds.

1. Frank was proud of (finish) _____ the project.

2. The children enjoyed (visit) _____ the farm last week.

3. His Russian seems (get) _____ better after a year in Moscow.

4. The office staff disliked (work) _____ last Sunday.

5. Lola was glad (won) _____ the prize in the opera competition.

(3 points each) _____ / 15

E. Complete the sentences with the passive voice of the infinitives or gerunds.

1. The class likes (invite) _____ to the governor's mansion.

2. The floors need (clean) _____; there's dirt all over the house.

3. Timothy is unhappy about (transfer) _____ to another state.

4. The house needs (paint) _____; it looks terrible.

5. The applicant was pleased about (offer) _____ the job.

(4 points each) _____ / 20

SCORE _____ / 100

Name: _____ Date: _____

A. **Choose the best answer, A, B, C, or D, to complete each sentence. Mark your answer by darkening the oval with the same letter.**

1. I think mathematics _____ more difficult than physics.

   A. is   Ⓐ Ⓑ Ⓒ Ⓓ
   B. are
   C. be
   D. have been

2. All the majors at that university _____ related to science.

   A. be   Ⓐ Ⓑ Ⓒ Ⓓ
   B. are being
   C. is
   D. are

3. _____ the men or women going to cook at the barbecue tonight?

   A. Wasn't   Ⓐ Ⓑ Ⓒ Ⓓ
   B. Was
   C. Are
   D. Is

4. I think the cats or the dog _____ hiding under the sofa.

   A. are   Ⓐ Ⓑ Ⓒ Ⓓ
   B. is
   C. were
   D. have been

5. Every citizen _____ to vote in order to participate in a democracy.

   A. have   Ⓐ Ⓑ Ⓒ Ⓓ
   B. has
   C. are having
   D. having

6. The researcher, together with her assistants, _____ some important discoveries.

   A. having made   Ⓐ Ⓑ Ⓒ Ⓓ
   B. have made
   C. has made
   D. has making

7. The instructions for changing the oil in a car _____ easy to understand.

   A. is   Ⓐ Ⓑ Ⓒ Ⓓ
   B. was
   C. has been
   D. were

8. There _____ a thunderstorm and several tornadoes this past week.

   A. have been   Ⓐ Ⓑ Ⓒ Ⓓ
   B. has been
   C. has being
   D. have being

9. Twenty dollars _____ all his mother could give him.

   A. were   Ⓐ Ⓑ Ⓒ Ⓓ
   B. was
   C. has been
   D. have been

10. Some of the apples _____ bad so I threw them away.

   A. are   Ⓐ Ⓑ Ⓒ Ⓓ
   B. is
   C. were
   D. was

11. None of the cars _____ bought by the end of the day.

    A. are   Ⓐ Ⓑ Ⓒ Ⓓ
    B. is
    C. were
    D. was

12. To travel and _____ in other countries is his dream.

    A. worked   Ⓐ Ⓑ Ⓒ Ⓓ
    B. working
    C. to work
    D. works

13. The nurse said that eating well and _____ were necessary for good health.

    A. exercising   Ⓐ Ⓑ Ⓒ Ⓓ
    B. exercise
    C. to exercise
    D. exercises

14. The scientific method involves hypothesis, _____, and conclusion.

    A. to experiment   Ⓐ Ⓑ Ⓒ Ⓓ
    B. experimented
    C. experimentation
    D. experiment

15. The carpenter measured the _____, width, and height of the cabinet.

    A. longth   Ⓐ Ⓑ Ⓒ Ⓓ
    B. length
    C. long
    D. longing

(3 points each) _____ / 45

B. **Complete the sentences in parallel structure with words from the list.**

begging	compose	fair	living room	physics

1. She decorated the bedroom, bathroom, and _____ in green and blue.

2. The principal of the school was firm, kind, and _____ to the pupils.

3. Knowing about astronomy and _____ is vital for an astronaut.

4. Fetching balls, rolling over, and _____ for food were the dog's favorite tricks.

5. Shakespeare lived to _____ poetry and write plays.

(2 points each) _____ / 10

C. Complete the sentences with *both...and, not only...but also, either...or,* and *neither...nor.*

1. _____ Vanessa _____ Lilliana will win first prize for painting.

2. The philanthropist was _____ wealthy _____ generous with his money.

3. _____ the dolphin _____ the whale are mammals.

4. Be self-sufficient with your money; _____ a borrower

   _____ a lender be.

5. _____ Argentina _____ Chile are at the end of South America.

(4 points each) _____ / 20

D. Punctuate the sentences with commas and periods, and use capital letters where necessary.

1. whales are mammals like dolphins for they give birth to live young

2. baby whales weigh a few tons at birth and they drink milk from their mothers

3. whale milk is fifty percent fat so baby whales grow quickly

4. they usually swim in groups called pods but they sometimes swim alone

5. whales may be far from each other yet they can communicate sonically through water

(3 points each) _____ / 15

E. Fill in the correct form of the verb in parentheses. Use present tense verbs.

1. Only about half of the population of most countries (vote) _____ .

2. Five days (be/not)_____ much time for vacation.

3. The number of international students (decrease) _____ every year.

4. Some of the watermelon (be) _____ bad, so we can't eat it.

5. In the picture, the couple (run) _____ after the bus, but it's not stopping.

*(2 points each)*_____ / 10

SCORE _____ / 100

Name: _____ Date: _____

A. **Choose the best answer, A, B, C, or D, to complete each sentence. Mark your answer by darkening the oval with the same letter.**

1. I agree _____ accept more international students.

   A. we should that   Ⓐ Ⓑ Ⓒ Ⓓ
   B. that we should
   C. that should we
   D. should that we

2. _____ First Lady is intelligent is easy to see.

   A. That are   Ⓐ Ⓑ Ⓒ Ⓓ
   B. That is
   C. That's the
   D. That the

3. Tom: Do you think it's going to snow all night?
Pat: _____

   A. I hope not.   Ⓐ Ⓑ Ⓒ Ⓓ
   B. I hope don't.
   C. I don't hope.
   D. I hopen't.

4. The camp counselor wanted to know _____

   A. where they went.   Ⓐ Ⓑ Ⓒ Ⓓ
   B. where went they.
   C. went they were.
   D. went were they.

5. I'm not sure _____

   A. they how got there.   Ⓐ Ⓑ Ⓒ Ⓓ
   B. how there got they.
   C. how got they there.
   D. how they got there.

6. Sue: Shall we eat dinner a little later?
Amy: _____ I'm not very hungry now.

   A. I not guess.   Ⓐ Ⓑ Ⓒ Ⓓ
   B. I so guess.
   C. I guess so.
   D. I guess not.

7. Can you tell me _____

   A. where is the dog?   Ⓐ Ⓑ Ⓒ Ⓓ
   B. where the dog is?
   C. where dog is?
   D. were dog is?

8. The veterinarian will want to know _____

   Ⓐ Ⓑ Ⓒ Ⓓ

   A. how the dog has been.
   B. how has been the dog.
   C. how has the dog been.
   D. how has the been dog.

9. Her new employer will want to know _____

   Ⓐ Ⓑ Ⓒ Ⓓ

   A. why she her last job left.
   B. why left her last job she.
   C. why left she her last job.
   D. why she left her last job.

10. Do they know _____

   Ⓐ Ⓑ Ⓒ Ⓓ

   A. many people will be if hired?
   B. if will be hired many people?
   C. if many people will be hired?
   D. many people will be hired if?

11. I can't remember _____

                  Ⓐ Ⓑ Ⓒ Ⓓ
    A. I turned the lights out.
    B. whether I turned the lights out.
    C. whether the lights I turned out.
    D. whether the lights out I turned.

12. "Ask not what your country _____

    A. can do you for."   Ⓐ Ⓑ Ⓒ Ⓓ
    B. can do for you."
    C. for you can do."
    D. for you do can."

13. Benjamin Franklin believed _____

                  Ⓐ Ⓑ Ⓒ Ⓓ
    A. taxes were that too high.
    B. taxes that were too high.
    C. that taxes were too high.
    D. that were too high taxes.

14. Malia said _____ to the party on Saturday night.

    A. couldn't come she   Ⓐ Ⓑ Ⓒ Ⓓ
    B. couldn't she come
    C. she come couldn't
    D. she couldn't come

15. The salesperson was calling to remind you _____

                  Ⓐ Ⓑ Ⓒ Ⓓ
    A. that your TV had arrived.
    B. that TV had arrived.
    C. that arrived your TV.
    D. that arrived TV.

(3 points each) _____ / 45

B. Complete the sentences with words from the list.

desires	insisted	requires	suggested	recommended

1. The commander _____ that the soldiers march in the parade even though they didn't want to.

2. The counselor _____ that the student take the TOEFL three times, because most students' scores improve with practice.

3. The aging opera star _____ that the public listen to her again.

4. My boss _____ that I take a computer course because I can advance faster if I have better computer skills.

5. The university _____ that all students have a medical exam before starting classes.

(2 points each) _____ / 10

C. Complete the sentences with words from the list.

investigate	be	convince	develop	give

1. It is imperative that we _____ alternatives to fossil fuels.

2. It is critical that the government _____ grants to institutions.

3. It is vital that the committee _____ all possible solutions to the problem.

4. It is essential that sources such as wind _____ used as energy.

5. It is urgent that we _____ the public to use new energy sources.

(4 points each) _____ / 20

D. Punctuate the sentences with capital letters, commas, periods, and quotation marks where necessary.

1. Kennedy said ask what you can do for your country

2. give me liberty or give me death said the patriot, Patrick Henry

3. you have a beautiful voice said the fox to the crow

4. Thoreau stated men have become the tools of their tools

5. we didn't lose the game we just ran out of time said Coach Lombardi

(5 points each) _____ / 25

SCORE _____ / 100

Name: _____ Date: _____

A. Choose the best answer, A, B, C, or D, to complete each sentence. Mark your answer by darkening the oval with the same letter.

1. Mary Anderson, _____ invented the windshield wiper, made streetcars safer.

   A. whom   Ⓐ Ⓑ Ⓒ Ⓓ
   B. whose
   C. who's
   D. who

2. Adolf Fick, _____ contact lenses for animals were made of brown glass, was from Germany.

   A. which   Ⓐ Ⓑ Ⓒ Ⓓ
   B. whose
   C. that
   D. who

3. That's the police officer _____ caught the thief.

   A. that   Ⓐ Ⓑ Ⓒ Ⓓ
   B. that's
   C. whose
   D. whom

4. She's the minister to _____ the president spoke last night.

   A. that   Ⓐ Ⓑ Ⓒ Ⓓ
   B. whose
   C. whom
   D. which

5. That book of poetry, _____ she gave me for my birthday, is my favorite.

   A. how   Ⓐ Ⓑ Ⓒ Ⓓ
   B. who
   C. which
   D. what

6. Our professor, _____ from Calgary, is very strict about deadlines.

   A. whose   Ⓐ Ⓑ Ⓒ Ⓓ
   B. who's
   C. that's
   D. there's

7. I live near the house _____ John F. Kennedy was born.

   A. who's   Ⓐ Ⓑ Ⓒ Ⓓ
   B. whose
   C. where's
   D. where

8. The time will come _____ wise men will laugh like fools.

   A. where   Ⓐ Ⓑ Ⓒ Ⓓ
   B. when
   C. why
   D. that

9. The reason _____ I came for a visit is a secret.

   A. where   Ⓐ Ⓑ Ⓒ Ⓓ
   B. which
   C. when
   D. why

10. Louis Braille used the same instrument _____ blinded him to make the raised dots.

    A. that   Ⓐ Ⓑ Ⓒ Ⓓ
    B. which
    C. what
    D. when

11. My grandfather, _____ died recently, was an excellent golfer.

    A. which   Ⓐ Ⓑ Ⓒ Ⓓ
    B. that
    C. who
    D. whom

12. The banker, _____ our family trusted, was accused of fraud.

    A. for whom   Ⓐ Ⓑ Ⓒ Ⓓ
    B. in whom
    C. to whom
    D. with whom

13. The plane was late arriving, _____ worried the passengers.

    A. which   Ⓐ Ⓑ Ⓒ Ⓓ
    B. that
    C. what
    D. who

14. Do you recognize the actor _____ the limousine?

    A. gets out of   Ⓐ Ⓑ Ⓒ Ⓓ
    B. got out of
    C. gotten out of
    D. getting out of

15. The bus schedule _____ on the Internet wasn't up to date.

    A. finds   Ⓐ Ⓑ Ⓒ Ⓓ
    B. finding
    C. found
    D. having found

(3 points each) _____ / 45

B. **Complete the sentences with words from the list.**

    who   whom   whose   that   which

1. I recognized the woman _____ purse had been stolen.

2. He's the man _____ stands on the street and begs for money.

3. Mars is the closest planet to the earth, _____ means we may be able to land on it.

4. The professor from _____ I got a recommendation won a Nobel Prize.

5. The person _____ I most often ask for help is my mother.

(2 points each) _____ / 10

C. Complete the sentences with the present or past participle of verbs from the list.

cover   cry   hang   park   surround

1. The building _____ by guards is the State Capitol.

2. The statue _____ with canvas is being restored.

3. The painting _____ in the gallery is a Van Gogh.

4. The baby _____ on the airplane sounds like it's hungry.

5. The car _____ in the driveway is my neighbor's.

(4 points each) _____ / 20

D. Underline the relative clauses and rewrite them in reduced form with participles.

1. T. E. Lawrence was an English soldier who was famous for his courage.

_____

2. At first, he went to the Middle East as a scholar who was interested in archaeology.

_____

3. Then the War Office in London asked him to draw maps of the area, which were used for strategic planning.

_____

4. After that, Lawrence helped the Arab sheiks take back the land that was held by the Turks.

_____

5. His intelligence and bravery are shown in the movie "Lawrence of Arabia," which has been seen by millions of people.

_____

(5 points each) _____ / 25

SCORE _____ / 100

Grammar Form and Function   Unit 12 Quiz

Name: _____ Date: _____

A. **Choose the best answer, A, B, C, or D, to complete each sentence. Mark your answer by darkening the oval with the same letter.**

1. _____ I saw the actress in the restaurant, I recognized her.

   A. Soon   Ⓐ Ⓑ Ⓒ Ⓓ
   B. As soon
   C. As soon as
   D. Soon as

2. Lance stops to visit his grandmother _____ he is in her neighborhood.

   A. whichever   Ⓐ Ⓑ Ⓒ Ⓓ
   B. whoever
   C. however
   D. whenever

3. _____ Hiroko has been in this country, she's visited a dozen major cities.

   A. Since   Ⓐ Ⓑ Ⓒ Ⓓ
   B. Until
   C. Once
   D. By the time

4. Because of _____ , many streets were closed.

   A. flood   Ⓐ Ⓑ Ⓒ Ⓓ
   B. the flood
   C. it flooded
   D. there were floods

5. The train accident occurred at rush hour; _____ many people couldn't get home.

   A. because   Ⓐ Ⓑ Ⓒ Ⓓ
   B. as
   C. as a result,
   D. since

6. Letitia gets up at 6:00 _____ she can take a yoga class.

   A. so that   Ⓐ Ⓑ Ⓒ Ⓓ
   B. so what
   C. so long
   D. so soon

7. _____ Pablo had extra tutoring, he wasn't able to pass the exam.

   A. Because   Ⓐ Ⓑ Ⓒ Ⓓ
   B. Nevertheless
   C. However
   D. Even though

8. The students didn't get very high SAT scores; _____ they did well at a community college.

   A. while   Ⓐ Ⓑ Ⓒ Ⓓ
   B. nevertheless,
   C. only if
   D. even though

9. _____ the boxer practices every day, he won't be able to beat the champion.

   A. Nevertheless   Ⓐ Ⓑ Ⓒ Ⓓ
   B. Only if
   C. In case
   D. Even though

10. _____ you take vitamins, you'll be healthy if you eat well.

   A. Whether   Ⓐ Ⓑ Ⓒ Ⓓ
   B. Whether or not
   C. Even if
   D. Only if

11. You can have a piece of candy _____ you finish your dinner.

  A. whereas   Ⓐ Ⓑ Ⓒ Ⓓ
  B. even if
  C. unless
  D. only if

12. _____, the tickets sold out.

        Ⓐ Ⓑ Ⓒ Ⓓ

  A. While they waiting in line
  B. While waiting in line
  C. Waiting in line
  D. While they were waiting in line

13. Before _____ in New York, the students stopped in Philadelphia.

  A. arriving   Ⓐ Ⓑ Ⓒ Ⓓ
  B. they arriving
  C. arrived
  D. they arrive

14. _____ the pie, she offered it to her guests.

  A. Upon sliced   Ⓐ Ⓑ Ⓒ Ⓓ
  B. Upon slicing
  C. Has sliced
  D. Has slicing

15. _____ by the lake, Karen noticed the fisherman on the dock.

  A. If jogging   Ⓐ Ⓑ Ⓒ Ⓓ
  B. As jogging
  C. Jogged
  D. Jogging

(3 points each) _____ / 45

B. **Complete the sentences with words from the list.**

  once   while   by the time   until   whenever

1. The chef cried _____ chopping the onions.

2. _____ I logged on to the Internet, the ticket sale was over.

3. _____ he sees a dog, it barks at him.

4. _____ the spaghetti was done, we sat down to eat.

5. Melinda waited _____ everyone had left the office to lock up.

(3 points each) _____ / 15

C. Complete the sentences with *so...that* or *such...that* and a word from the list.

ancient   delicious   complex   destructive   relaxing

1. The tornado was _____ it destroyed fifty houses.

2. It was _____ statue _____ they took it to a museum.

3. The meal was _____ we all had second helpings.

4. The vacation was _____ we stayed an extra week.

5. It was _____ problem _____ they couldn't solve it.

(3 points each) _____ / 15

D. Underline the adverb clauses and rewrite them in reduced form with participles.

1. While she was in high school, Joan Benoit was the only female cross-country runner.

2. In 1979, when she was still in college, she ran the Boston Marathon and won.

3. After she recovered from leg surgery, she won the Marathon again in 1983.

4. Once she qualified for the Olympics, she won a gold medal in 1984.

5. Even after she had two children, Joan Benoit Samuelson qualified for the 1996 Olympic Trials Marathon.

(5 points each) _____ / 25

SCORE _____ / 100

Name: _____ Date: _____

A. **Choose the best answer, A, B, C, or D, to complete each sentence. Mark your answer by darkening the oval with the same letter.**

1. If you plant seeds in spring, you _____ flowers in summer.

   A. 'll have   Ⓐ Ⓑ Ⓒ Ⓓ
   B. had
   C. would have
   D. have had

2. If companies _____ good products, consumers buy them.

   A. will make   Ⓐ Ⓑ Ⓒ Ⓓ
   B. made
   C. make
   D. would make

3. If you _____ Amanda, tell her I'll call her.

   A. have seen   Ⓐ Ⓑ Ⓒ Ⓓ
   B. will see
   C. saw
   D. should see

4. If you don't stir the batter enough, it _____ lumpy.

   A. was   Ⓐ Ⓑ Ⓒ Ⓓ
   B. will be
   C. wasn't
   D. won't be

5. We _____ with school now if we had started classes earlier.

   A. would be done   Ⓐ Ⓑ Ⓒ Ⓓ
   B. will be done
   C. will done
   D. would done

6. I would drive you to the airport if I _____ a car.

   A. have   Ⓐ Ⓑ Ⓒ Ⓓ
   B. would have
   C. had
   D. could have

7. If I found a gold watch, I _____ it to lost and found.

   A. took   Ⓐ Ⓑ Ⓒ Ⓓ
   B. had taken
   C. have taken
   D. would take

8. If it _____, the company picnic would have been cancelled.

   A. had rained   Ⓐ Ⓑ Ⓒ Ⓓ
   B. rains
   C. raining
   D. would rain

9. If we had brought a DVD player with us, we _____ a movie now.

   A. could watching   Ⓐ Ⓑ Ⓒ Ⓓ
   B. could have watched
   C. could be watched
   D. could watch

10. If you had called the box office earlier, there _____ some tickets left.

    A. would   Ⓐ Ⓑ Ⓒ Ⓓ
    B. would have
    C. would have been
    D. would had been

11. It's very cold and cloudy. It looks _____ it is going to snow.

A. as if   Ⓐ Ⓑ Ⓒ Ⓓ
B. even if
C. like if
D. only if

12. The puppy is very alert. It looks _____ a good watchdog.

A. though it will be   Ⓐ Ⓑ Ⓒ Ⓓ
B. as it will be
C. if it will be
D. like it will be

13. _____ we weren't coming, they wouldn't have prepared dinner.

A. Have they known   Ⓐ Ⓑ Ⓒ Ⓓ
B. Had they known
C. They had known
D. They hadn't known

14. Maria didn't see Alfredo; _____ she would have greeted him.

A. without   Ⓐ Ⓑ Ⓒ Ⓓ
B. if not,
C. otherwise,
D. as though

15. Do you want any more soup? _____, I'll put it in the fridge.

A. As though   Ⓐ Ⓑ Ⓒ Ⓓ
B. As if
C. If so
D. If not

(3 points each) _____ / 45

B. **Complete the sentences with words from the list.**

if so   if not   otherwise   with   without

1. _____ your assistance, I'll complete the report on time.

2. The driver didn't see the other car; _____ , she would have stopped.

3. They say that now is a good time to buy a new computer. _____ , I should start looking.

4. The president couldn't have been elected _____ the support of his party.

5. Take the baby's temperature to see if he has a fever. _____ , you can take him to daycare.

(3 points each) _____ / 15

187

C. **Complete the sentences with forms of _wish_ or _hope_.**

1. The other students _____ you'd come to the party.

2. My father _____ my brother will be a doctor like him.

3. Most people _____ the war will be over soon.

4. The little girl _____ Santa Claus came more often.

5. Marco _____ he didn't have to work so hard.

(3 points each) _____ / 15

D. **Complete the sentences with the correct tense of the verbs in parentheses.**

1. If nuclear weapons (eliminate) _____ , the world (be)

_____ a safer place today.

2. We (not/be) _____ so dependent on oil-based fuels if we (develop)

_____ alternative sources of energy years ago.

3. If all the countries of the world (protect) _____ endangered animals

over the years, some of them (not/already/disappear) _____ .

4. There (not/be) _____ so many mudslides in tropical countries every

year if deforestation (prevent) _____ .

5. If genetically modified food (use) _____ ten years ago, there (be)

_____ more food in developing countries now.

(5 points each) _____ / 25

SCORE _____ / 100

Grammar Form and Function 3
Unit Quiz Answer Keys

Unit 1
A. 1. A **2.** B **3.** D **4.** C **5.** C **6.** B **7.** D **8.** A **9.** C **10.** B **11.** D **12.** A
  13. C **14.** A **15.** B
B. 1. is trying **2.** drives **3.** memorize **4.** is raining/is snowing **5.** are you watching
C. 1. never studies **2.** are always stopping/always stop **3.** is now **4.** sometimes dress
  5. rarely goes
D. 1. I have. **2.** they don't. **3.** he does. **4.** it has. **5.** they don't.
E. 1. What does JK Rowling do (for a few hours) every day? **2.** Who has/have played tennis
  for more than ten years? **3.** How many countries has Jacob traveled to (so far)?
  4. Why have they been saving money? **5.** When does the weather get warmer?

Unit 2
A. 1. A **2.** C **3.** D **4.** C **5.** A **6.** D **7.** B **8.** A **9.** D **10.** C **11.** B **12.** C
  13. D **14.** A **15.** B
B. 1. ironed **2.** were flying/flew **3.** were/playing **4.** didn't/did not know
  5. was playing/was marching; played/marched
C. 1. had already finished/came **2.** sometimes walked **3.** had seen **4.** hadn't eaten
  5. had never taken
D. 1. he was. **2.** he did. **3.** he wasn't. **4.** he had. **5.** he didn't.
E. 1. What had the boy shouted several times before? **2.** Who still conducted an orchestra
  even though he was deaf? **3.** When had the thieves stolen the limousine?
  4. Why did the Beatles break up? **5.** Where did Bruno use to live?

Unit 3
A. 1. C **2.** D **3.** A **4.** B **5.** D **6.** C **7.** A **8.** D **9.** B **10.** C **11.** B **12.** B
  13. A **14.** C **15.** D
B. 1. 'll/will call **2.** 's/is going to rain **3.** will be **4.** 's/is going to become
  5. 's/is going to be
C. 1. are going **2.** leaves **3.** 're/are staying **4.** begins **5.** 're/are coming
D. 1. I am/we are. **2.** I/we will. **3.** I'm/we're not. **4.** I/we won't. **5.** I am/we are.
E. 1. Who is/are planning to send another rover to Mars? **2.** What will the new rover collect?
  3. How will scientists control the rover? **4.** How much will this space mission cost?
  5. When are scientists hoping to send a manned spacecraft to Mars?

Unit 4

A. **1.** D **2.** B **3.** A **4.** C **5.** D **6.** B **7.** C **8.** A **9.** B **10.** B **11.** D **12.** A
13. C **14.** D **15.** C

B. **1.** knives **2.** aircraft **3.** children **4.** theses **5.** media

C. **1.** Arlene's **2.** friends' **3.** boyfriend's **4.** hairdresser's. **5.** limousine driver's

D. **1.** three-week vacation. **2.** five-year-old son. **3.** two-hour test. **4.** four-year program.
5. six-month course.

E. **1.** all **2.** One **3.** both **4.** Every **5.** Each

Unit 5

A. **1.** D **2.** B **3.** A **4.** C **5.** A **6.** D **7.** C **8.** B **9.** A **10.** B **11.** C **12.** D
13. B **14.** A **15.** D

B. **1.** X **2.** The **3.** X/X **4.** the **5.** X

C. **1.** a **2.** an **3.** X/X **4.** an **5.** X

D. **1.** A small/medium/large one. **2.** The jelly/sugar ones. **3.** The sesame/onion ones.
4. The Thai/Korean one. **5.** The digital/regular one.

E. **1.** the other **3.** Other **2.** another **4.** others **5.** the others

Unit 6

A. **1.** D **2.** B **3.** A **4.** C **5.** B **6.** D **7.** C **8.** A **9.** B **10.** C **11.** A **12.** B
13. D **14.** C **15.** A

B. **1.** can climb; are able to climb **2.** was able to speak **3.** can change; is able to change
4. Could you ride; Were you able to ride **5.** can reach; is able to reach

C. **1.** has to go; has got to go **2.** must stop **3.** do/have to have; must/have
4. Did/have to finish **5.** had to take

D. **1.** they do. **2.** he shouldn't. **3.** she must. **4.** you weren't. **5.** you should have.

E. **1.** Who ought to study acting? **2.** Where could they have gone? **3.** Why isn't Venus able
to play tennis? **4.** What has Thomas got to do before the deadline?
5. When had the tourists better go home?

Unit 7

A. **1.** A **2.** C **3.** D **4.** B **5.** A **6.** C **7.** B **8.** A **9.** C **10.** D **11.** B **12.** C
13. A **14.** B **15.** D

B. **1.** Why don't/Shall **2.** Let's **3.** Why don't/Shall **4.** What about/How about
5. what about/how about

C. **1.** prefers studying **2.** would rather drive **3.** prefer eating **4.** would rather live
5. prefers having

D. (Answers may vary.) **1.** you may/of course. **2.** you can't/it's not allowed.
3. I would/I'd love one. **4.** I can/I'd be happy to. **5.** I wouldn't/of course not.

E. **1.** It may/might/could rain. **2.** They must have just been playing tennis.
3. He may/might/could leave the company. He must be leaving the company.
4. She may/might/could/must be staying home with her baby. **5.** They
may/might/could/must have bought another house.

Unit 8

A. 1. B **2.** C **3.** D **4.** A **5.** C **6.** B **7.** D **8.** A **9.** B **10.** C **11.** D **12.** A
13. D **14.** C **15.** B

B. 1. exhausted **2.** boring **3.** shocking **4.** confusing **5.** impressed

C. 1. down **2.** up **3.** on **4.** off **5.** over

D. 1. about **2.** at **3.** in **4.** to **5.** on

E. 1. I didn't take it out. **2.** she dresses her up. **3.** they haven't worked it out yet.
4. he hung it up. **5.** I/we haven't taken them off.

Unit 9

A. 1. B **2.** C **3.** D **4.** A **5.** D **6.** C **7.** B **8.** A **9.** D **10.** B **11.** C **12.** A
13. D **14.** C **15.** B

B. 1. to buy **2.** taking **3.** to watch **4.** throwing **5.** telling

C. 1. too **2.** so **3.** enough **4.** so **5.** enough

D. 1. having finished **2.** having visited **3.** to have gotten **4.** having worked
5. to have won

E. 1. being invited **2.** to be cleaned **3.** being transferred **4.** to be painted
5. being offered

Unit 10

A. 1. A **2.** D **3.** C **4.** B **5.** B **6.** C **7.** D **8.** A (or B in informal English) **9.** B **10.** C
11. D (or C in informal English) **12.** C **13.** A **14.** C **15.** B

B. 1. living room **2.** fair **3.** physics **4.** begging **5.** compose

C. 1. Either / or **2.** both / and (OR not only / but also) **3.** Both / and (OR Not only / but
also) **4.** neither / nor **5.** Both / and (OR Not only / but also)

D. Complete the sentences with perfect infinitives or gerunds.
1. Whales are mammals like dolphins, for they give birth to live young.
2. Baby whales weigh a few tons at birth, and they drink milk from their mothers.
3. Whale milk is fifty percent fat, so baby whales grow quickly.
4. They usually swim in groups called pods, but they sometimes swim alone.
5. Whales may be far from each other, yet they can communicate sonically through water.

E. 1. votes **2.** isn't/is not **3.** decreased **4.** is **5.** is running

Unit 11

A. 1. B **2.** D **3.** A **4.** A **5.** D **6.** C **7.** B **8.** A **9.** D **10.** C **11.** B **12.** B
13. C **14.** D **15.** A

B. 1. insisted **2.** recommended / suggested **3.** desires **4.** recommended / suggested
5. requires

C. 1. develop / investigate **2.** give **3.** investigate **4.** be **5.** convince

D. 1. Kennedy said, "Ask what you can do for your country."
2. "Give me liberty or give me death," said the patriot, Patrick Henry.
3. "You have a beautiful voice," said the fox to the crow.
4. Thoreau stated, "Men have become the tools of their tools."
5. "We didn't lose the game. We just ran out of time," said Coach Lombardi.

Unit 12

A. 1. D **2.** B **3.** A **4.** C **5.** C **6.** B **7.** D **8.** B **9.** D **10.** A **11.** C **12.** B
13. A **14.** D **15.** C

B. 1. whose **2.** that/who **3.** which **4.** whom **5.** who/that

C. 1. surrounded **2.** covered **3.** hanging **4.** crying **5.** parked

D. 1. ~~who was~~ famous for his courage.
2. ~~who was~~ interested in archaeology.
3. ~~which were~~ used for strategic planning.
4. ~~that was~~ held by the Turks.
5. ~~which has been~~ seen by millions of people.

Unit 13

A. 1. C **2.** D **3.** A **4.** B **5.** C **6.** A **7.** D **8.** B **9.** D **10.** B **11.** D **12.** B
13. A **14.** B **15.** D

B. 1. while **2.** By the time **3.** Whenever **4.** Once **5.** until

C. 1. so destructive that **2.** such an ancient...that **3.** so delicious that **4.** so relaxing that
5. such a complex...that

D. 1. While ~~she was~~ in high school,
2. while ~~she was~~ still in college,
3. After ~~she~~ recover~~ed~~ing from leg surgery,
4. Once ~~she~~ qualified for the Olympics,
5. Even after ~~she had~~ having two children,

Unit 14

A. 1. A **2.** C **3.** D **4.** B **5.** A **6.** C **7.** D **8.** A **9.** D **10.** C **11.** A **12.** D
13. B **14.** C **15.** D

B. 1. With **2.** otherwise **3.** If so **4.** without **5.** If not

C. 1. wish / hoped **2.** hopes **3.** hope **4.** wished **5.** wishes

D. 1. were eliminated / would be **2.** wouldn't be / had developed
3. had protected / wouldn't have already disappeared **4.** wouldn't be / were prevented
5. had been used / would be

Grammar Form and Function
Workbook 3 Answer Keys

UNIT 1   THE PRESENT TENSES

1a The Simple Present Tense and The Present Progressive Tense

Workbooks 3 and 3A p. 1, Student Books 3 and 3A p. 2

1 **Practice**

1. never see
2. are you going
3. am running / 'm running
4. am trying / 'm trying
5. want
6. is
7. are
8. am working out / 'm working out
9. get up
10. do you do
11. jog
12. take
13. is becoming / 's becoming
14. is
15. Are
16. am
17. come
18. stay
19. is getting / 's getting
20. is / 's
21. am not / 'm not
22. don't like

2 **Practice**

1. are you feeling
2. am not doing / 'm not doing
3. is getting
4. is constantly hurting / constantly hurts
5. Are you taking
6. am not taking / 'm not taking
7. Do you exercise
8. don't usually have
9. sometimes play
10. is bothering
11. Does it hurt
12. doesn't
13. always feel
14. does your knee feel
15. is
16. usually see
17. is

3 **Practice**

1. a 2. f 3. e 4. c 5. b 6. d

4 **Practice**

1. I 2. I 3. C 4. I 5. C 6. I 7. C 8. I

5 Practice

Answers will vary. Sample sentences:

Simple Present
1. These women are friends.
2. Do they like to shop?
3. What do they like to buy?
4. They don't have any more money.

Present Progressive
5. The women are running.
6. The women are shopping.
7. One woman is smiling.
8. Where are these women going now?

1b Stative Verbs and Action Verbs

Workbooks 3 and 3A p. 5, Student Books 3 and 3A p. 8

6 Practice

1. are looking
2. is
3. is
4. requires
5. love
6. smells
7. doesn't taste / does not taste
8. seems
9. doesn't have / does not have
10. isn't / is not
11. appears
12. don't enjoy / do not enjoy
13. 'm trying / am trying
14. seem
15. costs
16. realize
17. are charging
18. prefer
19. fear

7 Practice

1. is thinking, thinks
2. is tasting, tastes
3. smells, is smelling
4. appears, is appearing
5. is, is being

1c The Present Perfect Tense and The Present Perfect Progressive Tense

Workbooks 3 and 3A p. 7, Student Books 3 and 3A p. 11

8 Practice

A.
1. have just graduated
2. have been attending
3. have been waiting
4. has been studying
5. has already found
6. has decided
7. hasn't gone
8. haven't said
9. still haven't removed
10. have been

B.
1. has been trying
2. have been improving
3. has been helping
4. has been studying
5. has been reviewing
6. has never been
7. hasn't earned
8. has always preferred
9. has just received

9 Practice

A. Robin: <u>*Did you borrow*</u> my new dress (last night)?
　　　　　　　　 1

Joanna: No, I <u>*didn't*</u>. I <u>*haven't borrowed*</u> your clothes (in a long time).
　　　　　　　　　 2　　　　　　　 3

(Ever since) I gained a few pounds, I <u>*haven't been able to*</u> fit into
　　　　　　　　　　　　　　　　　　　　　 4

your clothes.

Robin: That's strange. I <u>*thought*</u> I put the dress in my closet (right after) I
　　　　　　　　　　 5

<u>*came*</u> home (yesterday).
　　 6

B. Erica: I like your new car! (When) <u>*did you buy*</u> it?
　　　　　　　　　　　　　　　 1

David: I <u>*bought*</u> it (at 2:00 today). I <u>*'ve only had*</u> it (for a few hours)!
　　　　 2　　　　　　　　　　　 3

Erica: It's really bright. I <u>*'ve never seen*</u> you in such a colorful car.
　　　　　　　　　　　　 4

<u>*Have you ever owned*</u> a red car (before)?
　　　　　 5

David: No, this is my first. I <u>*'ve always preferred*</u> black cars.
　　　　　　　　　　　　　　 6

I <u>*'ve been driving*</u> a black car (since the day) I <u>*got*</u> my
　　　 7　　　　　　　　　　　　　　 8

driver's license.

Erica: So why <u>*did you decide*</u> to buy a red car?
　　　　　　　 9

David: This one <u>*was*</u> on sale!
　　　　　　 10

C. Samantha: <u>*Did you watch*</u> the baseball game (last night)?
　　　　　　　 1

Ron: No, I <u>*didn't*</u>. I <u>*'ve never liked*</u> baseball.
　　　　 2　　　　 3

Samantha: You're kidding! Baseball <u>*has been*</u> this country's most popular sport
　　　　　　　　　　　　　 4

(for almost 100 years)! Everybody likes baseball!

Ron: Not me. I prefer soccer. I <u>*'ve been*</u> a soccer fan (since I was a kid).
　　　　　　　　　　　　 5

And I <u>*'ve been playing*</u> the game (for about ten years).
　　　 6

<u>*Have you ever seen*</u> the World Cup on TV? Now that's exciting to watch.
　　　 7

Samantha: I <u>*watched*</u> the World Cup (two years ago). You're right; it <u>*was*</u>
　　　　 8　　　　　　　　　　　　　　　　 9

exciting to watch. I think Americans <u>*have been growing*</u> more
　　　　　　　　　　　　　　 10

interested in soccer (in recent years). But I still like baseball better.

10 Practice

1. Gina has **just** walked to work in her new shoes.
2. She has **never** worn such uncomfortable shoes.
3. It is only 9:00 in the morning, but her feet have **already** started to hurt.
4. She hasn't arrived at work **yet**.

11 Practice

1. Has Gina **just** walked to work in her new shoes?
2. Has she **ever** worn such uncomfortable shoes?
3. Have her feet **already** started to hurt?
4. Has she arrived at work **yet**?

12 Practice

1. I **2.** I **3.** I **4.** C **5.** C **6.** I **7.** I **8.** I **9.** I **10.** C

13 Practice

Answers will vary. Sample sentences:

1. Runner 1096 has just won the race.
2. He has been training for this event for months.
3. He didn't win last year.
4. He is very happy now.
5. He is holding up his arms in victory.
6. Have the other runners won before? / Have the other runners worked as hard?
7. How long have the athletes been running? / Where have these athletes been training?

Unit 1 Workbook Self-Test

Workbooks 3 and 3A p. 12

A. **1.** C **2.** B **3.** B **4.** D **5.** C **6.** C **7.** D **8.** B **9.** A **10.** C
B. **1.** C **2.** C **3.** B **4.** B **5.** D **6.** A **7.** C **8.** D **9.** B **10.** B

UNIT 2   THE PAST TENSES

2a   The Simple Past Tense and The Past Progressive Tense

Workbooks 3 and 3A p. 14, Student Books 3 and 3A p. 28

1 Practice

A. 1. reported
2. was waiting
3. realized
4. left

B. 1. was watering
2. heard
3. called
4. dropped
5. ran
6. saw
7. noticed
8. stopped

5. forgot
6. returned
7. was
8. were

9. was doing
10. let
11. turned
12. didn't seem
13. started
14. didn't want
15. came

9. asked
10. didn't see
11. were standing
12. said

16. yelled
17. was escaping
18. tripped
19. fell
20. was trying
21. arrived
22. arrested

2 Practice

1. loved
2. gave
3. was
4. competed
5. won
6. was training
7. felt
8. ignored
9. passed
10. wasn't going

11. was getting
12. were
13. thought
14. took
15. did
16. was fixing
17. called
18. asked
19. said
20. had

21. decided
22. promised
23. got
24. kept
25. recovered
26. began
27. was going
28. started
29. were participating/participated
30. raised

3 Practice

1. **Q:** Did Mike love bicycles as a child?
   A: Yes, he did.
2. **Q:** Did he win a lot of money from bicycle races?
   A: Yes, he did.
3. **Q:** Did Mike see a doctor as soon as he felt pain?
   A: No, he didn't.
4. **Q:** Were Mike's parents worried about him?
   A: Yes, they were.
5. **Q:** Was Mike riding his bike while he was sick?
   A: No, he wasn't.
6. **Q:** Was Mike riding his bike again by 2001?
   A: Yes, he was.

4 Practice

1. When did Mike's parents give him a bicycle?
2. When did he first feel a pain in his chest?
3. What did Mike's parents think was wrong with him?
4. What was Mike doing when the doctor called?
5. How soon after his recovery was Mike going on long rides again?
6. How much money did Mike's event raise in 2004?
7. Why did Mike start this event?

5 Practice

1. b **2.** a **3.** a **4.** b **5.** a **6.** a

6 Practice

1. While I was studying for the final exam, I didn't want to hear the TV or the phone.
2. I never had any free time while I was working at two jobs.
3. When they heard we were moving to another city, my friends were upset.
4. More than 100 guests came to Elizabeth's birthday party when she turned 16.
5. While Josh was applying to colleges, his parents hoped he would stay close to home.

7 Practice

1. I didn't want to hear the TV or the phone **while I was studying for the final exam**.
2. **While I was working at two jobs**, I never had any free time.
3. My friends were upset **when they heard we were moving to another city**.
4. **When Elizabeth turned 16**, more than 100 guests came to her birthday party.
5. Josh's parents hoped he would stay close to home **while he was applying to colleges**.

8 Practice

Answers will vary. Sample sentences:

1. I felt really embarrassed when I walked into the wrong class last week.
2. My brother was very afraid when he got lost in New York City.
3. When I didn't win the race, I was very sad.
4. When I won the race, I was extremely happy.

9 Practice

Answers will vary.

2b The Past Perfect Tense and The Past Perfect Progressive Tense

Workbooks 3 and 3A p. 20, Student Books 3 and 3A p. 36

10 Practice

1. felt
2. went
3. wanted
4. hadn't eaten
5. had just been
6. thought
7. asked
8. was
9. started
10. had never seen
11. was
12. didn't know
13. wondered
14. had ever happened
15. stopped
16. took
17. counted
18. couldn't believe
19. had thought
20. put
21. walked
22. wondered
23. had done
24. had been (OR) was
25. hadn't been (OR) wasn't
26. brought
27. told
28. had happened
29. had never heard
30. was
31. had returned
32. took
33. was
34. said
35. had enjoyed
36. had spent

11 Practice

She looked happy because . . .

1. . . . she had just gotten a new job.
2. . . . she had bought some new clothes.
3. . . . she had been working out during her lunch hour. (OR) . . . she had worked out during her lunch hour.
4. . . . she hadn't been listening to the bad news on TV.

(Answers to 5 and 6 will vary.)

12 Practice

1. When did you make this movie?
2. Had you ever been in an action movie before?
3. What kinds of movies had you acted in before?
4. Why hadn't you ever done action movies?
5. Where did they film this movie?
6. Had you visited either of those countries before?
7. What had you been doing before you made this movie?
8. Where had you been living before you moved to New York?
9. How long had you been working in L.A.?
10. How many movies had you starred in?

13 Practice

Answers will vary.

14 Practice

1. have been packing
2. had been packing
3. have been wanting

4. had been complaining
5. had been moving
6. had been looking

2c *Used To* + Base Verb and *Would* + Base Verb

Workbooks 3 and 3A p. 24, Student Books 3 and 3A p. 44

15 Practice

A. 1. used to smoke
   2. did people use to
   3. would smoke
   4. didn't use to think

   5. started
   6. had
   7. used to light

B. 1. used to "court"
   2. would bring
   3. would try
   4. won
   5. asked

C. 1. used to dress
   2. used to wear
   3. wouldn't leave
   4. wouldn't wear

   5. used to walk
   6. used to go
   7. would work
   8. didn't use to go

16 Practice

1. Businesspeople in the past used to type or write by hand (**OR** would type or write by hand), but now they write on computers.
2. Today, businesspeople work from anywhere (like home), but in the past, they only used to work (**OR** would work) in the office.
3. Businesspeople didn't use to have good phone service, but these days they talk on cell phones with improved technology.
4. Now, businesspeople don't always meet the people they do business with; in contrast, in the past, they used to do (**OR** would do) a lot of business in person.
5. Businesspeople used to write (**OR** would write) letters; however, today they send and receive email.
6. These days, businesspeople often wear informal clothes, whereas in the past, they didn't use to dress informally.

17 Practice

Answers will vary. Sample sentences:

In the 1980s . . .

1. People used to listen to Michael Jackson and Madonna.
2. People used to pay only $5.00 to see a movie.
3. My friends and I would go roller-skating.
4. I used to like to go dancing.
5. I would wear a lot of hairspray before going out with my friends.
6. I didn't use to think about college or work.

Unit 2 Workbook Self-Test

Workbooks 3 and 3A p. 28

A. **1.** C **2.** B **3.** D **4.** A **5.** B **6.** B **7.** A **8.** C **9.** D **10.** B

B. **1.** D **2.** B **3.** D **4.** B **5.** A **6.** C **7.** B **8.** D **9.** B **10.** A

UNIT 3   THE FUTURE TENSES

3a *Be Going To* and *Will*

Workbooks 3 and 3A p. 30, Student Books 3 and 3A p. 58

1 Practice

A.
1. 'll bake / will bake
2. will get
3. won't
4. 'll eat / will eat
5. 'll take / will take
6. won't find
7. won't be
8. 's going to snow / is going to snow
9. 'll be / will be
10. will keep

B.
1. Are you going to add
2. will break
3. won't break
4. 'm going to be / am going to be
5. 's going to spill / is going to spill
6. won't have
7. will be
8. 'll clean / will clean
9. 'm going to put / am going to put
10. 'm going to turn on / am going to turn on

2 Practice

A.
1. is going to offer
2. is going to meet / will meet
3. is going to teach
4. will learn
5. will show
6. won't make
7. will give
8. won't see
9. will feel
10. will help
11. is going to be

B.

1. **Q:** When is Yoga Journeys going to offer a free class?
   A: Yoga Journeys is going to (**OR** will) offer a free class on February 6, from 1:00-2:30.
2. **Q:** Where is the class going to meet? (**OR**) Where will the class meet?
   A: The class is going to (**OR** will) meet in the main studio on Linden Avenue.
3. **Q:** Who is going to teach the class?
   A: Donna Bliss, a master teacher, is going to teach the class.
4. **Q:** What will you learn in this class? (**OR**) What are you going to learn in this class?
   A: You'll learn the basics of yoga positions. You'll also learn how to breathe correctly.
5. **Q:** Will the teacher make you learn any complicated movements?
   A: No, she won't. This is an introductory class.
6. **Q:** Will a yoga class make you stronger and more flexible?
   A: Yes, a yoga class will make you stronger and more flexible (over time).
7. **Q:** Will you feel strong and flexible after just one class?
   A: No, you probably won't see instant results.
8. **Q:** How will you feel after just a few minutes of yoga?
   A: You'll feel more relaxed after just a few minutes of yoga.
9. **Q:** Why is yoga going to be an increasingly important way to manage stress?
   A: Yoga is going to be an increasingly important way to manage stress because our society is becoming more stressful.

3 Practice

Answers and topics will vary.

3b Time Clauses and Conditional Sentences in the Future

Workbooks 3 and 3A p. 34, Student Books 3 and 3A p. 63

4 Practice

1. i   I can't believe it! When this train stops, I'll be in Rome!
2. j   While I'm traveling to Rome, I'll write to you about my plans.
3. g   I'm going to leave my backpack at the hotel before I go sightseeing in Rome.
4. f   After I check in to my hotel, I'm going to visit the Coliseum.
5. a   I won't leave Rome until I see the Trevi Fountain.
6. h   I'll think of you both while I'm eating gelato on the Spanish Steps.
7. b   I'll buy nice gifts for everyone if I have enough money.
8. e   Unless I save some money, I won't be able to afford a ticket to Naples.
9. d   I'm going to take the train to Naples after I spend three days in Rome.
10. c   I'll write to you again as soon as I get to Naples.

5 | Practice

1. What is Marco going to do when he arrives in Rome?
   When Marco arrives in Rome, what is he going to do?
2. Where is Marco going to go after he leaves Rome?
   After Marco leaves Rome, where is he going to go?
3. When is Marco going to write to us after he visits Naples?
   After Marco visits Naples, when is he going to write to us?
4. What will Marco do if he spends all his money?
   If Marco spends all his money, what will he do?
5. How will Marco ask for help if he gets lost?
   If Marco gets lost, how will he ask for help?
6. If Marco becomes sick, who will he call?
   Who will Marco call if he becomes sick?

6 | Practice

Answers will vary.

 # 3c Present Tenses with Future Meaning

Workbooks 3 and 3A p. 37, Student Books 3 and 3A p. 67

7 | Practice

1. does the store open
2. open
3. start
4. are staying / 're staying
5. are having / 're having
6. am leaving / 'm leaving
7. is continuing
8. am going / 'm going
9. are you coming / do you come
10. return / am returning / 'm returning
11. am not working / 'm not working
12. Are you still selling
13. 're not / aren't
14. ends

8 | Practice

The time clause may be at the beginning or the end of the sentence. Possible answers:

1. Michael is picking Keiko up at home around 6:30.
2. At 7:00, they are eating dinner at the Boston Bistro.
3. The movie starts at 8:15.
4. At 10:00, the movie ends.
5. They are going out for coffee and dessert around 10:15.
6. After coffee and dessert, they are driving to a friend's party.
7. No later than 11:30, Michael is driving Keiko home.
8. Keiko works at 8:00 A.M. the next day.

3d The Future Progressive Tense

Workbooks 3 and 3A p. 39, Student Books 3 and 3A p. 70

9 Practice

1. Q: When will students and parents be arriving at the college?
   A: They'll (They will) be arriving at the college by 8:00.
2. Q: When will students and parents be eating breakfast?
   A: They'll (They will) be eating breakfast at 8:30.
3. Q: When will students and parents be registering for the open house?
   A: They'll (They will) be registering for the open house at 9:00.
4. Q: Where will the president be addressing new students?
   A: He'll/She'll (He/She will) be addressing new students in the auditorium.
5. Q: At what time will the morning activities be starting?
   A: They'll (They will) be starting at 10:00.
6. Q: Who will be giving tours of the campus?
   A: Students will be giving tours of the campus.
7. Q: What will be happening at lunch?
   A: Professors will be meeting with students and parents at lunch to talk about their classes.
8. Q: What will Dr. Hale be lecturing about?
   A: She'll (She will) be lecturing about the importance of college today.
9. Q: What will Dr. Mesler be leading a discussion about?
   A: He'll (He will) be leading a discussion about choosing a major.
10. Q: Who will be talking about financial aid?
   A: Kathleen Henry will be talking about financial aid.

10 Practice

1. will be starting
2. 'll go / will go
3. will be
4. 'll take / will take
5. Will you be going
6. will you be staying
7. 'll stay / will stay
8. won't get
9. 'll have / will have
10. 'll tell / will tell
11. 'll be going / will be going
12. won't see / won't be seeing

11 Practice

Answers will vary. Sample sentences:

1. On Saturday, January 15, you will be flying to St. Lucia at 8:00 A.M.
2. At 11:30 A.M., you will be checking in to your hotel.
3. You will be lying on a beach by this time tomorrow.
4. You will be hiking in the Grand Pitons in the afternoon.
5. In the evening, you will be dining by candlelight.
6. You won't be missing the snow and cold at the end of the day.

3e Other Expressions of the Future; The Future in the Past

Workbooks 3 and 3A p. 42, Student Books 3 and 3A p. 74

12 Practice

1. is about to finish
2. is about to paint
3. is to be
4. is to sell
5. is to help
6. is about to call
7. is about to become

13 Practice

1. was about to paint
2. was about to knock
3. was about to move
4. was about to laugh
5. were about to yell
6. were about to tell
7. was about to call
8. was about to start

14 Practice

Answers will vary. Sample sentences:

A. 1. They are about to leave for a business trip.
   2. Their flight was going to depart at 6:00, but it has been delayed.
   3. They plan to do some work while they wait.

B. 1. She is about to go out on a date.
   2. She wasn't going to go out with this person, but she changed her mind.
   3. She intends to have a nice time.

3f The Future Perfect Tense and The Future Perfect Progressive Tense

Workbooks 3 and 3A p. 45, Student Books 3 and 3A p. 77

15 Practice

1. will have graduated
2. will have seen
3. graduates, will have practiced
4. will have been wearing / will have worn
5. will have attended
6. will have received
7. will have sent her
8. won't have come
9. starts, will have been
10. will have worked, goes
11. quits, will have been saving
12. will have saved
13. what will her parents have been doing/have done
14. will have been preparing / will have prepared
15. will have finished

16 Practice

Answers will vary. Sample sentences:

1. I will have seen a lot of changes in technology.
2. I will have visited every country in the world.
3. I won't have lost my love of travel.
4. I will have been enjoying my children, grandchildren, and great-grandchildren.
5. I will have been learning new things all those years.
6. I won't have been worrying about getting old.

17 Practice

1. I   **2.** I   **3.** C   **4.** I   **5.** C   **6.** I   **7.** I   **8.** C   **9.** I   **10.** I

◆ Unit 3 Workbook Self-Test

Workbooks 3 and 3A p. 47

A. 1. C   **2.** A   **3.** D   **4.** D   **5.** B   **6.** A   **7.** C   **8.** A   **9.** D   **10.** B
B. 1. C   **2.** B   **3.** B   **4.** B   **5.** D   **6.** A   **7.** D   **8.** A   **9.** B   **10.** B

UNIT 4   NOUNS AND EXPRESSIONS OF QUANTITY

4a Regular and Irregular Plural Nouns

Workbooks 3 and 3A p. 49, Student Books 3 and 3A p. 90

1 Practice

1. people   **2.** men   **3.** children   **4.** waves   **5.** surfers   **6.** chairs   **7.** towels   **8.** feet
9. dogs   **10.** species

2 Practice

1. were   **2.** was   **3.** were   **4.** are   **5.** were   **6.** haven't

3 Practice

1. C   **2.** I   **3.** C   **4.** I   **5.** I   **6.** C   **7.** I   **8.** I   **9.** C   **10.** I

4 Practice

Answers will vary. Correct verb forms:

1. teeth–are   **2.** media–are, news–is   **3.** (student choice)–is   **4.** jeans–are
5. businesspeople–are   **6.** man–is   **7.** children–are

4b Possessive Nouns; Possessive Phrases with *Of*

Workbooks 3 and 3A p. 51, Student Books 3 and 3A p. 90

5 Practice

1. a. more than one   b. one
2. a. one   b. more than one
3. a. one   b. more than one
4. a. more than one   b. one
5. a. one   b. more than one
6. a. more than one   b. one

6 Practice

1. It's Scott's CD.
2. It's Leslie's car.
3. It will be the city's responsibility.
4. It's Cheryl's turn.
5. It was Alex's idea.
6. It was Patricia's locker. (OR) Patricia's locker was broken into.
7. It is the department's material. (OR) I'm using the department's material.
8. It will be accounting's database. (OR) We'll be accessing accounting's database.

7 Practice

1. neighbor's house   **2.** in the front of the house   **3.** electrical system of the house
4. her mother's jewelry   **5.** her children's photos

8 Practice

1. I   **2.** I   **3.** I   **4.** C   **5.** I   **6.** C   **7.** I   **8.** I

9 Practice

Following are the possessives. Student completions will vary.

1. The name of this book is *Grammar Form and Function*.
2. My best friend's name is _____.
3. My parents' taste in clothes is _____.
4. My instructor's name is _____.
5. My family's last vacation was _____.
6. The streets of my city are _____.
7. _____ is my favorite time of the year.
8. _____ is the name of my favorite book.

4c ◆ Compound Nouns

Workbooks 3 and 3A p. 54, Student Books 3 and 3A p. 97

10 Practice

1. f **2.** g **3.** e **4.** h **5.** b **6.** a **7.** c **8.** d

11 Practice

1. It was a three-hour tour.
2. She's a seven-year-old girl.
3. It's a 15-week-long semester.
4. It is a 600-page book
5. It was a 16-hour flight.
6. It was a three-course meal.
7. It was a six-dollar bottle of wine.
8. It's going to be a ten-page paper.
9. It's going to be a three-day weekend.
10. It's a four-star restaurant.

12 Practice

Nick had wanted to be a <u>race-car</u> driver ever since he was a <u>seven-year-old</u> boy. In <u>high school</u>, he worked <u>part time</u> as an <u>auto mechanic</u> while he took <u>driving lessons</u>. The day he got his <u>driver's license</u> was the happiest one of his life!

Nick bought an old car and worked on it in his <u>spare time</u>. He started racing other boys on <u>country roads</u> outside town. As he won more and more of these races, he became more and more confident. Pretty soon, Nick applied to drive on a professional <u>racetrack</u>.

The day of the race, there was a <u>rainstorm</u>. Huge <u>thunderclouds</u> made the sky black, and the race was cancelled. Nick was disappointed, but he now had a chance to double-check his car. It was a good thing. During his inspection, he noticed his <u>seatbelt</u> wasn't connected well to the base! If he had raced, it could have been very dangerous.

4d ◆ Count Nouns and Noncount Nouns

Workbooks 3 and 3A p. 55, Student Books 3 and 3A p. 100

13 Practice

1. I **2.** I **3.** C **4.** I **5.** C **6.** C **7.** I **8.** C **9.** C **10.** I

14 Practice

(Brownies)

$\frac{1}{2}$ (cup) <u>butter</u>

2 (squares) of <u>chocolate</u>

1 (cup) of <u>sugar</u>

2 (eggs)

1 (teaspoon) <u>vanilla</u>

$\frac{3}{4}$ (cup) <u>flour</u>

$\frac{1}{2}$ (cup) (nuts)

Melt the <u>butter</u> and <u>chocolate</u> together. Remove from <u>heat</u>. Stir in <u>sugar</u>. Add (eggs) and <u>vanilla</u>. Mix gently until combined. Add <u>flour</u> and (nuts). Put (mixture) in a square (cake pan) and bake for 30 (minutes) at 350˚.

 15 **Practice**

1. isn't **2.** is **3.** are **4.** are **5.** is **6.** is **7.** were **8.** goes **9.** has been **10.** are

 16 **Practice**

Answers will vary.

 17 **Practice**

A. **1.** many **2.** much **3.** Few **4.** little **5.** Many
B. **1.** much **2.** little **3.** Few **4.** many

 18 **Practice**

Answers will vary.

 4e *Some* and *Any*

Workbooks 3 and 3A p. 58, Student Books 3 and 3A p. 103

 19 **Practice**

1. some **2.** any **3.** any **4.** any (OR) some **5.** some **6.** some **7.** some **8.** some

 20 **Practice**

1. I **2.** C **3.** C **4.** I **5.** C **6.** I **7.** I **8.** I

 21 **Practice**

1. any **2.** some **3.** some **4.** any **5.** any **6.** some

 22 **Practice**

1. c **2.** a **3.** a **4.** c **5.** b **6.** a **7.** b **8.** c

4f *Much, Many, A Lot Of, A Few, Few, A Little,* and *Little*
Workbooks 3 and 3A p. 60, Student Books 3 and 3A p. 106

23 Practice
1. a lot of **2.** a little **3.** a lot of **4.** a few **5.** a little **6.** a little **7.** a few

24 Practice
1. a few **2.** much **3.** many **4.** much **5.** little **6.** a little **7.** few **8.** A lot of

25 Practice
Answers will vary. Possible answers:

1. Yes, you have some friends, but not a lot of friends.
2. Yes, but he doesn't have many friends.
3. They have almost no time to finish the project.
4. There is almost no one still working at this hour.
5. Yes, you can do laundry. There is not a lot of soap, but there is some left.
6. They did not find a lot of money, but they found some.
7. No, the proposal has not been changed a lot. It has not been changed much at all.
8. Not a lot of people will be at dinner.

4g *Each, Each (One) Of, Every, Every One Of, Both, Both Of, All,* and *All Of*
Workbooks 3 and 3A p. 62, Student Books 3 and 3A p. 110

26 Practice
1. every **2.** Every **3.** each **4.** both of **5.** All **6.** Every one of **7.** both of

27 Practice
1. Both **2.** Every **3.** all **4.** Every **5.** all **6.** both **7.** all **8.** Both **9.** Every **10.** All

28 Practice
Answers will vary.

Unit 4 Workbook Self-Test
Workbooks 3 and 3A p. 64

A. 1. D **2.** A **3.** B **4.** A **5.** C **6.** B **7.** C **8.** A **9.** B **10.** D
B. 1. B **2.** A **3.** D **4.** D **5.** C **6.** A **7.** D **8.** B **9.** D **10.** B

UNIT 5   PRONOUNS AND ARTICLES

 5a **Subject and Object Pronouns; Possessive Adjectives; and Possessive Pronouns**

Workbooks 3 and 3A p. 66, Student Books 3 and 3A p. 120

☐1☐ **Practice**

A. 1. your   **2.** mine   **3.** my   **4.** yours   **5.** her
B. 1. He   **2.** them   **3.** knows   **4.** he   **5.** His
C. 1. She   **2.** her   **3.** theirs   **4.** They   **5.** them
D. 1. our   **2.** our

☐2☐ **Practice**

A. 1. mine   **2.** my
B. 1. Her   **2.** hers   **3.** her   **4.** her
C. our
D. 1. mine   **2.** mine   **3.** his
E. their
F. 1. our   **2.** theirs   **3.** ours
G. 1. his   **2.** mine
H. 1. your   **2.** mine   **3.** yours   **4.** my

☐3☐ **Practice**

1. It's   **2.** It's   **3.** Its   **4.** Its   **5.** its   **6.** Its   **7.** its   **8.** it's   **9.** its   **10.** It's

☐4☐ **Practice**

Answers will vary.

☐5☐ **Practice**

1. C   **2.** I   **3.** I   **4.** C   **5.** I   **6.** C   **7.** C   **8.** I   **9.** C   **10.** I

☐6☐ **Practice**

1. b   **2.** a   **3.** b   **4.** a   **5.** c   **6.** b   **7.** c   **8.** a   **9.** b   **10.** c

5b Reflexive Pronouns

Workbooks 3 and 3A p. 70, Student Books 3 and 3A p. 128

7 Practice

A. yourself

B. 1. ourselves   **2.** himself   **3.** myself   **4.** ourselves

C. 1. yourself   **2.** myself   **3.** yourself   **4.** myself

8 Practice

1. On the first day of school, the young friends said, "We can walk to school **by ourselves.**"
2. They wanted to walk to school **by themselves.**
3. Some of the most important lessons we learn in life, we have to learn **by ourselves.**
4. She's doing this exercise **by herself.**
5. He doesn't want to go to the party **by himself.**
6. My three-year-old son wants to get dressed **by himself.**
7. I don't like living with roommates. I like living **by myself.**
8. Victor and Carol are nervous about driving to Florida **by themselves.**
9. You are too dependent on your friends. You should do more things **by yourself.**
10. Father to his two children: Please, go out to the back yard and play **by yourselves** for a few minutes.

9 Practice

Correct reflexive pronouns are circled. Sentences with incorrect reflexive pronouns have been rewritten.

1. I didn't invite him! He invited him! *He invited himself.*
2. Our daughter wrote us from Mexico. She's enjoying (herself.)
3. Chen cut (himself) shaving this morning.
4. It's an all-you-can-eat-buffet. Help (yourselves.)
5. I me will help you. *I'll help you myself.*
6. Our dog taught (herself) how to open the door to the refrigerator.
7. The accident was our fault. We blame us. *We blame ourselves.*
8. The children locked (themselves) in the bedroom. We had to call the fire department.
9. Anne promised her to quit smoking. *Anne promised herself to quit smoking.*
10. Patrick painted the room him. *Patrick painted the room himself.*

10 Practice

Answers will vary.

5c   *Another, Other, Others, The Other,* and *The Others*

Workbooks 3 and 3A p. 72, Student Books 3 and 3A p. 130

 Practice

1. others   **2.** other   **3.** other   **4.** others   **5.** other   **6.** others, others   **7.** other, others

 Practice

1. the others   **2.** another   **3.** another, another, another   **4.** the other   **5.** another
6. the other   **7.** the others   **8.** the others

 Practice

1. A B C D E F G H I
2. Sunday, Tuesday, Thursday, Saturday
3. 1998, 1999, 2000, 2001, 2002, 2003, 2004, 2005, 2006
4. January, March, May, July, September, November

 Practice

1. I   **2.** C   **3.** I   **4.** C   **5.** I   **6.** C   **7.** C   **8.** C

5d   The Indefinite Articles *A* and *An; One* and *Ones*

Workbooks 3 and 3A p. 74, Student Books 3 and 3A p. 133

 Practice

1. I   **2.** C   **3.** C   **4.** I   **5.** I   **6.** C   **7.** I   **8.** C   **9.** I   **10.** C

 Practice

1. a   **2.** one/a   **3.** a   **4.** an   **5.** a   **6.** a   **7.** a   **8.** one   **9.** an   **10.** one

17 **Practice**

1. No, thanks. I already have **one**.
2. My teacher likes the old designs better than the new **ones**.
3. Tom: I don't know. I don't have **one**.
4. Vicky: She got the red **one**.
5. My inbox was filled with messages, so I deleted the old **ones**.
6. Sadiq: It was the worst **one** I've ever been to!
7. Tyra: Use the **one** at the library.
8. Tim: Okay. I failed the first test, but passed the other **ones**.
9. Salesperson: The earrings on the counter are full price, but the **ones** in the basket are on sale.

18 Practice

Answers will vary.

5e The Definite Article *The*

Workbooks 3 and 3A p. 76, Student Books 3 and 3A p. 138

19 Practice

1. Everyone should drink _____ water.
2. __The__ water in our city doesn't taste very good.
3. Frank went to __the__ store.
4. I got some fruit. Please put __the__ bananas on the counter.
5. Ben and his friends are planning a trip to _____ Europe.
6. Look at __the__ stars! They're beautiful tonight.
7. Neil Armstrong was __the__ first person to walk on __the__ moon.
8. My sister's family has a rabbit, a cat, and a dog. __The__ rabbit and __the__ dog get along well, but __the__ cat doesn't like anyone!
9. Manuel loves _____ animals.
10. __The__ animals on our rescue farm get good care.

20 Practice

Cross out "the" in # 1, 4, 5, 7, 9, 10.

~~The~~ surfing originated in <u>the</u> Hawaiian Islands. <u>The</u> first European to record a
  1   **2**   **3**

description of it was ~~the~~ Lieutenant James King. ~~The~~ surfing is called "<u>The</u> Sport of
                        4   **5**   **6**

Kings." Hawaiian royalty had beaches and surfboards that were different from everyone

else's. Hawaiian culture had strict rules, but as more and more ~~the~~ Westerners came to
                                                                    7

Hawaii, <u>the</u> traditions and culture changed. ~~The~~ surfing on ~~the~~ Hawaii fell off, but
          8   **9**   **10**

never died out completely. In <u>the</u> 1850s, surfing began to gain in popularity again.
                                11

21 Practice

Answers will vary.

22 Practice

1. We're having **a** test next week. **The** test will cover chapters 6, 7, and 8.
2. I need to get **a** new printer. **The** one I have now is too old.
3. Do you know **a** good babysitter? **The** guy we usually call is busy on Saturday.
4. **The** sun was really hot today! Vince got **a** bad sunburn.
5. Leon has to write **a** book report. I've never heard of **the** book he's chosen.
6. We took **a** taxi yesterday, and I left my sunglasses in **the** cab.
7. Bring **a** sweater with you this weekend. **The** nights can be really cold at our cabin.
8. Rachel had **a** problem with her car. The mechanic says **the** problem is in **the** fuel line.
9. Host: Do you have **a** reservation?
   Guest: Yes, **the** reservation is for 7:00 for four people.

23 Practice

1. an   **2.** a   **3.** an   **4.** a   **5.** a   **6.** the   **7.** a   **8.** the   **9.** the   **10.** the   **11.** the
12. a   **13.** the   **14.** the   **15.** the   **16.** the

24 Practice

Answers will vary.

◆ Unit 5 Workbook Self-Test

Workbooks 3 and 3A p. 80

A. 1. B   **2.** A   **3.** B   **4.** C   **5.** C   **6.** B   **7.** D   **8.** B   **9.** D   **10.** D

B. 1. B   **2.** A   **3.** A   **4.** C   **5.** A   **6.** D   **7.** C   **8.** A   **9.** B   **10.** C

UNIT 6   MODALS I

 6b *Can, Could,* and *Be Able To* to Express Ability

Workbooks 3 and 3A p. 82, Student Books 3 and 3A p. 151

1   Practice

1. couldn't (OR) wasn't able to
2. was able to
3. Will you be able to (OR) Could you (OR) Can you, won't be able to (OR) can't
4. can, can't
5. will be able to
6. simple past: were you able to, was able to (**OR** simple present: are you able to, am able to)
7. simple past: couldn't (OR) weren't able to (**OR** simple present: can't)
8. could (OR) was able to, isn't able to
9. simple past: was able to (**OR** simple present: can), can
10. was able to

2   Practice

Answers will vary. Sample answers:

1. Yes, I can write html code.
2. No, I'm not able to wiggle my ears.
3. No, I couldn't whistle using my fingers when I was a child.
4. Yes, I'm able to touch my nose with my tongue.
5. Yes, I could do magic tricks when I was younger.
6. No, I can't flip my eyelids inside out.
7. No, I wasn't able to curl my tongue.
8. No, I won't be able to walk on my hands if I practice.
9. Yes, I will be able to change a flat tire if you show me how.
10. Yes, I could run fast as a child.

3   Practice

Answers will vary. Bonus answer:

Turn on one switch and let it stay on for an hour or so. Turn it off and flip a different switch. Go into the room with the lights. Find the light that's hot and that one is connected to the first switch. The light that's on goes to the second switch and the cool light that is off goes with the third switch.

4 | Practice

Answers will vary. Examples:

1. The Mayans could/were able to tell time.
2. They could predict eclipses and understand the lunar cycle.
3. They were able to clear the jungle to make farmland and grow food.
4. They could use three calendar systems.
5. They were able to use a writing system which combined pictographs and sound characters.

6c *Must, Have To,* and *Have Got To* to Express Obligation and Necessity

Workbooks 3 and 3A p. 85, Student Books 3 and 3A p. 154

5 | Practice

1. e **2.** d **3.** b **4.** f **5.** g **6.** h **7.** c **8.** a

1. You must stop completely at red lights.
2. You have to change your oil every 2,500 miles.
3. You have to/must step on the clutch to change gears.
4. You must turn your headlights on when driving at night.
5. You must get insurance when you buy a car.
6. You have to/must signal before you turn.
7. You must wear seatbelts at all times.
8. You have to look behind you when you back up.

6 | Practice

1. had to
2. must
3. had to
4. have to / have got to
5. will have to
6. had to
7. will have to
8. has got to / must / has to
9. will have to
10. had to
11. have got to / have to
12. will have to

7 | Practice

Answers will vary. Examples:

1. You have to be ready to take care of one for about ten years before you get one.
2. You must clean their cages every three or four days.
3. You have to move slowly around them.
4. You have got to give them clean water every day.
5. A guinea pig has to have a safe place to sleep.

8 Practice

1. Billy **has got to** stop missing so many classes.
2. Sorry, I **have got to** get going.
3. What did we **have to** do?
4. We **had to** empty the trash.
5. Deborah **has to** get up at 3:00 A.M. every morning.
6. Yuichiro and Emiko **will have to** study before they'll be able to do anything else!

9 Practice

Some answers may vary. Note the following tenses for each.

1. All answers are in the past:
  a. I had to get up at 6:00.
  b. I had to brush my teeth.
  c. I had to shower.
  d. I had to get dressed.
2. All answers are in the future:
  a. My friends will have to arrange for a petsitter.
  b. They will have to book their flights.
  c. They will have to make hotel reservations.
  d. They will have to take their exams.
3. All answers are in the past:
  a. People had to use candles for light.
  b. They had to grow their own food.
  c. They had to use horses for transportation.
4. All answers are in the present:
  a. Lucy has to buy textbooks.
  b. She has to find a part-time job.
  c. She has to rent an apartment.
  d. She has to set up her computer.

6d *Not Have To* and *Must Not* to Express Prohibition and Lack of Necessity

Workbooks 3 and 3A p. 89, Student Books 3 and 3A p. 157

10 Practice

1. d **2.** a **3.** f **4.** e **5.** c **6.** b

11 Practice

1. have to **2.** have to **3.** mustn't **4.** mustn't **5.** have to **6.** have to **7.** mustn't
8. mustn't **9.** have to **10.** have to

Practice
1. had to   2. don't have to   3. had to   4. had to   5. don't have to   6. won't have to
7. won't have to   8. had to   9. won't have to

 Practice
Answers will vary.

 Practice
Answers will vary.

6e *Should, Ought To,* and *Had Better* to Give Advice
Workbooks 3 and 3A p. 92, Student Books 3 and 3A p. 159

 Practice
Answers will vary.

 Practice
Answers will vary.

 Practice
Answers will vary.

 Practice
Answers will vary.

6f *Should Have* and *Ought to Have* to Express Regret or a Mistake
Workbooks 3 and 3A p. 95, Student Books 3 and 3A p. 161

 Practice
1. They didn't tell you when they were coming back, and now you feel it was a mistake.
2. I ate too many cherries. That was a mistake.
3. We didn't spend enough time on our presentation. It wasn't very good.
4. My brother didn't return the library book, and that was a mistake.
5. You didn't introduce yourself to our new neighbors. That was a mistake.
6. I answered the phone. I didn't let the machine pick it up, and now I regret that.
7. The homeowners left the paint cans too close to the furnace. That was a mistake.
8. You're not a lawyer, but you argue like one. Maybe your career choice was a mistake.

20 Practice

A. Andy: Well, I should have gone to college when I had the chance. But I think it's too late now.

Regret: **Andy didn't go to college.**

And last year I gave my wife a vacuum cleaner for her birthday. I shouldn't have done that!

Regret: **He gave his wife a vacuum cleaner.**

B. Ms. Kim: Well, I should have accepted that job in Vietnam. It was a great opportunity.

Regret: **Ms. Kim didn't accept the job.**

And I shouldn't have started smoking again. It's so hard to quit!

Regret: **She started smoking again.**

C. Pierre: I should have checked my parking meter earlier. Look! I got a ticket.

Regret: **Pierre didn't check his parking meter before now.**

No, but seriously. I should have taken my family to the beach for our last vacation. We rented a cabin in the mountains, and it rained every day, and we were without power for most of the time. It was not fun.

Regret: **He went to the mountains on his vacation.**

D. Answers will vary.

21 Practice

1. You **should have** been there.
2. We **had** better get going.
3. Tommy **ought to have** moved to France.
4. We **could have** lent you the money.
5. Kirk **must have** gotten lost. Otherwise, he **would have** been here by now.
6. Do we **have to** do this right now?
7. Who **should have** done this?
8. Spock always **has to** solve the problems on the ship.

22 Practice

Answers will vary. Sample answers:

1. **a.** The crew must have done something wrong yesterday. (OR) They must not have fixed it.
   b. The fire could have spread to other houses.
   c. The crew should have made sure their work was finished yesterday.
2. **a.** They may have had an argument.
   b. She must be moving out.
   c. They should try to work it out.
3. **a.** She must be sick from the crab.
   b. She could be sick from eating something different.
   c. She should be more careful with seafood.
4. **a.** She must check the new program.
   b. She should contact her customers.
   c. She could fix the accounting software.

[23] Practice

Answers will vary.

 ## 6g *Be Supposed To* to Express Expectation

Workbooks 3 and 3A p. 99, Student Books 3 and 3A p. 161

[24] Practice

1. You're not supposed to put your elbows on the table.
2. You're supposed to wait until everyone is seated before starting to eat.
3. You're not supposed to chew with your mouth open.
4. You're not supposed to say you don't like something.
   You're supposed to leave it on your plate.
5. You're supposed to put your napkin in your lap.
6. You're supposed to cover your mouth and say "excuse me" if you burp.
7. You're not supposed to reach across the table to get something you want.
   You're supposed to ask someone politely to pass it to you.

[25] Practice

Answers will vary.

1. F **2.** T **3.** F **4.** F **5.** F

 ## Unit 6 Workbook Self-Test

Workbooks 3 and 3A p. 101

A. 1. B **2.** D **3.** A **4.** A **5.** C **6.** B **7.** D **8.** C **9.** C **10.** B
B. 1. A **2.** D **3.** B **4.** C **5.** B **6.** A **7.** C **8.** D **9.** B **10.** B

UNIT 7   MODALS II

 7a *Shall, Let's, How About, What About, Why Don't, Could,* and *Can* to Make Suggestions

Workbooks 3 and 3A p. 103, Student Books 3 and 3A p. 174

1 Practice

1. Shall   **2.** How about/What about   **3.** could/can   **4.** Shall   **5.** How about/What about
6. How about   **7.** could   **8.** How about   **9.** could/can   **10.** What about

2 Practice

1. How about/What about   **2.** Let's   **3.** could/can   **4.** could/can
5. How about/What about   **6.** Let's

3 Practice

1. How about turning on some music? (OR)
Let's turn on some music. (OR)
Why don't we/you turn on some music?
2. Why don't we/you order a pizza? (OR)
How about ordering a pizza? (OR)
Let's order a pizza.
3. Let's meet at my house. (OR)
How about meeting at my house? (OR)
Why don't we meet at my house?
4. Let's not take the highway. (OR)
How about not taking the highway? (OR)
Why don't we not take the highway? (correct but uncommon; usually used with emphasis on "not")
5. Why don't we/you take my car? (OR)
How about taking my car? (OR)
Let's take my car.
6. How about going now? (OR)
Let's go now. (OR)
Why don't we go now?
7. Why don't we take some more time before we decide? (OR)
How about taking some more time before we decide? (OR)
Let's take some more time before we decide.
8. Let's go to the lake this weekend. (OR)
How about going to the lake this weekend? (OR)
Why don't we go to the lake this weekend?

9. How about not playing card games for a change? (OR)
   Let's not play card games for a change. (OR)
   Why don't we not play card games for a change? (correct but uncommon; usually used with emphasis on "not")
10. Let's go out for dinner. (OR)
    How about going out for dinner? (OR)
    Why don't we go out for dinner?

 4 Practice

Answers will vary.

 7b *Prefer, Would Prefer,* and *Would Rather* to Express Preference

Workbooks 3 and 3A p. 106, Student Books 3 and 3A p. 176

 5 Practice

1. would rather **2.** would rather **3.** than **4.** prefer **5.** to **6.** prefer **7.** to **8.** would rather

 6 Practice

1. d **2.** a **3.** e **4.** b **5.** c

 7 Practice

Answers will vary.

8 Practice

Answers will vary. Samples:

1. Q: Would you rather study history or physics?
   A: I'd rather study physics than (study) history.
   Q: Do you prefer history to physics?
   A: No, I prefer physics (to history).
   Q: Do you prefer studying history to studying physics?
   A: No, I prefer studying physics (to studying history).
   Q: Do you prefer to study history?
   A: No, I don't.

2. Q: Would you rather work with numbers or work with people?
   A: I'd rather work with numbers than (work with) people.
   Q: Do you prefer working with numbers to working with people?
   A: Yes, I prefer working with numbers (to working with people).
   Q: Do you prefer to work with people?
   A: No, I don't. I prefer to work with numbers.

3. Q: Would you rather drive a car or ride a motorcycle?
   A: I'd rather ride a motorcycle than drive a car.
   Q: Do you prefer cars to motorcycles?
   A: No, I prefer motorcycles (to cars).
   Q: Do you prefer driving a car to riding a motorcycle?
   A: I prefer riding a motorcycle (to driving a car).
   Q: Do you prefer to drive a car?
   A: No, I don't.

4. Q: Would you rather garden or read?
   A: I'd rather garden than read.
   Q: Do you prefer gardening to reading?
   A: Yes, I prefer gardening (to reading).
   Q: Do you prefer to garden or to read?
   A: I prefer to garden.

5. Q: Would you rather talk about your problems with other people or solve them by yourself?
   A: I'd rather talk about my problems with other people than solve them by myself.
   Q: Do you prefer talking about your problems with other people or solving them by yourself?
   A: I prefer talking about my problems with other people (to solving them by myself).
   Q: Do you prefer to solve your problems by yourself?
   A: No, I don't. I prefer to talk about them with other people.

7c *May, Could,* and *Can* to Ask Permission
Workbooks 3 and 3A p. 109, Student Books 3 and 3A p. 180

9 Practice
A. 1. May/Could **2.** may/can **3.** may/could **4.** can't **5.** may/can
B. 1. Can/Could **2.** can't **3.** Can/Could **4.** can **5.** can
C. 1. could/can **2.** can **3.** Could/Can **4.** can **5.** can't
D. 1. May/Could **2.** can't **3.** may

10 Practice
1. b **2.** b **3.** a **4.** b **5.** b **6.** a **7.** a **8.** b **9.** b **10.** a

11 Practice
Answers will vary.

7d *Will, Can, Could, Would,* and *Would You Mind* to Make Requests

Workbooks 3 and 3A p. 111, Student Books 3 and 3A p. 184

 Practice

1. Could/Would   **2.** Could/Would   **3.** Would you mind   **4.** Could/Would   **5.** Could/Would
6. Would you mind   **7.** Would you mind   **8.** Could/Would   **9.** Would you mind

13 **Practice**

1. decline   **2.** accept   **3.** decline   **4.** accept   **5.** decline   **6.** accept   **7.** decline

Three people are going to help Jack move.

14 **Practice**

1. Would you mind ~~turn~~ *turning* down the music?

2. Would you *mind* going shopping with me?

3. A: Could you work late tonight?

   B: Yes, I ~~could~~ *can*.

4. A: Would you *mind* picking up some butter?

   B: Sure.

5. Would you mind ~~come~~ *coming* with me?

6. A: Could you lend me your MP3 player?

   B: No, I ~~couldn't~~ *can't*. Sorry.

7. A: Would you mind not ~~park~~ *parking* there?

   B: Oh, sorry!

8. A: Would you *mind* helping me with this exercise?

   B: No problem.

15 **Practice**

Answers will vary. Possible answers:
1. Could you teach me how to play guitar?
2. Would you mind giving me a ride to work?
3. Would you mind postponing the test?
4. Can you get the phone?
5. Would you please do the dishes?
6. Could you please not talk during the movie?
7. Could you please loan me $500?
8. Can I borrow your new sweater?
9. Could I get the restroom key, please?

7e *May, Might,* and *Could* to Express Possibility

Workbooks 3 and 3A p. 114, Student Books 3 and 3A p. 187

 16 **Practice**

1. b **2.** a **3.** a **4.** a **5.** a **6.** a **7.** b **8.** b **9.** a **10.** a

 17 **Practice**

Answers will vary.

 18 **Practice**

Answers will vary.

 19 **Practice**

Answers will vary.

7f *Should* and *Ought To* to Express Probability

Workbooks 3 and 3A p. 117, Student Books 3 and 3A p. 192

20 **Practice**

1. ought to feel/should feel
2. shouldn't be
3. should have stopped/
   ought to have stopped
4. should sleep/ought to sleep
5. should have tried/
   ought to have tried

6. shouldn't have been
7. should taste/ought to taste,
   should encourage/ought to encourage
8. should have sold/ought to have sold
9. should return/ought to return
10. shouldn't have failed

21 Practice

1. should have arrived / ought to have arrived
2. should have posted / ought to have posted
3. should have had / ought to have had
4. should have received / ought to have received
5. should have died down / ought to have died down
6. should have gotten / ought to have gotten
7. should have finished / ought to have finished
8. should have taken / ought to have taken

22 Practice

Answers will vary. Samples:

1. Normally at an opera, the audience arrives and is seated about 15 minutes before the opera begins. We expect this.
2. The students started the test 90 minutes ago. The class time is only 60 minutes long; therefore, we expect that they have already finished.
3. The trip from downtown only takes 40 minutes. It has been about 40 minutes now; therefore, we expect them to be back around now.
4. The mail usually arrives at noon. It is only 9:30, so we don't expect it to arrive until noon.
5. Jim was planning on leaving later than 7:30; therefore, since it is only 7:30 now, we expect that he hasn't left yet.
6. We don't have the agent's response to our offer on the new house yet. We expect to hear from the agent today.
7. Because the massage is so relaxing, we expect that you will feel good afterward.
8. Normally, students take a class in basic digital modeling before they take the advanced class; therefore, since you are taking the advanced digital modeling class, you should have learned the basics last semester.

7g *Must, Must Not,* and *Can't* to Make Deductions

Workbooks 3 and 3A p. 120, Student Books 3 and 3A p. 194

23 Practice

1. a 2. a 3. b 4. a 5. b 6. a 7. b 8. b 9. a 10. a

24 Practice

1. He must not know how to swim.
2. They must have a lot of money.
3. She must love animals.
4. She must not see us.
5. She must be afraid of them.
6. She must not worry too much about small issues.
7. They must be angry at each other.
8. He must not enjoy science fiction.

25 Practice

1. d **2.** c **3.** a **4.** e **5.** b

26 Practice

Answers will vary. Samples:

1. Armand must work out regularly. (OR) Armand must have started working out.

2. He must be married. (OR) He must have gotten married.

3. He must have a new job here. (OR) He must have gotten a new job here.

4. His twin sister must not live here. (OR) His twin sister must have moved away.

5. Armand must not wear glasses any longer. (OR) Armand must have gotten laser surgery on his eyes.

6. He must be more outgoing. (OR) He must have become less shy.

27 Practice

1. can't have seen (OR) couldn't have seen

2. can't have been (OR) couldn't have been

3. can't have waved (OR) couldn't have waved

4. can't have smiled (OR) couldn't have smiled

5. can't have said (OR) couldn't have said

7h The Progressive and Perfect Progressive Forms of Modals

Workbooks 3 and 3A p. 124, Student Books 3 and 3A p. 198

28 Practice

1. It's 4:00, so Irene and Ellen <u>should be doing their homework</u>.

2. It's 5:30, so Irene <u>should be watering the garden</u>.

3. From 5:15 to 5:45, Ellen <u>should be straightening the living room</u>.

4. At 6:00, Irene <u>could be cooking dinner</u>, or Ellen <u>could be cooking dinner</u>.

5. Then, from 7:15 to 7:30, Irene <u>could be washing the dishes</u>. (OR) <u>could be drying and putting away the dishes</u>.

6. At the same time, Ellen <u>could be drying and putting away the dishes</u>. (OR) <u>could be washing the dishes</u>.

7. From 7:30 to 9:30, they <u>could be watching TV</u>, <u>talking to friends</u>, <u>going online</u>, or they <u>could be visiting friends</u>.

29 Practice

1. Last Tuesday at 2:45, Irene and Ellen <u>should have been studying at school</u>.
2. At 3:45, they <u>should have been doing their homework</u>.
3. At 5:20, Ellen <u>should have been straightening the living room</u>.
4. At the same time, Irene <u>should have been watering the garden</u>.
5. At 6:00, Irene <u>could have been cooking dinner</u>, or Ellen <u>could have been cooking dinner</u>.
6. At 7:15, Ellen <u>could have been washing the dishes</u>. (OR) <u>could have been drying and putting away the dishes</u>.
7. At 8:00, they <u>could have been watching TV</u>, <u>talking to friends</u>, <u>going online</u>, or they <u>could have been visiting friends</u>.

30 Practice

1. could/may/might be walking 2. must have been surfing 3. must/could/may/might have been carrying 4. must/could/may/might be looking 5. must/could/may/might be racing 6. must/could/may/might have been running 7. must/could/may/might be stopping 8. must be having

31 Practice

1. C 2. I 3. C 4. I 5. C 6. I 7. C 8. I 9. C

32 Practice

Answers will vary.

Unit 7 Workbook Self-Test

Workbooks 3 and 3A p. 127

A. 1. B 2. D 3. D 4. C 5. D 6. C 7. A 8. B 9. D 10. A
B. 1. D 2. A 3. A 4. D 5. A 6. A 7. B 8. B 9. B 10. D

UNIT 8   THE PASSIVE VOICE, CAUSATIVES, AND PHRASAL VERBS

8a The Passive Voice: Overview

Workbook 3 p. 129, Workbook 3B p. 1, Student Book 3, p. 212, Student Book 3B p. 2

1 Practice

1. A 2. A 3. P 4. P 5. P 6. A 7. P 8. P

2 Practice

1. N 2. N 3. N 4. U 5. N 6. U 7. U 8. U 9. U 10. U

3 Practice

A. Welcome to Island Tours! We have a few guidelines to give you. First, **passengers are requested** to carry their identification at all times. **Passengers are also expected** to take their boarding passes with them whenever they leave the boat. If anyone loses their boarding pass, **they will be charged** a $15.00 replacement fee. Finally, **passengers are asked** to be very careful on the upper deck. **The upper deck has just been washed**. The wood is very slippery right now.

B. Yesterday, **the cross-country skiing championship was won by Lars Larsen**. This is the third year that **the race has been won by the champion skier from Norway**. But two days ago, no one believed **this race would be won by Lars. His left knee had been injured** six months before the big event. He had surgery on that knee in October. Early in this race, **Lars was troubled by** the knee injury. **It was thought that** he was going to drop out of the race. However, **Lars was encouraged by thousands of fans in Norway.** Hundreds of people came all the way to Utah to support him in this race. Lars said that **he was motivated to win by his fans.** After a while, **the pain was forgotten. A rival skier**, Italy's Marco Bernini, **was passed**. Once again, **Lars was awarded** the Golden Ski.

C. Much of Watertown, Ohio has been destroyed by major floods. The problems began last week when **the water level in the river was raised by heavy rains**. In addition, **the river wall had already been damaged by construction in the area. Great efforts were made** to stop the flooding. **Walls were built** out of sandbags all along the river. But the rains continued, and the river water continued to rise and move towards the town. **Windows of homes and businesses were boarded up. Important belongings were moved** to the rooftops. Eventually, **homes were vacated by most residents. People were relocated (by the National Guard)** to shelters in nearby towns. **Some people were taken by helicopter** from their rooftops and **were flown** to the shelters. **Nearly $3 million in damage was caused by the flood. Emergency aid will be requested** from federal funds.

8b The Passive Voice of Modals and Modal Phrases
Workbook 3 p. 133, Workbook 3B p. 5, Student Book 3 p. 219, Student Book 3B p. 9

4 Practice

1. can be found
2. can be seen
3. should be told
4. ought to have been informed
5. has to be cut
6. must be emptied
7. must not have been emptied
8. ought to be washed
9. ought to have been washed
10. were supposed to have been cleaned
11. had to have been paid
12. could be disconnected
13. will be informed
14. had better be moved

5 Practice

1. I **2.** C **3.** I **4.** I **5.** C **6.** I **7.** C **8.** I

8c The Passive Voice with *Get; Get* + Adjective

Workbook 3 p. 134, Workbook 3B p. 6, Student Book 3 p. 222, Student Book 3B p. 12

6 Practice

1. gets depressed
2. is getting older
3. is getting younger at heart
4. got tired
5. get bored
6. is getting excited
7. got worried/scared
8. got scared/worried
9. get hurt
10. get delivered
11. has gotten involved
12. get delivered
13. will get exhibited
14. got married
15. had gotten divorced

7 Practice

1. B 2. B 3. B 4. B 5. B 6. B 7. B 8. B 9. B 10. 0 11. B 12. 0 13. 0

14. 0 15. 0

8 Practice

Answers will vary. Possible adjectives pictured:

1. anxious, worried, scared

2. angry, frustrated, exasperated

3. bored, tired

8d *It* + a Passive Voice Verb + a *That* Clause

Workbook 3 p. 137, Workbook 3B p. 9, Student Book 3 p. 226, Student Book 3B p. 16

9 Practice

1. It is said that my friend Luke is a genius.
   My friend Luke is said to be a genius.
2. It is reported that his software company is the most successful new business of the year.
   His software company is reported to be the most successful new business of the year.
3. It is estimated that his sales will double next month.
   His sales are estimated to double next month.
4. It is believed that his products are changing people's lives.
   His products are believed to be changing people's lives.
5. It is known that starting a new business is difficult in today's economy.
   Starting a new business is known to be difficult in today's economy.
6. It is thought that Luke is especially successful because he is only twenty-seven.
   Luke is thought to be especially successful because he is only twenty-seven.

10 Practice

Answers will vary. Sample sentences:

1. It is believed that teenagers today want to communicate with their parents.
2. It is reported that life may have existed on the planet Mars.
3. It is estimated that nearly 50% of current college students will take five years or more to graduate.
4. It is known that cigarettes can cause cancer.
5. It is feared that violent movies have an impact on young viewers.
6. It is thought that yoga is good for mental health as well as physical health.

8e Present and Past Participles Used as Adjectives

Workbook 3 p. 138, Workbook 3B p. 10, Student Book 3 p. 228, Student Book 3B p. 18

11 Practice

1. disappointing 2. disappointed 3. exciting 4. boring 5. confusing 6. interesting
7. surprised 8. impressive 9. amazing 10. amused 11. frightened 12. exhausting
13. interesting 14. tiring

12 Practice

Answers will vary.

8f Causative Sentences with *Have*, *Get*, and *Make*: Active Voice

Workbook 3 p. 140, Workbook 3B p. 12, Student Book 3 p. 231, Student Book 3B p. 21

13 Practice

1. have my brother paint (OR) get my brother to paint
2. had him paint (OR) got him to paint
3. get him to agree
4. make us repaint
5. have her replace
6. make her take
7. get the neighbors to move
8. got the landlord to give
9. have a housekeeper clean (OR) get a housekeeper to clean
10. had anyone clean
11. make you see
12. have someone else do (OR) get someone else to do

8g Causative Sentences with *Have* and *Get*: Passive Voice

Workbook 3 p. 141, Workbook 3B p. 13, Student Book 3 p. 234, Student Book 3B p. 24

14 Practice

Answers will vary. Sample sentences:

1. **a.** I always get/have my prescriptions filled at the same pharmacy.
   b. I always get the same pharmacy to fill my prescriptions.
   (OR) I always have the same pharmacy fill my prescriptions.
2. **a.** Linda has gotten/had her résumé edited by a career counselor a few times this year.
   b. Linda has gotten a career counselor to edit her résumé a few times this year.
   (OR) Linda has had a career counselor edit her résumé a few times this year.
3. **a.** Noel is having/getting his checks cashed at the bank.
   b. Noel is having the bank cash his checks.
   (OR) Noel is getting the bank to cash his checks.
4. **a.** James usually gets/has his hair cut by a family friend.
   b. James usually gets a family friend to cut his hair.
   (OR) James usually has a family friend cut his hair.
5. **a.** Sandy got/had her nails painted by her favorite manicurist last Friday.
   b. Sandy had her favorite manicurist paint her nails last Friday.
   (OR) Sandy got her favorite manicurist to paint her nails last Friday.
6. **a.** Rachel should have/get her teeth looked at by the dentist soon.
   b. Rachel should have the dentist look at her teeth soon.
   (OR) Rachel should get the dentist to look at her teeth soon.
7. **a.** Midge has just had/gotten her cat checked by Dr. Neuman.
   b. Midge has just had Dr. Neuman check her cat.
   (OR) Midge has just gotten Dr. Neuman to check her cat.
8. **a.** Maryam had her laundry done at the laundromat last week.
   b. Maryam had the laundromat do her laundry last week.
   (OR) Maryam got the laundromat to do her laundry last week.
9. **a.** I will have/get my apartment redecorated by an interior designer next summer.
   b. I will have an interior designer redecorate my apartment next summer.
   (OR) I will get an interior designer to redecorate my apartment next summer.
10. **a.** Ellen is having/getting the film editing program explained to her by Marcus.
   b. Ellen is having Marcus explain the film editing program.
   (OR) Ellen is getting Marcus to explain the film editing program.

15 Practice

Answers will vary.

8h Phrasal Verbs

Workbook 3 p. 143, Workbook 3B p. 15, Student Book 3 p. 236, Student Book 3B p. 26

16 Practice

1. up **2.** out **3.** up **4.** up **5.** into **6.** up **7.** off **8.** off **9.** out **10.** off
11. down/off/over **12.** up **13.** up **14.** on **15.** on **16.** down **17.** up **18.** over
19. over **20.** off **21.** with **22.** up **23.** across **24.** down **25.** about

17 Practice

1. I **2.** I **3.** I **4.** S **5.** I **6.** I **7.** S **8.** S **9.** S **10.** I **11.** I **12.** S **13.** I
14. S **15.** I **16.** I **17.** S **18.** S **19.** I **20.** S **21.** I **22.** I **23.** I **24.** I **25.** I

18 Practice

1. John picked her up after work.
   John picked up Emily after work.
2. They are going to tear that old building down.
   They are going to tear it down.
3. inseparable verb
4. Where should I drop the books off?
   Where should I drop them off?
5. I don't know how to set my new computer up.
   I don't know how to set it up.
6. inseparable verb
7. Somebody used all the sugar up.
   Somebody used it up.
8. inseparable verb

8i Prepositions Following Verbs, Adjectives, and Nouns; Other Combinations with Prepositions

Workbook 3 p. 146, Workbook 3B p. 18, Student Book 3 p. 244, Student Book 3B p. 34

19 Practice

1. need for **2.** contribute to **3.** disappointed with **4.** tired of **5.** fond of
6. complained about **7.** shouting at **8.** solution to **9.** According to **10.** impact on
11. cost of **12.** responsible for **13.** opposed to **14.** essential to **15.** fight for

Unit 8 Workbook Self-Test

Workbook 3 p. 148, Workbook 3B p. 20

A. 1. A **2.** A **3.** C **4.** D **5.** B **6.** D **7.** C **8.** A **9.** B **10.** C
B. 1. C **2.** C **3.** A **4.** B **5.** B **6.** B **7.** B **8.** D **9.** D **10.** A

UNIT 9   GERUNDS AND INFINITIVES

9a Gerunds as Subjects and Objects; Verbs Followed by Gerunds

Workbook 3 p. 150, Workbook 3B p. 22, Student Book 3 p. 256, Student Book 3B p. 46

1 Practice

1. G   2. V   3. G   4. G   5. G   6. V   7. V   8. G

2 Practice

1. snowboarding   2. being   3. swimming   4. surfing   5. skiing   6. going (OR traveling)
7. traveling (OR going)   8. taking   9. Keeping   10. falling   11. giving up   12. standing
13. riding   14. learning   15. exercising

3 Practice

1. reading   2. buying   3. published   4. finished   5. want   6. leaving   7. waiting
8. Discussing   9. arguing   10. going   11. is   12. enjoys   13. reading   14. hopes
15. writing   16. reading

4 Practice

Answers will vary. Sample sentences with gerunds as subjects and objects:

1. **a.** Dancing is difficult for my boyfriend.
   b. My boyfriend doesn't enjoy dancing very much.
2. **a.** Listening to jazz annoys me.
   b. I can't stand listening to jazz.
3. **a.** Studying for a math test is impossible without the book.
   b. I suggest studying for the math test with the math book.
4. **a.** Traveling without a map can be risky.
   b. I wouldn't risk traveling without a map.
5. **a.** Watching reality TV shows is a waste of time.
   b. We can't help watching reality TV shows even though we know they're a waste of time.
6. **a.** Cooking every day takes a lot of time and energy.
   b. My sister quit cooking every day after she got a new job.

9b Gerunds as Objects of Prepositions; Gerunds after Certain Expressions

Workbook 3 p. 153, Workbook 3B p. 25, Student Book 3 p. 260, Student Book 3B p. 50

5 Practice

1. to **2.** on **3.** in **4.** of **5.** in **6.** from **7.** for **8.** at

6 Practice

Answers will vary. Sample sentences using gerunds after prepositions and expressions:

1. These days I'm busy studying for the TOEFL.
2. I have difficulty keeping papers organized.
3. I don't have trouble speaking in class.
4. I'm also good at preparing for tests.
5. I'm tired of writing essays.
6. I think memorizing information is a waste of time.
7. A teacher once tried to stop me from dropping a class.
8. I look forward to graduating soon.

9c Verbs Followed by Infinitives

Workbook 3 p. 154, Workbook 3B p. 26, Student Book 3 p. 263, Student Book 3B p. 53

7 Practice

1. Mr. Torres agreed to make breakfast for Alex.
2. Mrs. Torres reminded Alex to brush his teeth after breakfast. (OR)
   Mrs. Torres reminded Alex not to forget to brush his teeth after breakfast.
3. Alex asked his mother to bring him a picture of her office.
4. Mrs. Torres told Alex to be good and to do everything his father asked.
5. Alex wanted his mother to come home early.
6. Mrs. Torres promised to call her son and her husband at lunch.
7. Alex hoped to watch TV while his mom was at work.
8. Mrs. Torres warned her husband not to let Alex watch more than one hour of TV.
9. Mr. Torres expected his wife to be back home by 5:30.
10. Mrs. Torres encouraged him to call Kevin next door if he needed any help.

8 Practice

1. I **2.** C **3.** I **4.** I **5.** C **6.** C **7.** I **8.** I

9d Verbs Followed by a Gerund or an Infinitive

Workbook 3 p. 156, Workbook 3B p. 28, Student Book 3 p. 265, Student Book 3B p. 55

9 Practice

1. driving/to drive **2.** to ask **3.** driving **4.** asking/to ask **5.** to read **6.** to tell
7. to bring **8.** planning **9.** to get **10.** seeing **11.** traveling/to travel

10 Practice

1. acting **2.** to take **3.** to try **4.** acting **5.** acting **6.** spending **7.** to be
8. standing **9.** rehearsing **10.** to learn **11.** remembering **12.** to do **13.** to say
14. to tell **15.** to invite **16.** to see

9e Infinitives after Certain Adjectives, Nouns, and Indefinite Pronouns

Workbook 3 p. 158, Workbook 3B p. 30, Student Book 3 p. 268, Student Book 3B p. 58

11 Practice

1. to tell **2.** to hear **3.** to visit **4.** to drive **5.** to let **6.** to practice **7.** to go
8. to find **9.** to borrow **10.** to do **11.** to run **12.** to stop **13.** to pick up
14. to have

12 Practice

1. It's important to obey traffic laws.
2. It's necessary to understand how your car works.
3. It's disappointing to fail a driving test.
4. It's frustrating for some teenagers not to have a car.
5. It's illegal to drive without insurance.
6. It's dangerous not to wear a seatbelt.
7. For young people, it's very exciting to get their driver's license.
8. It can be expensive to own and to maintain a car.
9. It isn't easy for everyone to save money for a car.

9f *Too* and *Enough* Followed by Infinitives

Workbook 3 p. 160, Workbook 3B p. 32, Student Book 3 p. 270, Student Book 3B p. 60

13 Practice

1. **a.** In Jared's psychology class, there are too many people for everyone to have a chair.
   b. In his psychology class, there aren't enough chairs for everyone to sit on.
   c. In his English class, there are enough chairs for everyone to sit on.
2. **a.** The professor in his psychology class speaks too softly for the students in the back to hear.
   b. In his psychology class, the professor doesn't speak loudly enough for the students in the back to hear.
   c. In his English class, the professor speaks loudly enough for everyone to hear.
3. **a.** The psychology professor speaks too quickly for Jared to take notes.
   b. The psychology professor doesn't speak slowly enough for Jared to take notes.
   c. The English professor speaks slowly enough for Jared to take notes.
4. **a.** In the psychology classroom, the windows are too high to open.
   b. In the psychology classroom, the windows aren't low enough to open.
   c. In the English classroom, the windows are low enough to open.
5. **a.** In the 8:00 A.M. psychology class, the students are too tired to pay attention.
   b. In the 8:00 A.M. psychology class, the students aren't awake enough to pay attention.
   c. In the 10:00 A.M. English class, the students are awake enough to pay attention.
6. **a.** The psychology students are too lazy to do the homework.
   b. The psychology students aren't motivated enough to do the homework.
   c. The English students are motivated enough to do the homework.

14 Practice

1. enough **2.** not enough **3.** very **4.** too **5.** too **6.** enough **7.** very **8.** not enough
9. enough **10.** too

15 Practice

Answers will vary. Sample sentences:

1. The couch is too big to fit in the van.
2. There isn't enough room to put the couch in the van.
3. The couch is too heavy for one person to lift.
4. There are enough people to lift the couch.
5. There isn't enough space to carry anything else in the van.

9g The Infinitive of Purpose

Workbook 3 p. 162, Workbook 3B p. 34, Student Book 3 p. 273, Student Book 3B p. 63

16 Practice

1. **a.** David went to the library to locate a book about Spain.
   b. David went to the library in order to locate a book about Spain.
2. **a.** David wanted to visit Spain to see his relatives there.
   b. David wanted to visit Spain in order to see his relatives there.
3. **a.** He studied the book to find information about his family's town.
   b. He studied the book in order to find information about his family's town.
4. **a.** He got a summer job to earn travel money.
   b. He got a summer job in order to earn travel money.
5. **a.** He signed up at the community center to take Spanish classes.
   b. He signed up at the community center in order to take Spanish classes.
6. **a.** He used the Internet to buy a cheap airplane ticket to Spain.
   b. He used the Internet in order to buy a cheap airplane ticket to Spain.

17 Practice

Answers will vary. Sample sentences:

1. She must go to the furniture store to buy furniture.
2. She must call the telephone company in order to start her telephone service.
3. She must go to the hardware store to buy some paint for the walls.
4. She must go to the grocery store for food.
5. She must call or email everyone to tell them her new address.
6. She must have a housewarming party for fun.

18 Practice

1. You should sit near the front of the class in order not to miss anything the teacher says.
2. You should review your notes in order not to forget information.
3. You should buy file folders in order not to lose your papers.
4. You should allow plenty of time to get to class in order not to be late.
5. You should buy a day planner or a PDA in order not to waste time.
6. You should get enough sleep and exercise in order not to get sick.
7. You should join student clubs in order not to feel lonely.
8. You should ask your teachers for help in order not to fall behind.

9h Perfect Infinitives and Perfect Gerunds; Passive Voice of Infinitives and Gerunds

Workbook 3 p. 165, Workbook 3B p. 37, Student Book 3 p. 275, Student Book 3B p. 65

19 Practice

1. having woken up   **2.** Having been warned   **3.** to have remembered   **4.** not having looked   **5.** having left   **6.** having missed   **7.** having run   **8.** to have arrived   **9.** not to have been noticed   **10.** to have been called   **11.** having taken

20 Practice

1. a. The papers need filing.
   b. The papers need to be filed.
2. a. The 28 voicemail messages need deleting.
   b. The 28 voicemail messages need to be deleted.
3. a. Three meetings need scheduling before 4:00.
   b. Three meetings need to be scheduled before 4:00.
4. a. The computer needs servicing.
   b. The computer needs to be serviced.
5. a. The copy machine needs repairing.
   b. The copy machine needs to be repaired.
6. a. Her assistant needs replacing.
   b. Her assistant needs to be replaced.

9i Gerunds and Base Verbs with Verbs of Perception

Workbook 3 p. 167, Workbook 3B p. 39, Student Book 3 p. 279, Student Book 3B p. 69

21 Practice

1. moving   **2.** crawling   **3.** coming   **4.** walk   **5.** stop   **6.** happening   **7.** watching   **8.** put   **9.** reaching   **10.** shout   **11.** remove   **12.** run   **13.** being

9j ◆ Person + Gerund

Workbook 3 p. 168, Workbook 3B p. 40, Student Book 3 p. 281, Student Book 3B p. 71

22 Practice

1. **a.** I don't like Beth talking on her cell phone when we go out for coffee.
   b. I don't like Beth's talking on her cell phone when we go out for coffee.
2. **a.** I can't stand her friends calling and interrupting our conversation.
   b. I can't stand her friends' calling and interrupting our conversation.
3. **a.** I don't approve of them not asking her if she's free to talk on the phone.
   b. I don't approve of their not asking her if she's free to talk on the phone.
4. **a.** I appreciate my boyfriend turning his phone off in restaurants.
   b. I appreciate my boyfriend's turning his phone off in restaurants.
5. **a.** I respect him not wanting to hear the phone ring in public places.
   b. I respect his not wanting to hear the phone ring in public places.
6. **a.** On the other hand, sometimes I'm annoyed by him not answering the phone when I call.
   b. On the other hand, sometimes I'm annoyed by his not answering the phone when I call.
7. **a.** I'm tired of Beth ignoring me when her friends call.
   b. I'm tired of Beth's ignoring me when her friends call.
8. **a.** She doesn't hear me politely asking her to get off the phone.
   b. She doesn't hear my politely asking her to get off the phone.

23 Practice

1. I **2.** I **3.** C **4.** I **5.** C **6.** C **7.** I **8.** I

◆ Unit 9 Workbook Self-Test

Workbook 3 p. 170, Workbook 3B p. 42

A. 1. B **2.** C **3.** A **4.** D **5.** D **6.** B **7.** B **8.** A **9.** C **10.** A
B. 1. C **2.** B **3.** D **4.** B **5.** B **6.** C **7.** C **8.** A **9.** D **10.** C

UNIT 10 AGREEMENT AND PARALLEL STRUCTURE

◆ 10a Subject-Verb Agreement: General Rules Part 1

Workbook 3 p. 172, Workbook 3B p. 44, Student Book 3 p. 292, Student Book 3B p. 82

1 Practice

1. have **2.** is **3.** is **4.** contains **5.** is **6.** have **7.** has **8.** were **9.** are **10.** are
11. are **12.** is **13.** replaces **14.** have **15.** work **16.** stop **17.** is **18.** are **19.** are
20. is **21.** are **22.** show

2 Practice

Answers will vary. Sentences should take the following verb forms:

1. *all:* plural verb
2. *most:* plural verb
3. *some:* plural verb
4. *each:* singular verb
5. *every:* singular verb

6. *everyone:* singular verb
7. *not everyone:* singular verb
8. *any:* singular verb
9. *almost all:* plural verb

◆ 10b Subject-Verb Agreement: General Rules Part 2

Workbook 3 p. 174, Workbook 3B p. 46, Student Book 3 p. 295, Student Book 3B p. 85

3 Practice

1. is **2.** was **3.** are **4.** is **5.** is **6.** are **7.** are **8.** is **9.** were **10.** were **11.** was
12. is **13.** are **14.** is **15.** are **16.** is **17.** are **18.** are **19.** are **20.** is **21.** is
22. is **23.** are **24.** is **25.** is

4 Practice

Answers will vary. Sample sentences:
A. 1. All of these people are trying to fit into the doorway.
   2. One of these people is sitting.
   3. All of these people are smiling.
   4. Almost all of these people have brown hair.
   5. Half of these people are male.
B. 1. All four of these boys like to play basketball.
   2. Two of the boys are older (OR younger).
   3. The small boy in the striped shirt is making a funny face.
   4. One of the older boys is holding the ball.
   5. The challenge for three of the boys is to get the ball.
C. 1. The little girl together with her parents is reading.
   2. Everyone in this family enjoys reading.
   3. The parents of the little girl are teaching her to read.
   4. The exciting thing for her parents is watching her learn to read.

10c Subject-Verb Agreement with Quantity Words

Workbook 3 p. 176, Workbook 3B p. 48, Student Book 3 p. 297, Student Book 3B p. 87

5 Practice

1. are **2.** plan **3.** want **4.** have **5.** attend **6.** increases **7.** work **8.** have **9.** have
10. is **11.** is **12.** makes **13.** misses **14.** is

6 Practice

1. C **2.** I **3.** I **4.** C **5.** I **6.** C **7.** I **8.** I **9.** C **10.** I

10d Parallel Structure

Workbook 3 p. 178, Workbook 3B p. 50, Student Book 3 p. 301, Student Book 3B p. 91

7 Practice

1. adjectives	thick, heavy
2. nouns	South America, Asia, North America
3. gerunds	learning, winning
4. nouns	a domino with many dots, a domino with fewer dots
5. verbs	place, shuffle
6. gerunds	placing, matching, decreasing
7. infinitives	to play, to have
8. nouns	block games, draw games
9. verbs	play, eliminate
10. verbs	take, don't stop
11. adjectives	exciting, strategic
12. adjectives	regional, national, international

8 Practice

The sentences should be corrected and the parallel structures identified as follows:

1. nouns — Backgammon, a game for two players, requires a backgammon set, two sets of dice, and ~~you need~~ thirty checkers.

2. verbs — The backgammon board has twenty-four triangles which lie in four quadrants and ~~alternating~~ *alternate* in color.

3. nouns, no errors — A bar down the center of the board separates the players' "home board" and "outer board."

4. infinitives — The objects of the game are to move all of your checkers around the board, to bring them to your own home board, and ~~taking~~ *to take* them off the board.

5. infinitives, no errors — The first player to move all of his or her checkers and to take them off the board wins the game.

6. verbs   Players must roll the dice again if a die ~~fallen~~ *falls* outside the board, hits a checker, or does not land flat.

7. adjectives   If a player's move is unfinished or ~~illegality~~ *illegal*, the opponent is allowed to accept that move.

9   Practice

Answers will vary. Sample sentences:

1. My three favorite subjects in school are chemistry, math, and art.
   (Three nouns should be listed, and there should be a comma before the last noun.)
2. The three adjectives that best describe me are adventurous, hard-working, and kind.
   (OR) I am an adventurous, hard-working, and kind person.
   (Three adjectives should be listed, and there should be a comma before the last adjective.)
3. Every morning I eat breakfast and brush my teeth.
   (OR) Two things that I do every morning are eating breakfast and brushing my teeth.
   (Either verb phrases or gerunds can be used; there should be no comma, as there are only two parts using parallel structure.)
4. Three chores around the house that I dislike doing are vacuuming the rugs, taking out the garbage, and making the bed.
   (OR) I dislike vacuuming, taking out the garbage, and making the bed.
   (Three gerunds should be listed, and there should be a comma before the last gerund.)
5. In the future, I want to earn an MBA, own my own business, and give money to my parents.
   (Three verb phrases should be listed, and there should be a comma before the last verb.)
6. In the future, I don't want to owe money or forget my friends.
   (Two verb phrases should be joined with "or," and there should be no comma as there are only two parts using parallel structure.)
7. The three most useful activities for relieving stress are exercising, talking to friends, and sleeping.
   (Three gerunds should be listed, and there should be a comma before the last gerund.)
8. The two biggest causes of stress among people my age are job worries and relationship problems.
   (Two nouns or noun phrases should be used; there should be no comma as there are only two parts using parallel structure.)
9. I speak English slowly but correctly.
   (Two adverbs should be used, and they can be joined by "and" or "but"; no comma should be used, as there are only two parts using parallel structure.)
10. If someone visits my city, they should shop at Quincy Market, walk the Freedom Trail, and visit the Museum of Fine Arts.
    (Three verb phrases should be used; there should be a comma before the last verb.)

10   Practice

Answers will vary.

10e Coordinating Conjunctions

Workbook 3 p. 181, Workbook 3B p. 53, Student Book 3 p. 304, Student Book 3B p. 94

11 Practice

1. Alicia wants to buy fruit, **but (OR yet)** she doesn't know what kind.
2. The grapefruit looks ripe, **and** the plums look very fresh.
3. Apples are on sale today, **so** she should buy a lot of them.
4. She could use fresh fruit in a dessert, **or** she could use it in a salad instead.
5. The strawberries look delicious, **but (OR yet)** they are too expensive.
6. She should shop at the farmer's market, **for** the prices are lower, **and** the fruit is fresher.
7. Alicia would like to bake an apple pie, **but** she doesn't know how.
8. If she wants to bake a pie, she should buy a baking dish, **for** she doesn't have one.

12 Practice

Answers will vary. Sample sentences using each coordinating conjunction:

1. The living room has many windows, so the light can come in.
2. The rooms are clean and bright.
3. The ceilings are high, for the house is modern.
4. The rooms are large yet cold.
5. The floors are made of wood or tiles.
6. The house is very grand, but I wouldn't want to live there.

13 Practice

1. I; Change *so* to *but* or *yet*.
   My sister was always good at math, **yet/but** I was always better at English.
2. I; Change *for* to *but* or *yet*.
   Jacob applied for six jobs, **but/yet** he didn't get any of them.
3. C
4. I; Add a comma before *yet*.
   The actor was seventy years old, yet he was still very handsome.
5. I; Add a comma before *or*.
   You can leave a voicemail message, or you can call back later.
6. I; Change *and* to *but* or *yet*.
   They tried to take notes, **but/yet** they couldn't hear the teacher.
7. C
8. I; Change *or* to *but* or *yet*.
   The movie was so bad that we wanted to leave, **but/yet** we stayed and watched until the end.

10f Correlative Conjunctions: *Both . . . And;*
Not Only . . . But Also; Either . . . Or; Neither . . . Nor

Workbook 3 p. 183, Workbook 3B p. 55, Student Book 3 p. 307, Student Book 3B p. 97

14 Practice

1. are **2.** plan **3.** want **4.** prefer **5.** is **6.** thinks **7.** interests **8.** interests
9. offers **10.** are

15 Practice

1. Both Roger and Brandon play basketball.
2. Not only Roger but also Brandon plays basketball.
3. Neither Roger nor Brandon likes math.
4. Roger enjoys neither history nor math.
5. Roger doesn't enjoy either history or math.
6. Brandon either works on the weekends or he goes out with his friends.
7. Brandon likes either fixing cars or repairing electronic equipment for fun.
8. Both the twins and their parents like spending time with each other.
9. Not only Roger's mother but also Roger's father wants the boys to choose a college close to home.
10. Roger's mother not only wants the boys to visit often, but also wants her sons to be independent.

16 Practice

A. Answers will vary. Sample sentences:
1. Both vets and medical doctors need to study medicine.
2. Not only medical doctors but also vets want to help others get well.
3. Neither vets nor medical doctors can practice without a license.
4. Vets and medical doctors can either work for a large office or have their own private practice.

B. Answers will vary. Sample sentences:
1. Both chefs and waiters work in restaurants. (OR) Chefs and waiters can work in both expensive restaurants and inexpensive restaurants.
2. Not only chefs but also waiters have to know something about food. (OR) Chefs and waiters not only work in the evenings, but also they work on the weekends.
3. Neither chefs nor waiters are happy when customers complain about the food.
4. If you like what you eat in a restaurant, you can tell either the waiter or the chef.

C. Answers and job choices will vary.

◆ Unit 10 Workbook Self-Test

Workbook 3 p. 187, Workbook 3B p. 59

A. 1. B **2.** A **3.** B **4.** D **5.** C **6.** A **7.** B **8.** C **9.** D **10.** C

B. 1. A **2.** C **3.** B **4.** A **5.** A **6.** C **7.** C **8.** C **9.** B **10.** D

UNIT 11   NOUN CLAUSES AND REPORTED SPEECH

11a Noun Clauses Beginning with *That*

Workbook 3 p. 189, Workbook 3B p. 61, Student Book 3 p. 318, Student Book 3B p. 108

☐1☐ Practice

1. C **2.** C **3.** I **4.** C **5.** I **6.** C **7.** C **8.** I **9.** C **10.** I

☐2☐ Practice

Noun clauses are underlined as follows:

   Christopher Columbus, originally from Genoa, Italy, was an explorer who knew <u>the world was round</u>. He predicted <u>he could find a trade route to Asia by sailing west</u>. He had a very difficult time raising money for his voyage, so he finally appealed to Queen Isabella and King Ferdinand of Spain. They decided <u>that Columbus might be right</u>, and <u>it would be in the best interest of Spain to find out</u>. Columbus set out to prove <u>that he was right</u>.

   On his first voyage in 1492, he arrived in the Bahamas and established a settlement there, but he thought <u>he had arrived in Asia</u>, and when he went back to Spain, he told the king and queen <u>that he had</u>. Many people doubted <u>that this was true</u>. On his second trip, Columbus discovered <u>his original settlement had been destroyed</u>, and he had to spend most of his time governing instead of exploring. He was an unfit governor, and although he made a total of four trips to the New World, he died regretting <u>he had never found the route to Asia that he was convinced existed</u>.

☐3☐ Practice

1. 'm afraid not **2.** hope not **3.** don't think so **4.** guess not **5.** don't believe so

6. – 10. Answers will vary.

4 | Practice

Answers will vary. Sample answers:

1. Matt thought <u>that he'd made his house safe.</u>
2. Sasha knew <u>that they were in trouble / that something was wrong.</u>
3. Matt discovered <u>that the roof was gone.</u>
4. He observed <u>that the roof was being blown off.</u>
5. He realized <u>that they needed to leave the house.</u>
6. He decided <u>that they had to go to a neighbor's house.</u>
7. Matt and his family believe <u>that Sasha saved them.</u>

5 | Practice

Answers will vary.

11b Noun Clauses Beginning with Wh- Words (Indirect Wh- Questions)

Workbook 3 p. 192, Workbook 3B p. 64, Student Book 3 p. 321, Student Book 3B p. 111

6 | Practice

1. I **2.** C **3.** I **4.** C **5.** C **6.** I **7.** I **8.** C **9.** C **10.** I **11.** I **12.** C

7 | Practice

1. I know how I should take care of him.
2. I know what he eats.
3. I know when he sleeps.
4. I know what kind of toys he likes.
5. I know when I should take him to the vet.
6. I know what other equipment I need.
7. I know when I should feed him.
8. I know how long he will live.
9. I know what else I should know.

8 | Practice

1. What did she say?
2. When are we supposed to be there?
3. What should we bring?
4. When does the party start?
5. Who did she invite?
6. Where does she live?
7. How can we get there from here?

9 Practice

Answers will vary. Sample answers:

A. **1.** Your mother/father and I would like to know where you met her.
2. Your mother/father and I would like to know where she went to school.
3. Your mother/father and I would like to know who her family is.
4. Your mother/father and I would like to know where she's from.
5. Your mother/father and I would like to know what she does for a living.
6. Your mother/father and I would like to know when we can meet her.

B. **1.** Could you tell me where we'll be able to do a little shopping?
2. Could you tell me if any special activities are scheduled for today?
3. Could you tell me what cities we're going to?
4. Could you tell me what historical sites we'll visit?
5. Could you tell me about the local architecture?
6. Could you tell me when we'll be eating?

C. **1.** Do you know what we should do with our files during the move?
2. Do you know how long the move will take?
3. Do you know what my responsibilities are during the move?
4. Do you know when we're moving?
5. Do you know where we're moving to?
6. Do you know why we're leaving?

D. **1.** Tell us where you were last night at 9:00.
2. Tell us how you know the victim.
3. Tell us what you were doing when the crime was committed.
4. Tell us where you were when the crime was committed.
5. Tell us who you were with last night.

11c Noun Clauses Beginning with *If* or *Whether* (Indirect Yes/No Questions)

Workbook 3 p. 196, Workbook 3B p. 68, Student Book 3 p. 324, Student Book 3B p. 114

10 Practice

1. C **2.** I **3.** I **4.** C **5.** I **6.** C **7.** C **8.** C

11 Practice

Answers will vary. Sample answers:

1. I want to know if this plant needs a lot of light.
2. Could you tell me if I should water these plants every day?
3. Do you know whether or not I need to prune these plants often?
4. Could you tell me whether I plant these in the spring or the fall?
5. I want to know whether they will grow in containers or not.
6. Do you know if they will attract butterflies or not?
7. I want to know whether these plants need a lot of care or not.
8. Do you know if I should fertilize them every week?
9. I want to know if they will come back next year or not.

12 Practice

1. Is she having a good time?
2. Has she met any cute guys?
3. Has she been to Waikiki yet?
4. Is she coming back soon?
5. Has she tried surfing?
6. Has she bought us any souvenirs?

13 Practice

Answers will vary.

11d Quoted Speech

Workbook 3 p. 198, Workbook 3B p. 70, Student Book 3 p. 327, Student Book 3B p. 117

14 Practice

1. Q   **2.** R   **3.** Q   **4.** Q   **5.** R   **6.** Q   **7.** R   **8.** Q

15 Practice

Hotel clerk:	"Hello?"
Todd:	"Hello. I was wondering if you have a vacancy for this weekend."
Hotel clerk:	"Yes, we do."
Todd:	"Great. Could we get a room with a queen size bed?"
Hotel clerk:	"Sorry. The only rooms left are ones with two double beds. Will that work?"
Todd:	"That's fine."
Hotel clerk:	"Could I have your credit card number to hold the room?"
Todd:	"Here you are. It's 333 2121 4646 0000."
Hotel clerk:	"Thank you, sir. We'll see you this weekend."

16 Practice

1. e   **2.** d   **3.** a   **4.** b   **5.** c

Answers will vary. Samples:

1. Abraham Lincoln said, "Most folks are as happy as they make up their minds to be."

2. "I think, therefore, I am," said Rene Descartes.

3. "Everyone will be famous," said Andy Warhol, "for 15 minutes."

4. Lao Tzu said, "Give a man a fish and you feed him for a day. Teach him how to fish and you feed him for a lifetime."

5. "A journey of a thousand miles," said Confucius, "begins with a single step."

17 Practice

Answers will vary.

11e Reported Speech: Statements

Workbook 3 p. 200, Workbook 3B p. 72, Student Book 3 p. 328, Student Book 3B p. 118

18 Practice

1. Q **2.** R **3.** R **4.** Q **5.** Q **6.** R **7.** R **8.** Q **9.** R **10.** Q

19 Practice

1. His girlfriend told us that she hated James Smith and that he had ruined her life. She told us that she wished he were dead.
2. His son told us that he didn't have a father. He said that his father had left his sister and him when they had been young and had only come around once or twice a year. He said he hoped he stayed missing.
3. His ex-wife told us that she hadn't seen him since their divorce had become final many years ago. She said that she didn't know where he was or what he was doing and that she didn't care.
4. His butler told us that he wasn't sure what his plans had been that day, but that he was a very private man and rarely confided in him. He said that James had left the house yesterday morning and hadn't returned. That was why he called us.

20 Practice

Note: *that* may be included or omitted in the following reported speech. Both are correct.

1. Stephanie told me that the year before they had spent their vacation in Thailand. She said that they had thought about going back this year, but that they had decided to go camping instead. She said that they weren't leaving that day, but that they were probably going to leave the next day.
2. Did you hear the news last night? The announcer said that millions of gallons of water had flooded farms yesterday morning. He said that a levee had given way and engineers had been studying the problem to determine a cause for the collapse. Workers had been working nonstop since yesterday morning.
3. Melanie said that she had seen me talking with Chad. I said I hadn't been talking with him, but that he had been talking with me. She told me he was her boyfriend, and she wanted me to stay away from him. I told her I wasn't interested! I said that I had just been giving him the English homework assignment and that she needed to get a life.
4. Doug said that he had to drop out of school because his parents' business wasn't doing very well, and he needed to get a job. He said he would finish the semester, and then he was going to move back home. He told me that he wished he could continue studying, but that he couldn't.

21 Practice

A. 1. The Andersons said, "We are so sorry! We can't come because one of our children is sick."
2. Ms. Washington explained, "I have already made plans with my daughter."
3. The neighbors said, "We are going to be out of town."
4. Nancy told Bob, "I have a headache, and I'm not feeling well."

B. 1. Dale said, "Ted, your work hasn't been up to par, and we hired you because of your previous experience. We need you to be much more proactive."
2. Dale then said, "We will revisit this issue in three months and reevaluate at that point."

C. 1. Stan said, "Things have been bad for a while, and I think we should break up."
2. Angie said, "I know things are bad, but I think they will get better."
3. Stan then said, "I'm not sure about that, but we can take a break and see what happens."

22 Practice

Answers will vary.

23 Practice

Answers will vary.

11f Reported Speech: Questions

Workbook 3 p. 205, Workbook 3B p. 77, Student Book 3 p. 334, Student Book 3B p. 124

24 Practice

1. She asked me what I was doing tonight.
2. She asked me where the party was going to be.
3. Then she asked who was going to be there.
4. She asked if there were going to be parents at home during the party.
5. She asked when I was coming home.
6. She asked if I was going to wear this.
7. She asked if I didn't have something more appropriate to wear.

25 Practice

A. Answers will vary. Sample test questions:
1. Where did the Vikings come from?
2. Where does the word *Viking* probably come from?
3. What was the difference between the Vikings from Sweden and the Vikings from Denmark and Norway?
4. When did the Vikings make their most famous voyages?
5. Why were the Vikings able to conquer Europe so easily?
6. What is the stereotype of the Vikings?
7. Were the Vikings dependent on trade for survival?
8. Were they farmers as well as warriors?
9. What did their boats look like?
10. What is Yggdrasil in Viking mythology?
11. Who is Oden?

B. Answers will vary. Sample answers:
1. I asked them where the Vikings had come from.
2. I asked them where the word *Viking* probably comes from.
3. I asked them what the difference was between the Vikings from Sweden and the Vikings from Denmark and Norway.
4. I asked them when the Vikings made their most famous voyages.
5. I asked them why the Vikings were able to conquer Europe so easily.
6. I asked them what the stereotype of the Vikings is.
7. I asked them if the Vikings were dependent on trade for survival.
8. I asked them if they were farmers as well as warriors.
9. I asked them what their boats looked like.
10. I asked them what Yggdrasil was in Viking mythology.
11. I asked them who Oden was.

26 Practice

1. Jeff said he couldn't believe he'd found me and asked me where I was.
2. I told him I was in Washington and asked him where he lived.
3. He said that he lived in Washington, too, and that he had just moved there from Colorado.
4. I asked him what city he was in.
5. He told me he was in Seattle now and asked what city I was in.
6. I said that I was in Seattle, too, but that I lived in Ballard.
7. He thought I was kidding him and said that he lived there, too. He asked me what my address was.
8. I told him it was 313 Main.
9. He couldn't believe it. He asked me if I was serious or if I was messing with him.
10. I said that of course I wasn't and asked him why.
11. He told me that that was where he lived.
12. Then I asked him if *he* was for real and what his apartment number was.
13. He said he was in 406B.
14. Then I said I was in 503D and then asked him if he was at home.
15. He said that he was.
16. So I said I was coming down to meet him. *I still can't believe it!*

11g Reported Commands, Requests, Offers, Advice, Invitations, and Warnings

Workbook 3 p. 209, Workbook 3B p. 81, Student Book 3 p. 336, Student Book 3B p. 126

27 Practice

1. My trainer advised me to warm up every day on the treadmill for 15 minutes.
2. She advised me to do some arm work every other day.
3. She suggested we focus on abs every day.
4. She warned me not to push myself too much at the beginning.
5. She warned me not to continue if my knees started hurting.
6. She told me to follow her directions carefully so I wouldn't get hurt.
7. She advised me to try drinking a glass of water before we started.
8. She asked/told me to tell her if I didn't understand something.
9. She invited me to come watch her in a marathon next month.
10. She promised to help me look and feel 100% better in just six weeks.

28 Practice

Answers may vary slightly. Possible answers:

1. "Stop hanging around friends who are a bad influence on you."
2. "Improve your grades, or we'll have to take your computer away."
3. "We can get you a tutor to help you improve your grades."
4. "Don't do drugs!"
5. "Be home by 10:30 during the week and by 12:00 on Fridays and Saturdays."
6. "If you make these changes, we promise to pay for college."

29 Practice

1. The recipe says to put two large tomatoes in boiling water for one minute.
2. It says to take them out and remove the skins.
3. It says to squeeze out the seeds and to cut up the flesh into small pieces.
4. Then it says to put one or two jalapeño peppers over a gas flame or in the broiler.
5. It warns us not to let them burn.
6. It warns us to take them off the flame when they turn black.
7. It says to peel the jalapeños and to cut them into small pieces.
8. It says to remove their seeds and ribs.
9. It says to wash your/our hands immediately.
10. It warns you/us not to touch your/our eyes.
11. It says to peel and cut up an/one onion.
12. It says to put the tomatoes, onion, and peppers into a bowl.
13. It says to cut up a large clove of garlic and add it to the bowl.
14. It says to add some cilantro, lime juice, salt, and pepper.
15. Then it says to serve the salsa with chips and to enjoy it!

30 Practice

Answers will vary.

11h The Subjunctive in Noun Clauses

Workbook 3 p. 212, Workbook 3B p. 84, Student Book 3 p. 338, Student Book 3B p. 128

31 Practice

You have never seen a skin cream like this before, and using this line is so easy! The makers suggest <u>that you apply the lotion once in the morning and once before bedtime for best results</u>. We promise you will be amazed. We ask <u>that you try the product free for 30 days</u>, and if you decide this skin care line is not for you, we simply request <u>that you notify us, but keep the product as our gift to you</u>!

32 Practice

1. The owner insists that you be out there early.
2. The fans demand that you give 110%.
3. I recommend that you hit them hard.
4. Your teammates expect that you not let up.
5. The offensive coach advises that you remember their defense is weak.
6. Your competitive spirit requires that you go for this win!

33 Practice

Answers will vary.

Unit 11 Workbook Self-Test

Workbook 3 p. 214, Workbook 3B p. 86

A. 1. A **2.** D **3.** D **4.** C **5.** C **6.** A **7.** B **8.** C **9.** D **10.** A

B. 1. A **2.** B **3.** D **4.** D **5.** B **6.** B **7.** C **8.** C **9.** B **10.** C

UNIT 12   ADJECTIVE CLAUSES

12a Adjective Clauses with Subject Relative Pronouns

Workbook 3 p. 216, Workbook 3B p. 88, Student Book 3 p. 350, Student Book 3B p. 140

1 Practice

1. Ally is a woman who/that suffers from allergies.
2. Athletes are people who/that exercise regularly.
3. That is the company that/which allows its employees to work at home.
4. He is a man that/who listens to all kinds of music.
5. That is the laptop which/that uses the new operating system.
6. Bad drivers are people that/who run red lights and don't use their turn signals.
7. That is the apartment that/which has high ceilings.
8. You are a person that/who watches a lot of movies.
9. You are people that/who watch a lot of TV.
10. That book is the book that/which sits on the top shelf.

2 Practice

Answers will vary. Sample answers:

1. Sherry is the woman who is sitting on the chair.
2. Tina is the woman who is standing behind Sherry.
3. Anabelle is the woman who is holding a glass.
4. Kevin is the man who's the farthest away from the camera.
5. John is the man who is wearing white pants.
6. David is the man who's nearest the stereo.
7. Ellen is the woman who's between David and Karen.
8. Karen is the woman who is wearing a blue dress.

12b Adjective Clauses with Object Relative Pronouns

Workbook 3 p. 218, Workbook 3B p. 90, Student Book 3 p. 353, Student Book 3B p. 143

3 Practice

1. That's the man __that__ stole my wallet.   subject
2. It was the wallet _____ my roommate gave me.   object
3. The police officer __that__ took the report   subject
   eventually found my wallet.
4. Can I borrow the notes for the class _____ I missed today?   object
5. She's the same teacher __that__ teaches art history.   subject
6. Why aren't you wearing the blouse _____ you bought yesterday? object
7. The one __that__ has the red flowers? It's too hot.   subject
8. No, the one __that__ was in the window.   subject
9. The people __that__ shop at that mall must be wealthy.   subject
10. I don't remember the last time _____ my roommate did the dishes. object

4 Practice

Answers will vary. Sample answers:

1. A bracelet is something that/which a person wears on his or her wrist.
2. A masterpiece is something that/which an artist creates with great skill.
3. A speech is planned words that/which a speaker says in a public setting.
4. A decision is a determination that/which you make after carefully thinking about it.
5. A watermelon is a large fruit that/which people eat in the summer.
6. A crown is a piece of jewelry that/which a queen or king wears on his or her head.
7. A parachute is a device that/which skydivers rely on to get to the ground safely.
8. A water tank is a container that/which a town uses to store water.
9. A landmark is an object that/which travelers use to mark a location.
10. A bestseller is an item that/which customers buy a lot of.

5 Practice

Answers will vary.

12c Adjective Clauses with *Whose*

Workbook 3 p. 219, Workbook 3B p. 91, Student Book 3 p. 356, Student Book 3B p. 146

6 Practice

1. My friend lives in Los Angeles. His/her son attends the academy.
2. We've studied the philosopher. His ideas were revolutionary for his time.
3. They fired the executive. His/her salary was the highest.
4. She married a man. His first language is Spanish.
5. Karina doesn't get along with some people. Their politics are different from hers.
6. That's the model. His/her face is on every magazine cover this month.
7. Justin met the neighbors. Their dog keeps barking all the time.
8. Peter is my friend. His life was saved by a kidney transplant.
9. The jury convicted the defendant. His greed got him caught in the first place.

7 Practice

1. I am running against an opponent **whose** attitude bothers me.
2. This is an opponent **whose** lack of foresight has lead this country into near bankruptcy.
3. This is an opponent **whose** continued disregard for the public's welfare is shocking and **whose** denials of any wrongdoing trouble me, and they should trouble you.
4. I am the candidate **whose** only interest is seeing everyone in this community enjoying economic prosperity.
5. I am the candidate **whose** leadership skills will move us to that end.
6. I am the candidate **whose** team of experts has assured me that we have a very good chance of beating the incumbent.
7. You are the people **whose** opinion matters to me.
8. You are the people **whose** vote is very important.

8 Practice

Answers will vary. Possible answers:

1. The woman **who** was fired may have done it because she's angry.
   (OR) The woman **who** trained Joe may have done it because she's angry.
2. The man **who(m)** Joe borrowed money from may not have done it because he's been in his office since early this morning.
   (OR) The man **who(m)** Joe yelled at may have done it because he felt that Joe shouldn't have yelled at him in front of the team.
3. The woman **whose** project Joe took credit for may have done it because Joe made her look less productive than she actually is.
   (OR) The woman **who(m)** Joe cut out of an important conference call may have done it because she's angry that Joe's trying to make her look bad at work.
4. The man **whose** main account Joe stole may have done it because Joe has made him look less productive than he actually is.
   (OR) The man **who(m)** Joe asked to work late may have done it because he felt it wasn't fair that he had to work while Joe left early.

9 Practice

Answers will vary.

12d *When, Where, Why,* and *That* as Relative Pronouns

Workbook 3 p. 222, Workbook 3B p. 94, Student Book 3 p. 358, Student Book 3B p. 148

10 Practice

1. **a.** We visited the battlefield **where** thousands of soldiers died.
   b. We visited the battlefield **that** thousands of soldiers died **on**.
2. **a.** We saw the house **where** the religious leader was born.
   b. We saw the house **that** the religious leader was born **in**.
3. **a.** This is the clock tower **where** we had our picture taken.
   b. This is the clock tower **that** we had our picture taken **at**.
4. **a.** We chose a small town **where** fewer tourists were.
   b. We chose a small town **that** fewer tourists were **in**.
5. **a.** We stayed at a hotel **where** the royal family had stayed the week before.
   b. We stayed at a hotel **that** the royal family had stayed **in/at** the week before.
6. **a.** This is the restaurant **where** our friends took us.
   b. This is the restaurant **that** our friends took us **to**.
7. **a.** This is the square **where** we lost our traveler's checks.
   b. This is the square **that** we lost our traveler's checks **at/in**.
8. **a.** Next year we'd like to go to a place **where** the weather is a little warmer.
   b. Next year we'd like to go to a place **that** the weather is a little warmer **in**.

11 Practice

Answers will vary.

12 Practice

1. That was the party **where** I met my wife.
   That was the party **that** I met my wife **at**.
2. It was the fall **when** I started teaching at the university.
   It was the fall **that** I started teaching at the university.
3. We got married in the same place **where** we met.
   We got married in the same place **that** we met **at**.
4. That is the reason **why** we went to the same place on our second honeymoon.
   That is the reason **that** we went to the same place on our second honeymoon.
5. We moved to the city **where** her family is.
   We moved to the city **that** her family is **in**.
6. It is the reason **why** we moved to the city.
   It is the reason **that** we moved to the city.

13 Practice

Answers will vary.

12e Defining and Nondefining Adjective Clauses

Workbook 3 p. 225, Workbook 3B p. 97, Student Book 3 p. 361, Student Book 3B p. 151

14 Practice

1. ND 2. D 3. ND 4. D 5. D 6. ND 7. D 8. ND 9. ND 10. D

15 Practice

1. Toys, which can help children learn, have changed dramatically in the last 100 years.
2. Toys that have very small parts should not be given to very young children.
3. Guacamole, which is made from avocados, lime, cilantro, garlic, salt, and pepper, is very popular in Mexican restaurants.
4. The guacamole which my husband makes is out of this world!
5. The grammar exercises which are in this book are fun and easy!
6. Grammar exercises, which are designed to help people learn language, involve rules.
7. Garlic, which some people believe has medical properties, is easy to grow.
8. The garlic which you can buy crushed in a jar has a different taste from fresh garlic.

Practice

Some of the earliest ways to measure time were the use of obelisks in Egypt. Obelisks, which are tall four-sided towers, cast shadows, which people could use to measure different times of day. Later, people used water clocks, which measured time by how long it took for water to leak from one container to another. Water clocks, which didn't depend on the sun, moon, or stars, had markings in them to indicate time periods as the containers filled with the water. Candles, which were also used to mark the passage of time, burned to marks made along the side. In the 1400s, mechanical clocks, which use a mainspring and balance wheel, were introduced. In 1657, Christiaan Huygens built the first clock that used a pendulum. In 1884, many countries adopted Greenwich, England as the Prime Meridian, which indicates zero degrees longitude. In the 1920s, quartz clocks were developed. Quartz crystals, which can produce regular electric pulses, were found to be more accurate in keeping time than clocks which contained gears.

12f Using *Which* to Refer to an Entire Clause

Workbook 3 p. 227, Workbook 3B p. 99, Student Book 3 p. 364, Student Book 3B p. 154

17 **Practice**

1. Martha is in really good shape, **which** makes her happy.
2. Martha's running partner, Julia, has entered them in a triathlon for this fall, **which** has surprised Martha.
3. Martha and Julia are going to have only five months to train before the triathlon, **which** makes Martha a little nervous.
4. She and Julia have run races together, but they haven't done swimming or cycling before, **which** worries her.
5. Julia has done several triathlons, **which** is why she knows that they can do it.
6. Martha is an excellent swimmer, **which** will be when she makes good time in the race.
7. Julia has organized training rides to get Martha ready for the cycling part of the race, **which** will build Martha's cycling stamina.
8. After the triathlon, they are going to take a vacation for two weeks, **which** is just long enough to recover!

18 **Practice**

Answers will vary.

19 **Practice**

Answers will vary.

12g Reduced Adjective Clauses

Workbook 3 p. 228, Workbook 3B p. 100, Student Book 3 p. 367, Student Book 3B p. 157

20 Practice

Before the existence of money, barter, <u>the exchange of goods and services for other goods and services</u>, was the primary means of acquisition. In China, from approximately 9000 to 6000 B.C., cattle and grain were used for barter. From about 1200 B.C., many cultures used cowry shells, <u>the shell from an animal found in the Pacific and Indian Oceans</u>. This practice lasted for many hundreds of years. In 1000 B.C., China started producing coins <u>made of metal</u>, typically <u>having a hole in them</u> so as to be put on a string. In the country of Lydia, <u>now part of Turkey</u>, the first modern coins, <u>made from silver</u> and <u>having a round shape</u>, were manufactured. In China in 118 B.C., leather money appeared. This leather strip was the predecessor for paper notes, <u>also appearing for the first time in China</u>. In North America in the 1500s, "wampum," <u>strings of shell beads</u>, was used by the Native Americans for trade, as gifts, and other purposes. In later years, England and the United States adopted the gold standard, <u>abandoned in the United States after the Great Depression</u>. Today people rely on bank cards <u>representing how much money a person has</u> for many of their daily transactions.

21 Practice

1. On November 7, 1940, the Tacoma Narrows Bridge, <u>the third longest bridge in the world</u>, collapsed after only four months.
2. The bridge, <u>located on the Tacoma Narrows</u>, was light and flexible.
3. The bridge, <u>called "Galloping Gertie,"</u> would move when the wind blew at relatively low speeds.
4. No one thought the bridge, <u>designed by a well-known engineer</u>, was dangerous.
5. On November 7, 1940, the wind, <u>having a speed of about 42 miles per hour</u>, caused the bridge to oscillate violently.
6. The people <u>driving in the two cars</u> that were on the bridge at the time of its collapse got away safely.
7. The collapse, <u>seen and documented by many people</u>, taught engineers about the unique properties of suspension bridges.

22 Practice

1. People **who are** thinking about going on a low-carb diet should talk to their doctors first.
2. The light **which/that comes** into the west window keeps the living room warm in the afternoon.
3. People **who are** unhappy in their current careers should seek advice from a counselor.
4. Do you see the men **who are** talking on the corner?
   The one **who is** on the right is my boss.
5. Buildings **that/which were** built before the 1900s are protected under landmark status in this town.
6. I can't eat products **which/that are** made with peanuts.
7. My dad doesn't listen to any music **which/that was** recorded after 1990.
8. Merchants **who sell** jewelry on the street must have a permit.
9. Does anyone know what happened to the money **that/which was** left on the table?
10. The people **who were** living in the downstairs apartment just moved out.

261

23 Practice

Answers will vary.

 ## Unit 12 Workbook Self-Test

Workbook 3 p. 232, Workbook 3B p. 104

A. 1. B **2.** A **3.** D **4.** C **5.** D **6.** D **7.** A **8.** D **9.** C **10.** B
B. 1. A **2.** C **3.** B **4.** A **5.** C **6.** B **7.** B **8.** D **9.** A **10.** D

UNIT 13 ADVERB CLAUSES

13a Adverb Clauses of Time

Workbook 3 p. 234, Workbook 3B p. 106, Student Book 3 p. 380, Student Book 3B p. 170

1 Practice

A. 1. d **2.** e **3.** a **4.** b **5.** c
B. 1. e **2.** a **3.** d **4.** c **5.** g **6.** b **7.** f

2 Practice

1. I (There should be a comma before *please*.)
As soon as you get home, please give me a call.
2. C
3. C
4. I (Two adverb clause markers are used—*the first time* and *when*; *when* should be deleted.)
Were you worried the first time you traveled alone?
5. I (*Whenever* should be replaced with *when*; *whenever* suggests a repeated action, but *the first time* means only once.)
When I saw that movie the first time, I was very scared.
6. I (*Until* is the wrong adverb after *only*.)
The workers may go home only after the job is finished.
(OR) The workers may not go home until the job is finished.
7. I (No comma is needed.)
Amy has gone to the theater every weekend since she moved to New York.
8. C
9. I (Two adverbs are used; *while* or *when* should be deleted.)
While Susan was talking on the phone, her dog ran out the door.
(OR) Susan was talking on the phone when her dog ran out the door.
10. I (No comma is needed.)
Everyone watched in horror as the dancer fell off the stage.

3 Practice

Answers will vary.

13b Adverb Clauses of Reason and Result

Workbook 3 p. 237, Workbook 3B p. 109, Student Book 3 p. 383, Student Book 3B p. 173

4 Practice

1. because **2.** because **3.** so **4.** so **5.** because **6.** consequently **7.** as a result
8. so **9.** because of **10.** therefore

5 Practice

1. a. The restaurant was so new that almost nobody else was there.
   b. It was such a new restaurant that almost nobody else was there.
2. a. The service was so slow that they waited thirty minutes for their food.
   b. It was such slow service that they waited thirty minutes for their food.
3. a. The view was so beautiful that Erin and Paul didn't mind the slow service.
   b. It was such a beautiful view that Erin and Paul didn't mind the slow service.
4. a. The afternoon was so warm that they did not need to wear jackets.
   b. It was such a warm afternoon that they did not need to wear jackets.
5. a. The pasta was so delicious that they ate every bite of it.
   b. It was such delicious pasta that they ate every bite of it.
6. a. The dessert was so sweet that Erin couldn't eat all of it.
   b. It was such sweet dessert that Erin couldn't eat all of it.
7. a. The bill was so expensive that Paul thought there must be a mistake.
   b. It was such an expensive bill that Paul thought there must be a mistake.
8. a. The restaurant was so romantic that Erin and Paul decided to eat there again someday.
   b. It was such a romantic restaurant that Erin and Paul decided to eat there again someday.

6 Practice

1. The firefighter was very brave, and so he won an award.
2. Since I must go to work so early, I decided to go to bed early.
3. Gil didn't understand his math homework; therefore, he found a math tutor.
   (OR) Gil didn't understand his math homework. Therefore, he found a math tutor.
4. No punctuation is needed.
5. My sister is allergic to bees; as a result, she has to carry medicine with her.
   (OR) My sister is allergic to bees. As a result, she has to carry medicine with her.
6. Because of the earthquake, many homes were damaged.
7. No punctuation is needed.
8. Our flight was delayed, and as a result we did not leave until the next day.
9. Beth bought the wrong size dress, so she'll have to return to the store.
10. The company had to close; consequently, many people lost their jobs.
   (OR) The company had to close. Consequently, many people lost their jobs.

13c Adverb Clauses of Purpose

Workbook 3 p. 240, Workbook 3B p. 112, Student Book 3 p. 387, Student Book 3B p. 177

7 | Practice

1. b **2.** a **3.** b **4.** b **5.** a **6.** b

8 | Practice

1. Therefore, **2.** so that **3.** in order to **4.** in order to **5.** ; therefore, **6.** so that
7. Therefore, **8.** so that

9 | Practice

Answers will vary.

13d Adverb Clauses of Contrast

Workbook 3 p. 241, Workbook 3B p. 114, Student Book 3 p. 389, Student Book 3B p. 179

10 | Practice

1. when **2.** in order to **3.** because **4.** because of **5.** whereas **6.** however
7. though **8.** So that **9.** Once **10.** when **11.** before **12.** Because of **13.** while
14. so that **15.** in order to **16.** though **17.** Therefore **18.** Although **19.** so that
20. While **21.** nevertheless

11 | Practice

1. a. Although my city, Montreal, is very cold in the winter, there are many fun things to do outside.
   b. My city, Montreal, is very cold in the winter; however, there are many fun things to do outside.
2. a. You can go ice-skating in the park, although sometimes it is too cold for that.
   (OR) Although you can go ice-skating in the park, sometimes it is too cold for that.
   b. You can go ice-skating in the park; nevertheless, sometimes it is too cold for that.
3. a. While many people like to go shopping in the underground malls, others prefer visiting museums. **(OR)** Many people like to go shopping in the underground malls, while others prefer visiting museums.
   b. Many people like to go shopping in the underground malls; others prefer visiting museums, though. **(OR)** Many people like to go shopping in the underground malls, though others prefer visiting museums. **(OR)** Though many people like to go shopping in the underground malls, others prefer visiting museums.

4. **a.** Even though the streets can be slippery with ice, some people think it's romantic to ride in a horse and carriage.

  b. The streets can be slippery with ice; however, some people think it's romantic to ride in a horse and carriage.

5. **a.** Although it's a long drive, it's fun to go to Quebec City for the winter festival.

  b. It's a long drive; nevertheless, it's fun to go to Quebec City for the winter festival.

6. **a.** My husband always wants to go somewhere warmer in the winter, whereas I prefer to stay in Canada. **(OR)** Whereas my husband always wants to go somewhere warmer in the winter, I prefer to stay in Canada.

  b. My husband always wants to go somewhere warmer in the winter; I prefer to stay in Canada, though. **(OR)** My husband always wants to go somewhere warmer in the winter, though I prefer to stay in Canada. **(OR)** Though my husband always wants to go somewhere warmer in the winter, I prefer to stay in Canada.

12 Practice

Answers will vary. Sample sentences:

A. While one house is finished, the other is still under construction.
One house is being built; however, it should be finished soon.
One house is completely built. It might need repairs, though.
One house is pictured from the outside, whereas the other is seen from the inside.

B. The woman in the chair looks tired, whereas the woman in the bath looks relaxed.
The woman in the chair is resting; nevertheless, she doesn't look very relaxed.
Although the woman in the bath looks relaxed, she might be worried about something.
Both of these women might be tired from their jobs, though they might have different ways of relaxing.

◆ 13e Adverb Clauses of Condition

Workbook 3 p. 246, Workbook 3B p. 118, Student Book 3 p. 391, Student Book 3B p. 181

13 Practice

1. Unless it is a special promotion day, all employees must wear black pants and a green shirt to work.
2. Even if you washed your hands before coming to work, you must wash them again before handling food.
3. Hair must be tied back and worn under a cap unless it is above your shoulders.
4. Personal phone calls are permitted only if it is an emergency.
5. You should talk to your supervisor in case you have problems with your schedule.
6. All requests for vacation time must be in writing whether or not you have talked to your supervisor first.
7. You may have one free meal on your shift even if you work only a five-hour shift.
8. Food can only be consumed in the employee kitchen unless the restaurant is closed. (In that case, you may eat in the dining room.)

Practice

1. **a.** I can buy a used car only if I save $2,000.
   b. Only if I save $2,000 can I buy a used car.
2. **a.** I can save $2,000 only if I stop buying things I don't need.
   b. Only if I stop buying things I don't need can I save $2,000.
3. **a.** I will stop buying lunch every day only if I make my lunch at home.
   b. Only if I make my lunch at home will I stop buying lunch every day.
4. **a.** I will quit drinking expensive coffee only if I stop walking past that new cafe on my way to work.
   b. Only if I stop walking past that new cafe on my way to work will I quit drinking expensive coffee.
5. **a.** I will cancel my cable TV service only if I start reading more.
   b. Only if I start reading more will I cancel my cable TV service.
6. **a.** I can get books from the library instead of the bookstore only if I pay my library fine.
   b. Only if I pay my library fine can I get books from the library instead of the bookstore.
7. **a.** I'll stop using my cell phone so often only if my friends start calling me at home.
   b. Only if my friends start calling me at home will I stop using my cell phone so often.
8. **a.** I could get a second job only if I had a car (in order to get from one job to the other).
   b. Only if I had a car could I get a second job.

15 **Practice**

Answers will vary.

13f Reduced Adverb Clauses

Workbook 3 p. 249, Workbook 3B p. 121, Student Book 3 p. 394, Student Book 3B p. 184

16 **Practice**

1. AP **2.** AP **3.** AC **4.** AC **5.** AC **6.** AP **7.** AP **8.** AC **9.** AC **10.** AC

17 **Practice**

1. After they had lived in their apartment for two years, Carl and Adene decided to make some changes.
2. Because they wanted to make some inexpensive changes, they decided to paint the walls.
3. Before starting the project, they looked at magazines to see what colors they liked.
4. Cannot be reduced. (The subject is not the same in each clause).
5. After arguing over different colors, they finally agreed to paint two walls of the living room blue and two walls yellow.
6. They prepared the walls with white primer before they applied colored paint.
7. While she painted, Adene secretly worried that the colors would look bad.
8. Cannot be reduced. (The subject is not the same in each clause).
9. Since redecorating the living room, they have gone on to change the kitchen.
10. Cannot be reduced. (The subject is not the same in each clause).

18 **Practice**

1. I **2.** C **3.** I **4.** I **5.** I **6.** C **7.** I **8.** C

19 **Practice**

Answers will vary.

Unit 13 Workbook Self-Test

Workbook 3 p. 252, Workbook 3B p. 124

A. 1. C **2.** D **3.** C **4.** B **5.** B **6.** A **7.** A **8.** C **9.** B **10.** C

B. 1. A **2.** D **3.** D **4.** B **5.** B **6.** C **7.** A **8.** D **9.** C **10.** C

UNIT 14   CONDITIONAL SENTENCES

14a Real Conditional Sentences in the Present and Future

Workbook 3 p. 254, Workbook 3B p. 126, Student Book 3 p. 406, Student Book 3B p. 196

1 **Practice**

1. e **2.** b **3.** a **4.** d **5.** c

2 **Practice**

1. Please hang up and dial again if you want to make a call.
2. Ms. Landry is out of the office on Mondays if you are trying to reach her.
   (OR) She is out of the office on Mondays if you are trying to reach Ms. Landry.
3. Your message will not be sent if you do not press "one" after leaving it.
4. Please call Denise Williamson at extension 4573 if you should need to speak with some one immediately.
5. Ms. Landry will return your call as soon as possible if you leave a message.

3 **Practice**

Answers will vary. Be sure that tenses are used correctly in the condition clause and the main clause. In all sentences, a comma should be used only after the conditional.

1. Present tense should be used in both clauses.
2. Present tense should be used in both clauses.
3. Present tense should be used in the condition clause, and future tense (*will* + verb) should be used in the main clause.
4. *Should* + verb should be used in the condition clause, and future tense (*will* + verb) should be used in the main clause.
5. Present tense should be used in both clauses; the main clause should use an imperative (no subject should be stated).

14b Unreal Conditional Sentences in the Present or Future

Workbook 3 p. 256, Workbook 3B p. 128, Student Book 3 p. 409, Student Book 3B p. 199

4 Practice

1. If Kimberly practiced her speech tonight, she wouldn't be nervous tomorrow.
2. If she delivered a good speech, she would receive a good grade.
3. What would happen if she forgot part of her speech?
4. She could look at her notes if she forgot part of her speech.
5. She would speak more confidently if she liked the topic.
6. If Kimberly practiced in front of her friends, they could give her feedback.
7. She would do a better job if she slept well tonight.
8. If her speech were too long or too short, the teacher would lower her grade.
9. She could practice more if she had the time.
10. If Kimberly were more prepared, she could enjoy giving this speech.

5 Practice

1. a **2.** b **3.** b **4.** b **5.** a **6.** a **7.** b **8.** b

6 Practice

Answers will vary.

14c Unreal Conditional Sentences in the Past; Mixed Conditional Sentences

Workbook 3 p. 259, Workbook 3B p. 131, Student Book 3 p. 412, Student Book 3B p. 202

7 Practice

1. If Raymond hadn't learned to ride a bike at an early age, he wouldn't be such an excellent bicycle messenger today.
2. If Raymond's uncle hadn't owned a bike messenger company, Raymond might not have gotten a job there.
3. Last week, if Raymond hadn't talked on his cell phone while riding, he wouldn't have gotten hit by a car.
4. If he hadn't been busy talking, he could have heard the car behind him.
5. If he hadn't been late meeting a customer, he wouldn't have had to call to apologize.
6. If the car hadn't been going slowly, Raymond could have been badly injured.
7. If Raymond's boss weren't his uncle, Raymond might have been fired from his job.
8. If Raymond were afraid to ride his bike in traffic, he couldn't have returned to work yesterday.

8 Practice

1. M **2.** UP **3.** UP **4.** UP **5.** UP **6.** UP **7.** M **8.** M

9 Practice

Answers will vary.

14d Conditional Sentences with *As If* and *As Though*

Workbook 3 p. 261, Workbook 3B p. 133, Student Book 3 p. 416, Student Book 3B p. 206

10 Practice

1. R **2.** U **3.** U **4.** R **5.** R **6.** U

11 Practice

1. You look as though you are tired.
2. It looked as if the sun were going to come out a little while ago.
3. She talks as if she will get the job.
4. The band sounds like they haven't practiced.
5. It looks as though we had too much food for the party.
   (**OR**) It looked as though we had too much food for the party.
6. It looks as if there were a big party down the hall.
   (**OR**) It looked as if there were a big party down the hall.
7. You look like you knew how to solve the problem.
   (**OR**) You looked like you knew how to solve the problem.
8. His mother sounds as if she's angry about something.

12 Practice

Answers will vary. Sample sentences:

A. 1. It looks as though the man isn't going to be hurt.
   2. It looks as if the bicycle tires have slipped in the sand.
B. 1. It looks like the boy is going to take some cookies.
   2. It seems as if his mother has left the room.
C. 1. It looks as though the rock climber will reach the top.
   2. It looks as if the rock climber has come a long way.
D. 1. It looks as though traffic isn't going to move for a while.
   2. It looks like traffic hasn't moved for a long time.

14e Conditional Sentences Without *If*

Workbook 3 p. 264, Workbook 3B p. 136, Student Book 3 p. 418, Student Book 3B p. 208

13 | Practice

1. **a.** Had Matthew known his parents were coming to visit, he would have cleaned his apartment.
   b. Matthew didn't know his parents were coming to visit. Otherwise, he would have cleaned his apartment.
2. **a.** Had he had more time, he would have washed the dishes in the sink.
   b. With more time, he would have washed the dishes in the sink.
3. **a.** Should his mother see the stains on the rug, she will be upset.
   b. His mother might see the stains on the rug. If so, she will be upset.
4. **a.** Had his friend not helped him, he wouldn't have finished cleaning in time.
   b. Without his friend's help, he wouldn't have finished cleaning in time.
5. **a.** Had the hotels not been full this weekend, they wouldn't have asked to stay with Matthew.
   b. The hotels were full this weekend; otherwise, they wouldn't have asked to stay with Matthew.
6. **a.** Should Matthew's parents arrive early, they'll take him out to dinner.
   b. Matthew's parent might arrive early. If so, they'll take him out to dinner.

14 | Practice

1. If I had known that the suitcase would break so easily, I never would have bought it.
2. If the handle hadn't broken, I wouldn't have had to travel around France with a rope tied to the suitcase.
3. It's true that if my suitcase weren't so full, the zipper might not have broken.
4. Your ad says that if the suitcase should get too full, the zipper will not break.
5. If the zipper hadn't broken, I wouldn't have lost some of my clothing.
6. If I had realized the fabric was so thin, I wouldn't have put anything in there.
7. If I were you, I would carefully test my product before giving false information about it.
8. If your company improves its products in the future, I will consider buying another Stimson suitcase.

14f **Wishes About the Present, Future, and Past;** *Hope*

Workbook 3 p. 267, Workbook 3B p. 139, Student Book 3 p. 422, Student Book 3B p. 212

15 **Practice**

1. d **2.** a **3.** b **4.** c

16 **Practice**

1. He wishes (that) he had a computer at home.
2. He wishes (that) he didn't have to use the library computer.
3. He wishes (that) the Internet connection weren't slow. / were faster.
4. He wishes (that) he could use the computer for more than thirty minutes. / could use the computer longer.
5. He wishes (that) his friend Joe weren't telling him jokes.
6. He wishes (that) he could print on the library computer.
7. He wishes (that) he hadn't left his floppy disk at home.
8. He wishes (that) he hadn't forgotten one of his books.
9. He wishes (that) he hadn't lost his library card.
10. He wishes (that) he could finish his assignment.

17 **Practice**

1. I hope (that) I have enough time to finish the assignment.
2. I hope (that) the librarian can help me.
3. I hope (that) I can buy my own computer.
4. I hope (that) my friend wrote down the assignment.
5. I hope (that) people will stop talking.
6. I hope (that) I brought money for the photocopy machine.

18 **Practice**

Answers will vary.

14g Conditional Sentences with *If Only*

Workbook 3 p. 270, Workbook 3B p. 142, Student Book 3 p. 425, Student Book 3B p. 215

19 Practice

1. If only I had a job right now.
2. If only I had an MBA.
3. If only I didn't have to work near my home.
4. If only I liked to wear suits.
5. If only I had finished college.
6. If only I could work on weekends.
7. If only I had learned to use a lot of computer programs.
8. If only the job that I wanted hadn't been given to someone else.
9. If only I had a suit to wear to a job interview.
10. If only I had started looking for jobs before last week. (OR earlier)
11. If only I weren't late paying the rent this month.
12. If only I hadn't lost my job last month.

20 Practice

Answers will vary.

◆ Unit 14 Workbook Self-Test

Workbook 3 p. 272, Workbook 3B p. 144

A. 1. D **2.** B **3.** A **4.** A **5.** D **6.** B **7.** C **8.** C **9.** A **10.** B

B. 1. D **2.** A **3.** B **4.** B **5.** C **6.** A **7.** C **8.** C **9.** C **10.** A